Theatre History Studies

2021 Volume 40

Edited by

LISA JACKSON-SCHEBETTA

PUBLISHED BY THE MID-AMERICA THEATRE CONFERENCE
AND THE UNIVERSITY OF ALABAMA PRESS

Template Design: Todd Lape / Lape Designs

Essays appearing in this journal are abstracted and indexed in *Historical Abstracts* and *America: History and Life*.

MEMBER
CELJ
Council of Editors of Learned Journals

Cover Art
Character exploration of Grizeld Bane from the Night Garden sketch series by Danielle Laurin, costume designer; *Witchcraft*, written by Joanna Baillie, produced by the Concordia University Theatre Department, November 2011, directed by Louis Patrick Leroux and Cristina Iovita. Used with permission

Cover Design
Todd Lape / Lape Designs

Please note: there was no issue published in 2013

Theatre History Studies is an official journal of the Mid-America Theatre Conference, Inc. (MATC). The conference is dedicated to the growth and improvement of all forms of theatre throughout a twelve--state region that includes the states of Illinois, Iowa, Nebraska, Kansas, Missouri, Minnesota, North Dakota, South Dakota, and Wisconsin. Its purposes are to unite people and organizations within this region and elsewhere who have an interest in theatre and to promote the growth and development of all forms of theatre.

Theatre History Studies is devoted to research in all areas of theatre studies. Manuscripts should be prepared in conformity with the guidelines established in the *Chicago Manual of Style* and emailed to Lisa Jackson-Schebetta at ths.editor@matc.us. Consulting editors read the manuscripts, a process that takes approximately four months. The journal does not normally accept studies of dramatic literature unless there is a focus on actual production and performance. Authors whose manuscripts are accepted must provide the editor with an electronic file, using Microsoft Word. Illustrations are welcomed and should conform with the instructions listed on the style guide on the website: http://matc.us/wordpress/wp-content/uploads/UAL-Press-Guidelines-Revised-2013.pdf

This publication is issued annually by the Mid-America Theatre Conference and The University of Alabama Press.

Subscription rates for 2021 are $25.00 for individuals, $35.00 for institutions, and an additional $10.00 for foreign delivery. Subscription orders and changes of address should be directed to Allie Harper, The University of Alabama Press, Box 870380, Tuscaloosa, AL 35487; (205) 348–1564, phone; (205) 348–9201, fax.

Any single current-year issue or back issue is $34.95 each if ordered through the Chicago Distribution Center. (Please note: there was no issue published in 2013.)

Theatre History Studies is indexed in Historical Abstracts and America: History and Life, Humanities Index, Humanities Abstracts, Book Review Index, MLA International Bibliography, International Bibliography of Theatre & Dance, Arts & Humanities Citation Index, IBZ International Bibliography of Periodical Literature, and IBR International Bibliography of Book Reviews, the database of the International Index to the Performing Arts. Full texts of essays appear in the databases of both Humanities Abstracts Full Text and SIRS.

CONTENTS

CONTENTS

PART II
Witch Characters and Witchy Performance

PART III
Essay From The Conference

The Robert A. Schanke Award-Winning Essay, MATC 2020

PART IV
Book Reviews

CONTENTS

CONTENTS

ILLUSTRATIONS

Introduction

—LISA JACKSON-SCHEBETTA WITH ODAI JOHNSON, CHRYSTYNA DAIL, AND JONATHAN SHANDELL

This editor's introduction takes a somewhat different form.

Stay with me, please.

There are three sections to it, which I leave intentionally unconnected by my prose, intentionally without transition, a structure reflective of my process/processing of this moment in which I write.

I.

As I write this editor's introduction in August 2020, two refrains continue to surface in my mind:

> Walter Benjamin: "The tradition of the oppressed teaches us that the 'state of emergency' in which we live is not the exception but the rule."[1]
> George Orwell: "Who controls the past controls the future."[2]

I am quite certain others also find their minds turning to these writings and writers. For me, over the last four years in the Americas, Orwell's and Benjamin's phrases and work have been constant, urgent, recurring companions, alongside Diana Taylor's conviction that "performances operate as vital acts of transfer, transmitting social knowledge, memory, and a sense of identity through reiterated actions."[3] If Benjamin and Orwell have helped me to remember—with colleagues, students, collaborators—that the stakes of participating in history and citizenship are *always* and *have always been* life or death, Taylor has loaned me faith when my own has faltered. That is, as a historian who works at the intersection of theatre history and performance studies, I have looked to Taylor as a compass: both theatre and scholarship are performances and, thus, both function as vital acts of transfer. Both offer means through which to participate in history and, by doing so, to contribute to the shape of the future, to the world(s) yet to be.

The articles I am proud to share with you, within these pages, are not only fine pieces of scholarly writing but also documents (acts of transfer) of our field's work in the midst of a global pandemic that has disproportionately affected Black, indigenous, and people of color communities in the United States, the Americas, and around the world, (re)exposing hemispheric and global inequities. These articles came to their final stages in late spring and summer 2020, in the midst of large-scale protests in the United States against the state's normalized, perpetual, and systemic violence against Black lives, a brutality deeply imbricated with this hemisphere's founding. The time/space of our geography *invented*—through colonialism and imperialism—as the "Americas" is founded upon transatlantic and trans-hemispheric violence that normalizes (indeed, depends upon) the disposability of Black, brown, trans, female, queer, disabled, indigenous, people of color, and immigrant bodies.[4]

In what ways does this moment teach us to mark and re-mark the absences in and of both archives and repertoires; to track and retrack the limitations, presumptions, and privileges of access and existence; to interrogate how archives and repertoires tell us which lives have mattered and which have not in the history of modernity/coloniality, issuing cautions as we make those decisions ourselves, in our work; and to confront us, via brute force, with the urgent need to continue to reimagine ways of writing history?[5] How does this moment demand that we catch and hold Benjamin's moment of danger, ruthlessly reminding ourselves that the state of emergency in which we live is *not new?* How does this moment demonstrate, in plain, naked sight, the urgency of Taylor's acts of transfer and how the scenario functions as both subject and object of performance, as well as historiographical method?

These preoccupations I offer are my own, but they have been deeply contoured by my work with authors in this volume. In "Un-Reading Voltaire: The Ghost in the Cupboard of the House of Reason," Odai Johnson invites the historian to (re)make space for what we deem the "nonrational." Moving through the poetic, theatrical, political, and historiographic imaginations of sixteenth- and seventeenth-century Europe, 500 BCE to 500 CE Greece, and nineteenth-century Egypt, Johnson returns us to a "sense of history and performance" in which "both [are] inexorably, inexpugnably shaped by nonrational experiences in cultures that found the supernatural—ghosts, and miracles—perfectly natural." In doing so, Johnson offers not only an intellectually and emotionally breathtaking itinerary but also a pointed and poignant provocation that recalls Hamlet's rejoinder to Horatio: "There are more things in heaven and Earth, Horatio, / Than are dreamt of in your philosophy."[6] I invite you to substitute "historian" for Horatio, and "method-archive-repertoire" for philosophy. In a field that often feels eager to dismiss sites such as the Renaissance and Enlightenment Europe in our desire to decolonize, Johnson reminds us that such sites are more complex than we might know (or care to recall). Johnson's exploration reveals that such sites remain inextricably connected to how we understand our present—and how we imagine our possible futures.

Jonathan Shandell and Scott Proudfit both interrogate white supremacy culture in historiographical methodology, historical record-keeping, and representations of historical memory. In "Caricatured, Marginalized, and Erased: African American Artists and Philadelphia's Negro Unit of the FTP, 1936–1939," Shandell examines three key productions of Philadelphia's Negro Unit of the Federal Theatre Project in order to expose how progressive white liberalism erases and excuses white chauvinism both within the theatrical practices of the FTP and in FTP histories. Proudfit, in "Stop Your Sobbing: White Fragility, Slippery Empathy, and Historical Consciousness in Branden Jacobs-Jenkins's *Appropriate*," deploys the concept, practice, and discourse of "white tears" in an analysis of Branden Jacobs-Jenkins's *Appropriate*. In doing so, Proudfit demonstrates how Jacobs-Jenkins's play illuminates the uniquely insidious functions of white *men's* tears in the United States from 2016 to 2020.

In the final article of the general section, "Asia and Alwin Nikolais: Interdisciplinarity, Orientalist Tendencies, and Midcentury American Dance," Angela K. Ahlgren challenges the binaristic and sedimented categories of appropriation, Orientalism, influence, presence, and absence. While acknowledging that choreographer Alwin Nikolais's work relied on Orientalist and appropriative actions, Ahlgren convincingly argues that Nikolais's work also depended on "the presence of Japanese, Chinese, Indian, Cambodian, and other artists in New York, as well as the circulation of instruments and other objects." Employing an interdisciplinary lens informed by musicology, dance, and theatre history, Ahlgren documents histories that would otherwise be erased while simultaneously demonstrating the need for historiographical methods that work across music, theatre, and dance. Looking ahead, the special section of volume 41 of *Theatre*

History Studies (2022), coedited by Ahlgren and Victoria Fortuna, will take up this methodological call. I look forward to the ways we will extend and expand this conversation in our next issue.

In the "Witch Characters and Witchy Performances" special section of this volume of *Theatre History Studies*, coeditors Jane Barnette and Chrystyna Dail illuminate the ways in which, as Dail writes in the section introduction, theatre and performance show how the "trope of the witch" functions as a stand-in for the "outsider" who is calling out, standing up to, or standing up for "her community." The articles in this section examine witch characters and witchiness in popular culture, historical account, site-specific contemporary performance, and classical texts. They offer a tour de force of theoretical analyses, historiographical interventions, and insightful, unabashed critique—they demand we attend and re-attend to the ways we ignore, dismiss, and narrate the outsider, gender, sexuality, race, and power in theatre practice and scholarship.

Finally, it is with great pleasure that I share the 2020 Robert A. Schanke Award-Winning Essay. In "New Conventions for a New Generation: High School Musicals and Broadway in the 2010s," Lindsey Mantoan demonstrates that a new genre in the US American musical has arrived: the high school musical. Focusing on *Bring It On* and *Mean Girls*, Mantoan argues that this new genre has moved far away from the social clique dramas of 1990s high school movies and television. The post-2010 high school musicals, Mantoan contends, "signal a shift in what constitutes a community, which individuals are valued, and what integration might truly mean."

II.

Some of the authors in this volume I am fortunate to know very well; others I am lucky to have gotten to know better. I am exceptionally humbled to be invited into their work and, quite frankly, their lives over the last eight months. I am grateful to them, as colleagues and writers, for the sustenance they have provided me.

When I sat down to write the editor's introduction to this volume, I felt lonely. Not alone. As a writer, I like being alone. I felt lonely. My exchange with the authors in this volume began in 2019, but our one-on-one work—my favorite work, in which I, as editor, am lucky to be invited to dance with the author and their ideas—took place in earnest between January and August 2020. In the midst of the global pandemic and national protests and demonstrations for racial justice, my work with these authors took on a new kind of sharp relief.

As I missed my students and colleagues, as I worried for my family, friends, and loved ones, as I homeschooled and took care and made career transitions, as I struggled to write my own articles . . . my work with these authors *held me* and created a gentle continuity to my life and practice. I felt lonely, sitting to write about *their* work without *them*. I issued a last-minute invitation to the authors and special section editors to ask if they would like to add their words to this volume's introduction.[7] I thought this might serve as a documentation of our field in this moment, and it certainly does. I should have known there would also be more, that these authors would bear gifts, again. Their reflective words are poignant documents of something much deeper than I anticipated. These reflections remind me—and I hope you, too—that our work as writers and scholars is deeply imbricated with our humanity. Something I sometimes forget. Something I need to remember. I share these with you, here.

An Expanding View by Chrystyna Dail

Friday, March 13, 2020. My older daughter can tell you the exact date that COVID-19 changed her life. We picked our daughters up from their respective schools, told them we would not be getting haircuts as planned, and awaited the ineluctable: an email from the district notifying parents and guardians that schools would be closing for the foreseeable future and all learning transitioned online.

The distraction of raising children during a pandemic can be helpful. I am forced to put the concerns of other people before my own. As a parent, spouse, and educator (and a middle child), it is a position I know well and with which I thought I had grown comfortable. Yet this constant giving of oneself has never been so laden with anxiety. As 2020 progressed, I felt increasingly responsible not only for the emotional and psychological well-being of my immediate family but also for the financial status of my employer, the overall quality of education students were receiving in an online environment, and the palpable mourning mixed with rage espoused by BIPOC friends and students. And then on May 10, while in the midst of New York social distancing and completing the teaching of thrown-together online courses, a colleague in another department, who in our few interactions always had a smile on her face and a supportive word, took her own life. And in doing so, she changed mine.

When every week is a year (a phrase my husband and I started sharing in early April), one finds time for—or more appropriately is forced into—introspection. In this looking inward, I realized that my anxiety, tinged with moments of melancholy, originated well before the COVID pandemic and was grounded in myopia and an overwhelming sense of assumed inevitability. My life had reached stagnation, yet I was too busy emptily serving others to take notice of my own emotional stalling out.

This pandemic and its integrated losses have changed me profoundly. The time spent cogitating my own stasis assisted in reconnecting me with the small joys I savored as an adolescent: playing games, singing, dancing, being outdoors, pleasure reading. But I believe the joy also stems from growing more comfortable with what Buddhist author Pema Chödrön calls "the in-between state." Chödrön writes, "Becoming intimate with the queasy feeling of being in the middle of nowhere makes our hearts more tender. . . . By not knowing, not hoping to know, and not acting like we know what's happening, we begin to access our inner strength."[8] Admitting to the unknown, or intentionally positioning oneself in a liminal space or at a crossroads, is a challenge for many parents and even more academics, but I am attempting it.

And the view is expanding.

Odai Johnson

In the big scheme of plagues, our pandemic may not be Florence 1348, or London 1665, or Marseilles 1720. It is not likely to carry off a quarter of the population in a summer of death. But it is our plague, and the loss is our loss. You are a very fortunate reader if you have not lost somebody or know somebody lost to COVID. Those who survive will be shaped by it, like Depression children were shaped by hunger. If this plague teaches us anything, it is, as Artaud suggested, that the sky can fall at any time. Academia, however, has always been a profession of deferment. Time begins later here because it is structured on a conceptual future. We stack up degrees first, in the promise of a future whose rewards will outweigh the deferment of the present. We train, for years, we pass through coursework, begin a dissertation, defend a dissertation, throw ourselves on the market, wait for the first job, endure it, wait for the second job, the book, tenure. And somewhere is the retching question, when does it begin? Or was that it, all that time behind us waiting? What COVID teaches is to defer deferring. With universities spiraling to bankruptcy, with every theatre in America closed, and we still training (remotely) for a profession that will likely be obsolete, what to do with our little time on earth becomes a more pressing question. Do what you love best. For me, it is writing. For others, it is not writing. Whatever it is, it must be its own reward. This pandemic is not a rain-delay anymore; from here out, we learn to play in the rain.

Jonathan Shandell

I'm lucky that I had concluded the research and first-draft writing of my article by January, months before the coronavirus pandemic hit. The mid-March maelstrom of pivoting to online teaching, supporting my children's online schooling, and attending the legions of meetings and other conversations brought on by COVID-19 left precious remaining energy or mental capacity for scholarship. But as I worked on revisions later in the spring in response to feedback from Lisa and the article reviewers (thank you, whoever you are!), I soon discovered that I was missing a key piece of evidence: a review of one of the Philadelphia Negro Unit's productions from the city's Black community newspaper the *Philadelphia Tribune*. Comparing critical responses to the Unit's three productions from Black and white reviewers is key to my purpose in the article, so the absence of this particular review from the online database (part of a gap of several months' worth of *Tribune* issues that I hadn't noticed in my initial research) was significant. In ordinary times, a quick trip into the microfiche drawers would have solved the problem. But after several months of waiting and hoping in vain for research libraries to reopen, we made the decision to proceed with the article (with the insertion of an apologetic explanatory footnote). Was this the right choice? It feels deeply unsatisfying, but so too would have been a full one-year delay in presenting a story I was eager to share with the scholarly community. High on the list of things I cannot wait to do again (along with hugging my parents, rescheduling the party for my daughter's bat mitzvah celebration, going to the theatre, and buying a good friend a drink at a bar) is finding this review and figuring out in what ways (if at all) it changes how the story of the Philadelphia Negro Units must be told.

III.

Chrystyna Dail's refrain reverberates with me, now, along with the others I noted at the outset of my introduction: "This pandemic and its integrated losses have changed me profoundly."

Another year will pass before these articles arrive in print to a wider audience. I will be writing the introduction to volume 41 of the journal. How will the world have changed? And how will it have not? How will I, as a scholar and an editor, have challenged myself to change not only the conversation of theatre history and historiography but also its very terms?[9] How will I have failed to do so? And where and how will our field have built space and time to reflect on our work, on where it has succeeded, and faltered, and on what our next steps will be?

Notes

1. Walter Benjamin, "Theses on the Philosophy of History," in *Illuminations*, ed. Hannah Arendt (New York: Shocken, 1969), 253–64, 257.
2. George Orwell, *1984* (Adelaide, Australia: University of Adelaide, 2016), 42. https://www.openrightslibrary.com/nineteen-eighty-four-1984-ebook/.
3. Diana Taylor, *Performance* (Durham, NC: Duke University Press, 2016), 25.
4. My formulation of "time-space" and the "invention" of the Americas comes from the work of Aníbal Quijano and Walter Mignolo. See Aníbal Quijano, "Coloniality of Power, Eurocentrism, and Latin America," *Neplanta: Views from the South* 1, no. 3 (2000): 533–80; Walter D. Mignolo, *The Idea of Latin America* (Malden, MA: Blackwell, 2005).
5. My references to archive, repertoire, and scenario come directly from Diana Taylor, *The Archive and the Repertoire: Performing Cultural Memory in the Americas* (Durham, NC: Duke University Press, 2003).
6. William Shakespeare, *Hamlet*, act I, scene 5, lines 167–68.
7. Not everyone had capacity to accept my invitation. As you read this, think back to your own position in fall 2020. I am humbled that any of the authors took me up.
8. Pema Chödrön, *The Places That Scare You: A Guide to Fearlessness in Difficult Times* (Boston: Shambhala, 2002), 120.
9. Again, I proceed here from the discourse of modernity/coloniality and, in particular, from Walter Mignolo's provocation that changing the terms of the conversation is not sufficient. We must change the conversation itself. See Walter Mignolo, *The Darker Side of Western Modernity: Global Futures, Decolonial Options* (Durham, NC: Duke University Press, 2011); Emily Sahakian, Christiana Molldrem Harkulich, and Lisa Jackson-Schebetta, "Hemispheric Historiography: Introduction to Special Section," *Theatre History Studies* 39 (2020): 117–22; Lisa Jackson-Schebetta, *Traveler, There Is No Road: Theatre, the Spanish Civil War, and the Decolonial Imagination in the Americas* (Iowa City: University of Iowa Press, 2016).

Editor's correction: Please note that volume 39 erroneously printed author Mike Sell's name as Michael Sell.

Part I

STUDIES IN THEATRE HISTORY

Un-Reading Voltaire

The Ghost in the Cupboard of the House of Reason

—ODAI JOHNSON

"We no longer believe in ghosts? Who says so?"
—G. E. LESSING, *HAMBURG DRAMATURGY*

"Even the Enlightened individual has not completely overcome the old belief."
—THEODOR ADORNO AND MAX HORKHEIMER, "ON THE THEORY OF GHOSTS," *DIALECTIC OF ENLIGHTENMENT*

I: The Great Extinction

When Gustav Flaubert was traveling in Egypt, in 1850, he wrote to his friend, the poet and playwright Louis Bouilhet, of his adventures (mostly in the brothel districts *avec ces dames*), but he also wrote of upright encounters on the Nile, like the miracles at Sheikh Sa'id, "a tomb-chapel built in honor of a Moslum saint where birds go of their own and drop food that is given to them—this food is then offered to poor travelers—(you and I, who have read Voltaire, don't believe this. But everyone is so backward here!)."[1] For those of us "who have read Voltaire," that is, we of the post-Enlightenment legacy, we the thoroughly disabused of such miracles, for us, birds don't feed pilgrims, and the cataloguing of such "miracles" in a travelogue is but to chuckle at the backwardness of these unenlightened Egyptians.

Until one day a bird drops something for you.

And you stand awhile on the threshold of incredulity and glimpse a little of all that's lost in a world where such things cannot be.

I want to cross back to that older side of this rational divide, where miracles and unnatural things still happen(ed). I want to un-read Voltaire, not to embrace the supernatural of witches and miracles and ghosts with a fulsome gullibility but to return to a sense of history and performance that were both inexorably, inexpugnably shaped by nonrational experiences in cultures that found the supernatural—ghosts and miracles—perfectly natural.

Because before this great extinction of the monstrous, before the Enlightenment reasoned away the supernatural, before we, in Freud's words, "surmounted" our older belief, much of performance's past lived in a more expansive haunted world that we would call prerational. It was peopled with ghosts and gods; it was storied with miraculous encounters, and there is a historic value to those stories and how they worked in that world. Not our world; theirs. Much of performance's long life was routinely structured around events that do not happen in a rational world (from the inexplicable gods of Euripides to the miracle at the tomb to the witches of Macbeth: visions, devils, hell and satyrs and allegories and vengeance-seeking ghosts of the un-biological dead), and the world for which these performances were made was far more comfortable with the irrational before witches were social outcasts, before accusing them was criminalized (Witchcraft Act of 1735), before ghosts were exposed, and before miracles were phenomenologically explained. For performance historians who tromp the farther past (the intrepid few who venture beyond the 1968 milepost, where search engines collapse and the path goes analog and weedy), it may require more than a passing gloss on *Macbeth* and *Daemonologie* to inhale seriously that comfort of a world with ghosts and witches; it may require more of a willing inhabiting of the mystery. I think this is what Paul Ricoeur called the "second naïveté," not the first flush of "medieval" gullibility that bit at every miracle but rather a reasoned, seasoned, mental accommodation of the unexplainable.[2]

Consider, for example, the mental poise of Banquo and how handily he processes his first supernatural encounter in the play *Macbeth*. In that imagined place of a blasted heath, three witches appear, not as an internal psychic disorder from a war-weary, PTSD, or pharmaceutically enhanced mind, like the indelible impression of blood on guilty hands we will see later. These two soldiers, Banquo and Macbeth, have not yet "eaten of the insane root"—all our modern explanations—but they meet witches with temporary substance, bodies, beards, gender, speech, and gestures. They are greeted by them—all hail—and their sudden discovery evokes an astonished wonder. They both are and are not of the earth, yet while here, they foretell a future for which there is no rational explanation. They are eerily correct in their prognostications, and then they vanish like substantial things cannot. They are, of course, in a play; it's always *just a play*. But it's the *how* of their reception that is the invitation: they were known as residents in the world of that play. That is, they were possible because they were known as residents in the world outside that play, composed as it was for a king who wrote at some length on the validity of such spirits, a world in which the supernatural cohabited with the natural in ways it does not for us.[3] About this strange encounter Banquo's initial astonishment quickly gives way to a sober possibility in a dense, troubling, deeply inviting but matter-of-fact statement about how the supernatural is trapped in the natural:

> "The earth hath bubbles as the water has
> And these are of them. Whither are they vanished?" (I iii, 79–80)

My question exactly: Wither have they vanished? I want to press this question beyond the pat response that they are simply conventions of a play for a patron who "believed" in witches and flogged that belief with royal authority. I want to probe awhile all that was lost in that extinction when the idea of the supernatural was "surmounted," when the bubbles of the earth ceased to exert any epistemological appeal. I am interested in the scars its excision left behind when it was cut away and in what to do with all that supernatural stumpage, all that material of our performance past that was deeply, sometimes structurally, obliged to it before its passing. Eschewing the ontological (do they exist?) or the epistemological (can we know them?), I see the problem of the supernatural as a historiographical and hence dramaturgical problem: how to authentically story a pre-Enlightenment world with post-Enlightenment habits of mind, a world in which miracles happened, where the earth hath bubbles, and the supernatural was once quite natural in ways it is not for us.

Lessing wrote of this problem early on in the *Hamburg Dramaturgy* (essay 11, continued in essay 12), discussing antiquity's belief in ghosts, before they lost materiality to become simply metaphors, but what makes Lessing's treatment of the problem so unlike his generation's rational itch for disenchanting the past is his appreciation of the dramaturgical efficacy of ghosts, and he folds that power into the discourse with the provocative line "We no longer believe in ghosts? Who says so?" Lessing's critique here is cogent because, unlike Voltaire, for example, he does not argue for or against ghosts, either ontologically or epistemologically. Rather, Lessing puzzles over their dramaturgical necessity.

Shakespeare, he suggested, could write terrifying ghosts (*Hamlet, Macbeth*) and Voltaire could not (*Sémiramis*) not because one was the better playwright but because the one lived in a world where ghosts were resident, and the other did not.[4] Voltaire could not reconcile the dismantling of spectrality as a philosopher while embracing it as a dramatist.

That world that Shakespeare and his royal patron wrote of, of witches and their "fearful abounding at this time, in this country," belonged to a deep genealogy of the supernatural. It was the world of Lope de Vega, of Hrotsvitha, of Euripides, a large and ancient world and, by Enlightenment standards, most of it irrational. "Rosthvitha, it must be remembered, believed in miracles," wrote apologetically the first English editor of her plays, "the average Englishman is skeptical," and this divide can extend to much of the prior world of gods and witches and visions and soothsayers and ghost-driven revenge plays, tempestuous spirits and all manner of paranormal experience that are not wholly explicable as fits, seizures, or hallucinations of a distempered mind, a world in which a body could be placed in a tomb and not be there when the stone was lifted.[5] Go and announce, quoth an angel who was another unnatural resident of the irrational prior, but Christian culture was not established without angels and miracles, virgin births and resurrection, nor was its theatre of faith in such "bubbles" of the earth.

What follows is not so much a séancing back of the vanished supernatural, or even a nostalgia for the world behind the stage that was wont to traffic in such imaginings, as a gravestone rubbing of what were once the bubbles of an older earth, a sounding of the absent presence of the miraculous *non est hic* of the once world, an attempt to chart its vanishing and to take some stock of the size of the cavity of what is missing. What follows is about all that is lost after the expulsion of the nonrational, all the Furies and witches and ghosts, the miracles, and all that extra-phenomenal supernatural presence-in-absence, the superstitious, super dramatic forces that were once at the heart of our long theatre history. And I should say from the opening, I kind of miss them. I rather like the idea of a world where birds carry food to pilgrims.

In the end, I hope to arrive at the suggestion that even for the most hardened enlightened mind, the theatre still functions, now as then, as something of a preserve where these refugees, the deported witches and ghosts, these alien exiles from the Enlightenment, and all that was lost, can still find a temporary reanimation. Even in the thick of rationalism, even by rationalists, the theatre remained the one place where the experiencing of the nonrational lived on unmolested by reason.

Sidebar: Probate

To get some sense of the scale of that great extinction, oblige me a brief inventory.

Item: one Dionysus, mystical, ecstatic, unhinging, ubiquitous from 500 BCE to 500 CE. Careful. Item: enumerable possessed maenadic ecstatic trance dancers, often chased by, item: priapic satyrs, hybridic crossbreeds, thought to be a crypto-species until the late eighteenth century, thereafter, fables (though possibly modulated into medieval devils for a second life); item: gods and demigods (dozens of them) and their agency that utterly dislodged human reason (love, lust, madness, vengeance); mortals touched by gods, prophets, and soothsayers (the blinded, second-sight bird-gut readers), mystic visionaries. Item: one large body of liturgical drama begun in the most egregious of miracles, with a story from virgin birth to resurrected death that was full monty start to finish biologically impossible, with various and sundry centuries of other equally impossible events staged (loaves and fishes, water-walking, dead-raising, bleeding hosts) in miracle plays, with attendant morality allegories. Item: one hellmouth, a metaphorical geography promoted to material place; item: wings for angels, still in the catalog of properties, 1620s. Shamans and Senecan ghosts, bands of wild men, Midsummer fairies, trance dancers from Bali to Africa to the Caribbean (is all our theatre on drugs?), none of which have any grounding in the rational experience of this natural world, nor, I might add, does performance history itself, that began with, item: one backward-looking Muse, Clio, as an inspired form to record other inspired forms derived from a sorority of irrational Muses who possessed poets and brought them words, like birds bring food to pilgrims, and all our rational treatments of the first twenty-four-hundred years of theatre history cannot wholly account for the power of that theatre if we cannot in some way reenter that nonrational space that produced it.

If historically theatre has been such an utterly irrational act, how can a rational history of theatre hope to authentically contain it? We may need witches more than we know. And ghosts.

We are back in Foucault's dilemma here, articulated in his study on the history of madness, namely, how to story with reason what we have diagnosed as madness. And it's critical not to get this entirely wrong—as Flaubert did to dismiss it utterly—because of all our losses in the long sweep of performance history, this may be our most costly loss, certainly among the deepest of our deep culture identity; we have lost more than faith if we have lost our capacity for faith; that is, the certainty, the in-your-bones knowledge of knowing what we cannot empirically know. If we have lost our capacity for the miraculous, the spectral, if there are not and indeed never were bubbles in this over-mapped and rational earth, the more loss for us, for then all our performative past has been but Flaubert's chuckle at backward peoples staging their own ignorant superstitions.

So, at the risk of un-reading Voltaire, can we stand a while on the edge of this parapet: "Has this thing appeared again tonight?"

II: The Excision Named "Fabulation"

The process of the excision has come to be called "fabulation." The word is Hayden White's creation, generated for a symposium on the irrational in the eighteenth century.[6] I like that the word itself is somewhat irrational, a not-quite-a-word word, invented as a process of exclusion, given a coat and tie but not fully admitted into the salon of polite usage. "Fabulation" leans on its quotes like a brace of crutches, because the unassimilated word stands on a threshold of its own liminality. It was crafted first to describe a kind of magical realism in fiction, like hair that continues to grow after death ("The stone shattered at the first blow of the pick-axe, and a stream of living hair, the intense color of copper spilled out of the crypt . . . spread out on the floor, the splendid hair measured twenty-two meters, eleven centimeters"), that is, used only to describe what doesn't actually happen on earth.[7] But Hayden White pressed it into historical service for an argument on meta-history to capture the process of something that did happen: the removal, the exclusion, of events that didn't happen from the walled and rational lexicon of history. He tapped it to speak on behalf of the eighteenth century's extradition of the excluded and now "irrational" forces of history, all those things not explicable by the laws of nature, like faith, visions, prophecy, inspiration, miracles, witches, ghosts, or the force of ecstatic religions; those fables, myths, marvels, outlandish crypto-species—what Carolus Linnaeus called "Paradoxa"—all the apocrypha that after the eighteenth century would no longer be allowed to account for historical causes. "Fabulation" would be the made-up word to speak for a made-up body of material, like miracle culture in the medieval annals. "The principal charge against the Enlighteners," writes White, "is that their militant rationalism short-circuited any impulse to entertain sympathetically and to judge tolerantly the many manifestations of the irrational that they found in the historical record, and especially records of the Middle Ages and remote antiquity."[8] Confronted with the irrational, the rational historians of Voltaire's generation, Linnaeus's generation, disenchanted the past. Turned it over, shook out the ghosts, the miracles, the witches and Wildmen. The excisions were rough, the removals brutal. Voltaire's *Philosophical Dictionary* ("The early annals of all our modern nations are no less fabulous; the prodigious and improbable things must sometimes be reported, but as proofs of human credulity") or David Hume's *Of Miracles* ("Miracles are a violation of the laws of nature") represent the milder end of this disenchantment. Thomas Woolston's *Six Discourses* was among the harsher criticisms, beginning with debunking Christian miracles and concluding with what was in his day the dangerous assertion that the resurrection was accomplished by disciples bribing the Roman soldiers and stealing the body.[9]

And yet, it is not the intention here to remap the texts of that Enlightenment disenchantment but rather to consider all that performance lost when the nonrational was disenchanted.

If history is what "stands in" for the past that was, witches abounded in early modern Europe and in its plays. Miracles abounded in medieval chronicles and medieval plays because they abounded in the medieval world, not as signs of unenlightened credulity but as potent shaping forces of the culture. Miracles explained faith; they were the "why" of why things happened. The excision of the nonrational cut out the period's accounting of their own world, and that accounting was an authentic part of the history. For example, the widespread "moral panic and violence" that tore through Europe at the start of the seventeenth century and all its attendant disorders—the Thirty Years' War, the Plague, the Little Ice Age, the crop failures, the economic collapse, the resulting displacements and impoverishments on a scale that seemed worldwide—also saw the most vigorous prosecution of witches. There were plenty of modern official causalities for what looked to be an apocalyptic global crisis, summarized by Peter Wilson in his history of the causes of the Thirty Years' War, but Wilson is also quick to note that this collapse had unofficial causes as well: "Many found these explanations wholly unsatisfactory, and preferred to attribute their misfortune to the supernatural or magical causes. Such beliefs were shared by many in power precipitating the European 'witch craze' that claimed its highest number of victims in the Empire between the 1580s and the 1630s."[10] That accounting of supernatural causes may be excluded as fable, dismissed as a pre-Enlightenment "craze," but the violence was real for the more than fifty thousand people who lost their lives to claims of witchcraft in that hysteria, and Shakespeare's staged encounter stands square in the middle of this violence. Some access to how witches worked in that world may be needed yet if we are to authentically story that world.

It's an odd thought, but whether miracles happened or not may be immaterial to the force they exerted in the medieval imaginary. Loaves and fishes may not work mathematically, but miracles are still what advanced Christianity through the long trough of its expansive centuries to become the social structure of Europe; miracles are an inexpungible part of that period's history, percolating down to its micro-histories of relics, shrines, and healing centers that grew up around such unexplainables. Consider one small quantum of the irrational that one finds ubiquitously in medieval annals: visions. We have, for example, some access to the effusively private world of a woman's life in a twelfth-century monastery because the "mystic" Hildegard of Bingen had "visions." She wrote because she needed to write down her visions, and the history that came to be preserved around her writing became the supporting apparatus of a thoroughly nonrational experience. Among her visions was the earliest morality play, her *Ordo Virtutum*, composed in 1151 (though "composed" implies more agency than she herself would acknowledge, who conceived of her work as a "visitation"). The play, she described, came to her; she "received" her visions—sometimes waking, sometimes asleep, often in prayer, and once in a sort of trance—in ways that are now all "fabulation."[11] If we dismiss her visions, we don't get her history. In this case, the modalities of both history and dramatic history share an originating impulse in a decidedly nonrational experience. Even our sense of the most basic kind of irrational experience—the "inspiration" that Hildegarde was prone to—has ceased to be the god-gift of the Muses, certainly as the Greeks understood it (*enthaiusistai*—to be full of gods), or how Shakespeare understood it, as he accused his rival poet (Marlowe?) three times in one sonnet, whose "spirits" or "affable ghost" elevated his work "above a mortal pitch."[12] "Inspiration" has ceased to be a divine receiving, as the poets, saints, and mystics understood it. Rather, now, "inspired" has become something rewritten ("inspired by real events") and less insipid than the host it was pilfered from. The idea that the beautiful forces of words, music, stories, and ideas existed first somewhat beyond and outside human agency ("Sing, through me, O Muse," poets once said), or the recognition of powerful forces at work in the world, like love as an abstract distraction, the sort visited upon poor Phaedra, or madness, or maenadic or Methodist ecstasy, sudden fits of possession, like were visited upon Dulcitius in the monastery pantry banging his pots in Hrotsvitha's play, or prophetic knowledge, prophetic dreams, all the altered states of inspiration in which visions, poems, or plays arrive and peck at the head of the poet (words, words, they always come like Hitchcock's *Birds*): that experience, I hope, has not entirely fallen into the camp of hallucinogens or temporary wine-induced mental disorders.

I suspect this exclusion of the irrational in so many of its historic forms has become part of our deep culture identity, which undervalues the unreasonable of the past. That is, we are shaped by an inheritance of an overproduced rational habit of mind that has excelled at mapping out the chimera and paradoxa of the world and the human psyche. It was, for good or ill, the legacy of the Enlightenment that disenchanted the world of the supernatural, and for good or ill, much of the historic past, including especially some of the best parts of performance's past; it was an excision that removed the most powerful elements of the performance culture and left its faith and fears, its abstracted forces, and its accounting for its world somewhat inaccessible. Our encounters have been rendered bereft by their loss. Making space for the nonrational affords a certain access to the *mentalités* of history, in this case, witchcraft and the disorders of the seventeenth century. Inventive productions, good scholarship, may curate the absence, may metaphorically invite us back to a world of witches and ghosts and possessed maenads, but we nonetheless remain imperfect outsiders, not initiates, plagued with the troubling post-Enlightenment thought: some kinds of knowledge used to come to us like the witches of *Macbeth*, and we may need witches to account for that knowledge still.

"Fabulation," as was undertaken in the eighteenth century, deported the nonrational, the supernatural, and represented a remapping of history, a process Hayden White saw as a certain kind of 'sciencing' of the discipline that narrowed its practice, its narratives, its voice, its liberties, especially the materials from which history would be built. History would now include circumscribed bodies of vetted and attested evidence, narratives, and causes, and excise others that were incapable of corroboration or rational explanation. "Fabulation" was the process of marking those narratives that would suffer an extradition out of history and back to the realm of myth, and that process de-rubricated much of the fabric of the medieval period, in the same way that the body of neoclassical tragedy represents a sort of textual fabulation where the gods have been cut out and ghost back like so many phantom limbs. The cutaway parts, the de-rubricated holes, remain legible texts of a century's compulsion to expulsion. Perhaps the greatest loss is how they accounted for their world, their own way, not ours, and that seems a vital part of history that performance history can still lean into.

Part of this new Enlightenment rigor is understandable in light of the discourse of the day. This disciplining of history not coincidentally occurred in the heyday of hoaxes, true enough, and that spate of new irrational material threw up a sharp assault on the agenda of reason. Spiritualism, what the eighteenth century termed "enthusiasm" with a nod back to the Greeks, and vision-based ecstatic religions—both as broad, popular movements and genres in the printing market, with hundreds of pamphlets purporting "narratives of spiritual visions" —abounded in the eighteenth century to such a degree that even the parodies of "enthusiasm" form a large canon.[13]

But once deported, the fabulation of ghosts and miracles and witches seems a deeper, more malicious act of mnemocide—a willful destruction of memory—because it erases the historic and generational retelling of nonrational experience, because it excludes and then *incredulates* the originating experience, disenfranchises the nonrational as a cultural voice. Fabulation became something of a hard border wall between the superstitious centuries and the "dare to think" modernists, defined as it is/was by the new attention to reason and a pronounced disenchantment with older mystery. "It is . . . notable how many histories of the period (from within it and subsequent to it) are invested in an account of progressive secularization as the narrative of modernity," succinctly writes Misty Anderson.[14] In the constructing of this divide (secular and religious), history as a discipline found itself squarely on the secular and scientific side, some have argued even triumphantly so.[15] Fabulation retired an older optic, like monocles, something they used to squint through but don't anymore. But that optic also afforded visibility to things we no longer see, the bubbles of the earth, and where does that deportation leave performance history that routinely relied on them? "As long as they identified the 'fabulous' with the 'unreal,'" writes Hayden White, they "failed to see that fabulation itself could serve as a means to the apprehension of the truth about reality."[16] I should be loath to lose everything that Euripides's *Medea* teaches us about citizenship in the classical world just because she comes with poisonous spells. And a dragon.

III: Miracle Culture (The Dramaturgy of Thaumaturgy)

In the thick of what has come to be called "The Age of Reason," we have a few marvelous windows into the formation of this hard divide, this extinction distinction, and the aggressive deportation of miracles and marvels.

Consider this imagined conversation from a tract published in 1770 in Paris that envisions a young scholar, a *philosophe* in the making, raised on reason and now visiting his old Catholic tutor (raised on faith, what the philosophes would call "fanaticism") debating a recent miracle that occurred (?) at the annual Procession of Corpus Christi when a paralytic girl prayed and was healed, threw off her crutches, and walked. It is a tutorial in Enlightenment thinking, from Louis Guidi's *Entretiens sur la religion entre un jeune incredible*, and the titular young man has some hard questions about the miracle: "How do I know if her paralysis was truly complete, if her recovery was sudden, and whether her health has sustained itself since? How do I know if the doctors followed the sick woman with attention, and if their capacity suffices to decide whether this sudden change was natural or supernatural? . . . How do I know that the witnesses you present to me are worthy of trust, that all of this is not but a show, that some spirit of partiality did not contrive this entire affair, that the vanity of the sick woman did not mislead her, or that the designs of interest did not lead to a maneuver that would perhaps make the most zealous partisans turn red if it was ever entirely unveiled?"[17] The young man clearly suspects fraud, and with good reason. The Age of Reason was also the age of frauds (think the Mechanical Turk, first displayed in 1770, or London's Cock Lane Ghost, 1762), and he may be right to ask all the skeptic's questions that a young historian of the period should ask. The conversation captures nicely that spirit of incredulity that fabulized miracles in an age of hoaxes. Sometimes the frauds of faith were so transparently fabricated in the first half of the eighteenth century that they were openly ridiculed in caricatures, essays, and novels and onstage. In England, writers and artists like William Hogarth, Joseph Addison, Samuel Foote, and Henry Fielding, in essay, play, and print, all took deep swipes at the ecstatic movement called "enthusiasm"—that excess of spirit that would people the world with ghosts, visions, and demons, the epitome of which were the early Methodists and Shaking Quakers.[18] Satires were present because there were frauds aplenty, reminding us that the great Age of Reason was also the great age of unreason. But for the man of faith (and he, too, is part of history) and all those faithful who witnessed the miracle (and they, too, are part of history), the young man's questions in no way undid the eventness of that miracle at the Corpus Christi. It had, for the Catholic faithful, still "happened," as it may have as well to the paralytic (?) girl who walked (?) away healed (?) and to those who gathered to witness and renew their faith. As a historical "truth," that also happened, and its happening was central to the performance and the endurance of Corpus Christi.

What might it mean to live in a world of faith and magic before such events were walled out, interrogated out? Documenting (and then staging) miracles had been part of the arsenal of the Church since its inception, and it would remain a potent force of faith. Staging miracles is at the core of medieval drama, because archiving miracles was at the core of Christianity, and that practice of celebrating the miraculous habituated the auditors to the naturalness of the supernatural. Making the miracle-making believable is no small accomplishment for performance. Suddenly alienating that experience, as the late eighteenth century did, could only have left a void in the psyche, and once emptied, once dislodged, that hole where faith once lived doesn't invalidate or empty the belief of the long centuries grounded in such experience. In the new rational accounting, the iconoclasm of miracles could still not wholly undo the miraculousness of the miracles.

Angela Haas, whom I credit for the above case study of the father and the philosophe, has shown how the critical apparatus around vetting the miraculous changed in the eighteenth century to accommodate the new rationalism but didn't go away. An apparatus of witness testimony and verification was erected around miraculous events, bolstered by clerical vetting. The requirements of miracles to be public, to be witnessed by clergy, were part of that accommodation and indeed part of an ongoing process of attestation that remains in place, at which we may scoff like sloppy journalists in an age of fake news, but the Vatican still employs these standards to vet miracles in, for example, the process of beatification (Pope John Paul II beatified more than 1,300 people and then was himself beatified). In spite of the accommodation to reason, miracles, by definition, remain irrational things that still happen. They may be, as David Hume famously noted, a violation of the laws of nature and thrive only among the most ignorant of nations, but they are still, to the faithful, happening.[19] At the close of that conversation between the young sceptic and the Catholic faithful, the man of faith sighs a world-weary sigh, because for him, if witnessing the miraculous, as he had, required a rational explanation, then it no longer had any validity as a miracle, which was for him—and more than a few others—the testimony of God's power to move out of nature. And if that was no longer possible, "From now on everything dissolves," sighed the old believer, "everything collapses, everything vanishes in society."[20]

IV: Vanishing, Banishing, and the Holes Left Behind

Given the theatre's long investment in miracle culture, the passing of it all is a poignant moment, if we can inhabit it authentically. That loss was part of a great reorientation that saw so much of the "fabulous" retired and so little of it replaced. But as is usually the practice, the erasure is never complete. There is always a poetry of knowing as well as a science of knowing. The incredulating of miracles and ghosts didn't wholly replace the belief in them. The science might sound like Freud's thoughts on the uncanny. Writing of ghosts: "Nowadays we no longer believe in them, we have surmounted these modes of thought; but we do not feel quite sure of our new beliefs, and the old ones still exist within us ready to seize upon any confirmation."[21] That is, ghosts are still ghosting in the psyche. The place where such belief once lived has been vacated but not emptied and remains somewhat haunted by its own absence, and the summoning up is closer to the skin. Here the poetry of knowing might get us closer to inhabiting that loss. What is a ghost but a thing that refuses to go away? Sometimes these cutaway portions of culture, like phantom limbs, beyond all reason, go on feeling still, insisting on their presence, lingering in preserves of reanimation. They refuse to be expunged from memory, and the theatre has colluded mightily in their preservation, accommodating the absent presence in a space somewhere between desire and reason, between metaphor and materiality—more than one, less than the other—but a presence summonable. The return is inevitable.

I've been considering largely eighteenth-century historiographical culture, as that is when the hard divisions were made, but as with any wall, there are tunnels. There are always tunnels. Consider the spectral turn of the late nineteenth century, with its popular infatuation with "spiritualism,'" seances, mediums, and ghost-rapping. Ibsen may be writing of metaphorical ghosts, but his contemporary William Yeats was hosting séances, and Strindberg, well, he wrote seriously and repeatedly about having sex with spirits.[22] The Rossetti household held séances for years, and among their circle of participants were the Brownings and John Ruskin (and if there ever was a thoroughly rational mind, it was Ruskin's).[23] The Victorian parlor séance was so widespread that even Prince Albert "communicated" to Queen Victoria through a medium. Before we reduce it all to fortified absinthe, we might recall how seriously these apparitions were taken, even to the point of impaneling government commissions, like the Cock Lane Ghost Commission of the eighteenth century, or, in the nineteenth century, the Seybert Commission of which the Shakespearean scholar H. H. Furness was a member, appointed to investigate the validity of "Spiritualism"—the communication with the dead.[24] They were, at the time, the subject of satire, true enough, but these were also, we should note, taken seriously enough to warrant government attention.

Doing ghosts, in all their myriad and period genres of ghosts, we might say, belonged to many generations, long after such supernatural were rationally retired, and each subsequent generation "spoke ghost" a little differently but carried an indebtedness to a past belief that had not wholly been surmounted. For the writers of the gothic revival of the nineteenth century, ghosts were an aesthetic requirement but different than those of the parlor séance. What makes plays like Conor McPherson's *The Weir*, or, for that matter, the annual adaptations of Dickens's *Christmas Carol*, is not a quotation of ghosts past but rather a ghosting of an older faith that hasn't entirely vacated the stage.

In the dramaturgy of thaumaturgy, ours may not be to ask *if* but *how* a particular historic generation did their ghosts. For Lessing, ghosts made perfect dramatic sense. They were, as classicists might say, good to think with, if one could keep them alive in the culture, as Voltaire could not. For us, at least in theatre scholarship since Marvin Carlson's enormously useful introduction of "ghosting," certain metaphorical presences are still available to enrich the memory in spaces, performances, even props, with prior lives, to which we should remain attuned, as niches attune us to the gone saints, but our generational application of "ghosting" is far thinner than even our early-twentieth-century antecedents.[25] Our ghosts have lost too much of their density, and we are in some need of a ghost to ghost through the modern metaphor of ghosting.

V: Sanctuary Cities of the Dead

Which brings me back to the idea of theatre as sanctuaries of the displaced.

For this, I begin anecdotally, because anecdotes have a way of recording both the laughter at the incredulity and the belief behind it. One can, for example, rationally argue against witches, as the Witchcraft Act of 1735 did, but throughout the eighteenth century, women and men continued to be accused and tried as witches, and the rational arguments in print did little to mitigate the hysteria in the village. For that, we need a villager.

This first anecdote is from Henry Fielding's novel *Tom Jones* (1749), one scene of which is set in the playhouse during a performance of *Hamlet*. The usual trope of introducing a provincial tourist to London, a villager uninitiated to the codes of London performance, breaks down utterly and documents its breakdown when the country schoolmaster Mr. Partridge watches David Garrick as Hamlet first encountering the ghost. The fear is so complete that Partridge, who cannot believe in ghosts, believes in *the fear of the ghost*, and hence, reluctantly, the ghost. "Persuade me to that, sir, if you can," Partridge begins cynically when first told of the ghost. He moves from his disbelief not in a leap to naivete but by degrees, and that is the process to track. His body responded first, his hands trembled, his knees started knocking. "I know it is but a play, and if it was really a ghost, it could do no one harm at such a distance . . . and yet, if I was frightened, I'm not the only person. If that little man there upon the stage is not frightened, I never saw any man frightened in my life . . . Oh! There he is again! No farther!" Later, upon reflection, the country schoolteacher allows his fear was real: "When I saw the little man so frightened himself, it was that which took hold of me" (book 16, chap. 5). Without ghosts somewhere still in the culture, the fear of one could never take hold.

Such tutorials in dismantling skepticism abound in this midcentury generation who were exiling their unexplainables and had nothing with which to replace them but kept the empty niche for their fears to occupy. Says Parson Adams in another Fielding novel, *Joseph Andrews*, "tho' I'm not afraid of Ghosts, I do not absolutely disbelieve them."[26] When belief and disbelief collided, it was frequently in the theatre. Performance, like Garrick's fear, revivified what had not wholly passed, still rattling about in the bones and closets of the disbelievers, knees knocking, in spite of their best reason.

A second anecdote reminds us of the power and persistence of the non-rational, even as it survives its own eradication. One of the more amusing critics of the English "craze" for ghosts related an experience that sought to aggressively expose, once and for all, the gullibility of those seduced by the supernatural, and it thoroughly failed, thankfully, I would add, because of the prior potency of the theatre, and that is exactly what I've been aspiring to recover, the theatre's role in preserving the "second naivete." "This nation," begins the anonymous contributor to a mid-eighteenth-century London newspaper the *Entertainer*, "has in all ages been more addicted to folly and superstition than any other what[so]ever," and so the writer sets about disabusing his readers with an account of visiting a friend whom he happened to interrupt while he was reading *Macbeth*—more precisely, at exactly the point in the play when Banquo's ghost appears a second time. The reader, deeply invested in the scene was so startled by the intrusion of his friend that he took his guest to be no less than Banquo's ghost itself and recited out loud at his appearance the very words of the play: "Avaunt and quit my sight! Let the earth hide thee!" And so on with the passage, all the while trembling, we are told, with terror. The visiting friend, startled by the curse but seeing that the fear he had inspired in his host was quite real, "recovered himself" and "accordingly vanished away by walking backwards to the door, as I had seen Mr. Ross do in that character; no sooner had I disappeared than I heard him say in a triumphant tone: 'now I am a man again.'" After a short while, the guest/ghost returned (as guest) but found his host still shaking, trembling with fear, and relating to his guest with broken speech the horror of the most recent visitation of Banquo's ghost, reminding us, like Mr. Partridge in the novel, bodies don't lie.

The anecdote attempted the debunking of a self-induced ghost story, but all parts of it were instead deeply indebted to the theatre as a homeland of spectral vision. It was Shakespeare who taught the host to expect the ghost and, once primed, to structure that fear in acts of known performance; it was Mr. Ross, the Drury Lane actor of Banquo's ghost, who taught the guest to enact the ghost that frightened the host. But all parties in the tale were not acting equally. The guest acted, staged his ghost entrance, but the host saw what the theatre had taught him to see, and it shook him to the bones. We may chuckle as Flaubert does, but we cannot say that what he saw was any less real to they who experienced the fear. And indeed, even afterward when the guest "endeavoured to disabuse him by relating the whole circumstance, but all in vain; it was impossible for him to believe me; and to this day he is fully convinced of the truth of the Apparition."[27]

The reader in his armchair had done exactly what all actors hope audiences can do: fully inhale the reality of the scene. He crossed over into the world of the play and in that world of witches and ghosts he saw what he saw, he trembled at the sight of it, and no one could tell him otherwise. I can admire the theatre's role in keeping ghosts alive.

Where Habermas, critiquing Adorno, saw the Enlightenment as a practice of disenchantment that led us out but not in ("The mythical world is not the homeland but rather the labyrinth from which one must escape"), the theatre insists on leading us back in. If the post-Enlightenment desolation of the banishing/vanishing, the profaning of the mythic, the disenchantment left elsewhere a landscape bereft of power, the theatre re-enchanted and remained a preserve of the irrational, a sanctuary city for the refugees of the Age of Reason.[28]

What I have come to (reluctantly) embrace in this meditation is the notion that the most meaningful parts of performance history remain its sangfroid comfort with the nonrational: of course birds drop food for pilgrims, and that is a comfort that its historians do not often share. What the extraordinary (even the outlandish) can tell us about the past is essential to the storying of the past. Such "archives in the fiction," to use Julie Crawford's apt phrase, open up aesthetic experiences in the world that are not otherwise available, and they are clearly not metaphorical uses of the nonrational but a violent thrust, over the wall, back into the labyrinth of a second naivete.[29]

VI: Until One Day a Bird Drops Something for You

And so finally (those blessed words, "in conclusion"), we cannot leave this elegy to the absented without checking back in on Gustave Flaubert's journey through Egypt and his journey out of Voltaire, over the wall. One troubling experience was how deeply he was "absorbed" by the power of some trance-dancing he watched, which was a start toward his unsettling. The dances he describes first as fraud: "Just the evening before, we had been in a monastery of dervishes where we saw one fall into convulsions from shouting 'Allah!' These are very fine sights, which would have brought many a good laugh from M. de Voltaire. Imagine his remarks about the poor old human mind! About fanaticism! Superstition! None of it made me laugh in the slightest, and it is all too absorbing to be *appalling.*"[30] As all good travel writing reveals, the real journey is psychic. Flaubert is being inducted into the metaphysics of "beyondness," an ancient state of ecstatic dancing that predated the festival of Dionysus, whirling still, full of gods, in Cairo, and Flaubert is not laughing anymore. The next day he watched these same dervishes reenact a miracle by laying their bodies down to form a plank road while a sheik on horseback "walked slowly over the bodies of more than two hundred men lying flat on the ground . . . no one was hurt."[31]

Toward the close of his Egyptian travel, Flaubert experienced one last inexplicable encounter that troubled his mind even more. Like Banquo and Macbeth, Flaubert met a shaman on the Nile who told his future. Many parts of it surprised him, as they were or came to be true. Flaubert must relate this in a letter to Louis Bouilhet as he did the pilgrim-feeding birds of Sheik Sa'id, and he begins of course by jeering at the precision of the fraud. He was told a bag of mail just arrived and awaited his company in Assuan, and for travelers who had been up the Nile and in the desert, this was welcome news. How he knew mail waited for them, he reasoned, well, such things the captain of the boat might have known, but then the shaman added that in all that bundle of foreign mail, all hail, there would be no letters for him. Flaubert chuckled as he wrote to his friend, until some days later he arrived in Assuan and there was indeed a large bag of mail for his company just delivered, and none of it for him, no letters, and now Flaubert had no explanation for it. The impulse to explain was the first retreat: "Several things were true of what he had told me, but Joseph could have told them to him after learning them from my servant." Still, some things remained unexplained: "At Assuan there is an enormous packet, but nothing for me . . . I took that very hard." In that small pause of wonder and uncertainty, I will leave Flaubert and this meditation. As Habermas would note, "the modern fully rationalized world is only seemingly disenchanted."[32]

Notes

Chapter epigraph. G. E. Lessing, *Hamburg Dramaturgy*, in *Selected Prose Works of G. E. Lessing*, trans. E. C. Beasley and Helen Zimmern (London: George Bell, 1885), 261–63.

Chapter epigraph. Theodor Adorno and Max Horkheimer, *Dialectic of Enlightenment*, trans. John Cumming (London: Verso, 1979), 215.

1. G. Flaubert to Louis Bouilhet, March 13, 1850, *Flaubert in Egypt*, trans. Frances Steegmuller (New York: Penguin, 1972).
2. This lovely but complex term warrants Ricoeur's own context: "In every way, something has been lost, irremediably lost: immediacy of belief. But if we can no longer live the

great symbolisms of the sacred in accordance with the original belief in them, we can, we modern men, aim at a second naiveté in and through criticism." See Emerson Buchanan, trans., *The Symbolism of Evil* (New York: Harper and Row, 1967), 352.

3. It has been the argument of Stephen Greenblatt, in "Shakespeare and Cultural Traditions," and of other authors that Reginald Scot's more benign treatment, *The Discoverie of Witchcraft* (1584), burned at the king's orders, may have survived to influence Shakespeare. That quarrel of which witch is immaterial here to the presence of witches. See Stephen Greenblatt, *Shakespeare Bewitched*, ed. Tetsuo Kishi, Roger Pringle, and Stanley Wells (Newark: University of Delaware Press, 1994), 17–42.
4. Lessing's line here is quite clear: "This difference arose beyond question out of the different points of view from which the two poets regarded ghosts. Voltaire looked upon the reappearance of the dead man as a miracle, Shakespeare as quite a natural occurrence." See G. E. Lessing, *Hamburg Dramaturgy*, in *Selected Prose Works of G. E. Lessing*, trans. E. C. Beasley and Helen Zimmern (London: George Bell, 1885), 261–63.
5. King James, *Daemonogie*, preface ("To the Reader"), 1597; Christopher St. John, trans., *The Plays of Rothsvitha* (London: Chatto and Windus, 1923), 29.
6. Hayden White, "The Irrational and the Problem of Historical Knowledge in the Enlightenment," in *Studies in Eighteenth-Century Culture: Rationalism in the Eighteenth Century*, ed. Harold E. Pagliaro (Cleveland, OH: Press of Case Western Reserve University, 1972), 303–21, 313. The argument was built around the loss of the irrational as a shaping force in eighteenth-century history.
7. The example is from Gabriel García Márquez, *Of Love and other Demons*, trans. Edith Grossman (New York: Vintage, 1995), 4.
8. White, "The Irrational and the Problem of Historical Knowledge in the Enlightenment," 304.
9. Voltaire, "History," Project Gutenberg's *Voltaire's Philosophical Dictionary* (Project Gutenberg, 2006), 158; David Hume, *An Enquiry Concerning Human Understanding* (London, 1748). For an overview of the seventeenth and eighteenth centuries' vexed relationship with miracles, from Sir Robert Boyle to H. E. G. Paulus's biography of the historical Jesus, see Colin Brown, "Issues in the History of the Debates on Miracles," in *The Cambridge Companion to Miracles*, ed. Graham Twelftree (Cambridge: Cambridge University Press, 2011), 273–90.
10. Peter Wilson, "The Causes of the Thirty Years War, 1618–1648," in *English Historical Review*, vol. 123:502 (Oxford: Oxford University Press, 2008), 554–86, 573. For a more detailed discussion of witchcraft in the Thirty Years' War, see Wolfgang Behringer, *Witchcraft Persecutions in Bavaria* (New York: Cambridge University Press, 1997).
11. Even her modern editors consider her a "mystic"; *The Journal of Hildegard of Bingen*, ed. Barbara Lachman (New York: Bell Tower, 1993), 4–5. Hrotsvitha, as well, writes of her own inspiration as a "divine gift"; see *The Plays of Rosvitha* (1923), preface, xxix.
12. William Shakespeare, Sonnet 86 ("Was it the proud full sail of his great verse . . .")
13. For the published accounts of visions, see Ann Kirschner, "'Tending to Edify, Astonish, and Instruct': Published Narratives of Spiritual Dreams and Visions in the Early Republic," in *Early American Studies*, vol. 1:1 (University of Pennsylvania Press, 2003), 198–229. For Spiritualism in the eighteenth century, including its many, many parodies in print, caricature, and onstage, see Misty Anderson, *Imagining Methodism in Eighteenth-*

Century Britain, Enthusiasm, Belief and the Borders of the Self (Baltimore: Johns Hopkins University Press, 2012).

14. Anderson, *Imagining Methodism in Eighteenth-Century Britain, Enthusiasm, Belief and the Borders of the Self*, 15.
15. This process is best charted in Charles Taylor, *A Secular Age* (Cambridge, MA: Harvard University Press, 2007). For "the triumphalist history of the secular," see Talal Asad, *Formations of the Secular: Christianity, Islam, Modernity* (Palo Alto, CA: Stanford University Press, 2003), 25.
16. Hayden White, "The Irrational and the Problem of Historical Knowledge in the Enlightenment," in *Irrationalism in the Eighteenth Century*, ed. Harold E. Pagliaro (Cleveland, OH: Case Western Reserve University Press, 1972), 303–22, 313.
17. I am indebted here to Angela Haas, trans., "Miracles on Trial: Wonders and Their Witnesses in Eighteenth Century France," in *Journal of the Western Society for French History* 38 (Ann Arbor: Michigan Publishing, 2010): 111–28.
18. Hogarth's *Enthusiasm Delineated* ("A Medley"), 1762; Addison, *Spectator* (Essay 110, July 6, 1711), has a useful étude on believing the unbelievable; see Anderson, *Imagining Methodism*, particularly chapter 4, "Actors and Ghosts," for the English satire. Haas has traced the satire on the stage in France of the miracle movement.
19. David Hume, *An Enquiry Concerning Human Understanding*. On the violation of nature, 114; existing for the most ignorant, 94.
20. Guidi, *Entretiens*, as translated by Haas, in "Miracles on Trial," 111–12.
21. Sigmund Freud, "On the Uncanny," in *The Standard Edition of the Complete Psychological Works of Sigmund Freud*, ed. and trans. James Strachey, vol. 17, 1917–1919 (London: Hogarth, 1953–1974): 247–48.
22. For useful applications of "Spectrality," see Karl Bell, "'Civic Spirits?' Ghost Lore and Civic Narratives in Nineteenth-Century Portsmouth," in *Journal of the Social History Society* 11 (London: Routledge, 2014), 51–68; Avery Gordon, *Ghostly Matters: Haunting and the Sociological Imagination* (Minneapolis: University of Minnesota Press, 1997). Strindberg writes in his "Occult Diary," "Harriot and I have, periodically, lived together telepathically, and have 'enjoyed' each other from a distance . . ."; August Strindberg, *From an Occult Diary*, ed. Torsten Eklunds (London: Secker and Warburg, 1965), 22.
23. Rossetti's brother, William Michael Rossetti, kept a séance diary of the events. For more on Rossetti's use of the dead, see Andrew Stauffer, "Speaking with the Dead, the Séance Dairy of William Michael Rossetti, 1865–68," in *Journal of Pre-Raphaelite Studies* 24 (Toronto, 2015): 35–43.
24. I am indebted here to Lezlie Cross for her work on Furness and the Commission. See Cross, "The Linguistic Animation of an American Yorick," in *Performing Objects and Theatrical Things*, ed. Marlis Schweitzer and Joanne Zerdy (London: Palgrave Macmillan, 2014), 70–73.
25. Marvin Carlson, *The Haunted Stage: The Theatre as Memory Machine* (Ann Arbor: University of Michigan Press, 2001).
26. Henry Fielding, *Tom Jones*, book 16, chapter 5; Fielding, *Joseph Andrews*, book 3, chapter 2. Henry Fielding, *Tom Jones* (New York: Penguin, 1994); Henry Fielding *Joseph Andrews*, ed. Adam Potkay (New York: Pearson, 2008).
27. *Entertainer*, London, November 12, 1754.

28. Jürgen Habermas, "The Entwinement of Myth and Enlightenment: Re-reading Dialectic of Enlightenment," in *New German Critique* 26 (1982): 12–30. Reprint (1996): 16.
29. Julie Crawford, *Marvelous Protestantism: Monstrous Births in Post-Reformation England* (Baltimore, MD: Johns Hopkins University Press, 2005).
30. *Flaubert in Egypt*, 94.
31. *Flaubert in Egypt*, 94.
32. Habermas, *The Entwinement of Myth and Enlightenment*, 1996, 110.

Caricatured, Marginalized, and Erased

African American Artists and Philadelphia's Negro Unit of the FTP, 1936–1939

—JONATHAN SHANDELL

In July 1937, Federal Theatre Project (FTP) leadership engineered what they hoped would be a distinct course correction for the project's Negro Unit in Philadelphia. The Unit's two earlier productions—variety shows titled *Truckin' Along* and *So What?*, mounted at the Drexel Hill Playhouse, in a suburb ten miles west of the city—had not lived up to the ambitions of the FTP. As Arthur R. Jarvis recounts, these performances were "crowd-pleasing effort[s] that made effective use of African-American talent" but amounted to little more than "buffoonery and low comedy"[1] that hearkened back to the legacy of the minstrel stage. In contrast, Negro Units in other cities were conducting substantive theatrical experiments by developing new dramas by African American writers (such as Frank Wilson's *Walk Together, Chillun* in New York, Theodore Ward's *Big White Fog* in Chicago, and Theodore Browne's *Natural Man* in Seattle) or by reviving classical plays with African American casts (New York's "voodoo *Macbeth*" being the most familiar example). So Hallie Flanagan—the FTP's idealistic national director—took action. She brought James Light, preeminent stage director and alumnus of the groundbreaking Provincetown Players, from New York to Philadelphia to be the Unit's new leader.

White leadership for African American companies was nothing new for the FTP's Negro Units. Actor John Houseman had helped led the New York Unit to prominence,[2] as did husband-and-wife team Burton and Florence James in Seattle. Elsewhere, white-led Negro "little theatres" had flourished in Chicago and Cleveland. Those precedents, along with Light's own artistic history, positioned the new director as a kind of "white savior" figure for African American theatre in Philadelphia. Light's stature as a director had been cemented through several high-profile collaborations with African American actors. He had directed Eugene O'Neill's race drama *All God's Chillun Got Wings*, a 1924 revival of *The Emperor Jones*, and a short-lived 1931 London engagement of *The Hairy Ape*—all starring Paul Robeson. These and other productions of spoken dramas with Black actors represented a challenge to the era's status quo of minstrel-derived stereotyping and established the young director as an integrationist trailblazer for the stage. Cheryl Black's study of Light's interracial collaborations across two decades—while emphasizing how this director's work with Black actors remained bound by "a theatre grounded in Eurocentric cultural experience"—demonstrates how this white artist's "pioneering efforts in interracial theatrical collaborations" helped foster a more "diverse and democratic" theatre for the United States.[3]

What would this change of leadership in Philadelphia portend for the artistic practice of the city's Black actors, playwrights, designers, and musicians? What would it mean for audiences and for the future of African American theatre? In this essay, I assess the three productions staged in Philadelphia under Light's directorship—*Jericho* by H. L. Fishel (1937), a new adaptation of Arthur Arent's "Living Newspaper" play *One-Third of a Nation* (1938), and the dance-drama *Prelude to Swing* (1939; staged and choreographed by Malvena Fried, with text by Carleton Moss). These three projects represented a distinct shift away from the "buffoonery and low comedy" that had preceded them. Even so, surviving evidence captures the persistence of racial inequities and a pervasive white chauvinism—typical of the wider American theatrical culture of the era—that compromised those efforts. These projects are case studies in how paternalistic white leadership (even if well-intentioned) has historically denigrated, excluded, or erased the African American creative praxis that it ostensibly seeks to serve. Furthermore, the same conditions that hampered the work of the Philadelphia Negro Unit persist in the archive, obscuring the voices and experiences of African American artists from our historiographical view today. While documentary records offer a few enticing glimpses of African American performance artistry, the archive mostly reflects (both in what it preserves and what is absent from it) how Black voices were caricatured, marginalized, and erased by the FTP in Philadelphia.

When Light arrived in Philadelphia in 1937, local conditions favored his mission to bolster African American cultural production and promote antiracist messages through the stage. Matthew J. Countryman writes: "During the second half of the 1930s, Philadelphia was a hotbed of left-wing antiracist activism."[4] Stanley Keith Arnold's analysis of the period is somewhat more sanguine: "The City of Brotherly Love has not always lived up to its name. . . . Yet its history also includes those who challenged accepted prejudices and sought to bridge these chasms of ignorance and hatred." The "interracial civil rights movement that emerged in the 1930s"[5] in Philadelphia arose in response to the influx of Southern migrants in the first decades of the twentieth century. The swelling of the city's Black population placed new demands on residential, educational, and civic resources and led to violent backlash from reactionary white residents. Growing tensions inspired activist groups, particularly from progressive Quaker and Christian religious communities, to organize and campaign for interracial harmony and understanding. Within such a civic landscape, a local Negro Unit could potently contribute to public conversations and might readily find an audience eager for such exploration. Philadelphia's historic identity as the "birthplace of America" and its proximity to New York could only amplify the impact of any worthy productions developed under Light's leadership.

But as with all the Negro Units of the FTP, racial politics were fraught. Rena Fraden describes the work of the Negro Units as "deeply circumscribed by history, tradition, and the dominant hegemony" of the United States. Though the FTP pursued a "noble aim" of fostering "an autonomous race theatre," the activities of local groups were frequently compromised by a thicket of "struggles and contestations . . . complications and contradictions"[6]—as hopes for authentic African American artistic expression clashed against a white federal bureaucracy and a trenchantly racist theatrical culture. Examining the three productions mounted under Light's directorship between 1937 and 1939, it becomes clear that dominant hegemony mostly prevailed over the progressive ambitions of advancing an autonomous race theatre. The Philadelphia Negro Unit's work helped create some new and welcomed opportunities for African American creative expression through performance but did so through problematic vehicles that mostly muted or distorted African American voices.

Jericho

Light's first project as leader of the Philadelphia FTP was to direct H. L. Fishel's play *Jericho* at the Walnut Street Theatre in the fall of 1937. This production transplanted the Unit's activities from its previously out-of-the-way suburban venue to an historic Center City playhouse and shifted its repertoire from vaudeville-style review to spoken drama. In advance of the opening, W. J. Hagerty (the

FTP's regional director for Pennsylvania) declared: "In producing *Jericho*, the first step is being taken towards establishing an important Negro theatre in this city. . . . Other fine plays will come if this effort succeeds."[7] As a transitional "first step" toward more ambitious and serious expression, *Jericho* offered African American performers of Philadelphia a much-needed opportunity for dramatic acting. There's no clear indication how or why Light chose this script to inaugurate his Philadelphia leadership, and its selection is curious in light of mixed assessments given by the FTP's play bureau. Some FTP play readers found it to be a worthy drama, animated by "a vital Negro psychology," "vividly indigenous dramatic and realistic motives," and an "authenticity of Negro dialect." Other evaluations are more circumspect: "The characters come through as either unscrupulous or ignorant clowns," one reader observed. "There is some coarseness and vulgarity of expression which does not approximate realism," complains another. "People do not talk like that in real life. But there is nothing in this play to make it seem authentic." One pointed report dismisses *Jericho* as a play geared toward "white audiences who like Negroes conceived in the image of white authors."[8]

These reports (completed prior to the Philadelphia production and preserved in the FTP's play file) do not identify the racial background of the reviewers; however, African Americans were mostly absent from administrative positions in the WPA's sprawling bureaucracy. Thus it seems likely that the evaluation of *Jericho* included no assessments of the play from African Americans. Surviving details about its author are scarce. H. L. Fishel worked as a play reader for the FTP at the time and has no other credits as a playwright to his name. No evidence survives to document how he came to write *Jericho* or what personal knowledge this author had (if any) about the play's setting or subject matter. Thus it seems possible, even probable, that the process that brought *Jericho* to the stage in Philadelphia was one that at every stage of development took African Americans for granted rather than into account.

Some of Light's own thoughts on *Jericho* survive in the director's report he composed for the FTP's production file. Here the director addresses some of the technical challenges posed by a script that contains several "quick changes and a large number of scenes" and that "alternates between comedy and melodrama." At times, Light betrays racial condescension in his reflections. He writes about the need for casting African American performers "who have the capacity of portraying spiritual exaltation" and the value in "tak[ing] advantage of the natural sense of comedy which the Negro actor has." At other moments, the director shows awareness of the danger that awaits if the staging "pushes the comedy . . . too far" or overemphasizes "the purely melodramatic effect of some scenes," which would risk alienating "the colored members of [the] audience against the production." Despite such concerns and the FTP's own skeptical evaluations, the FTP eagerly promoted *Jericho* to Philadelphia audiences as "A DISTINCT DRAMATIC ACHIEVEMENT" and "A beautiful story. . . . Containing a deep human interest that will linger long in your heart."[9]

The manuscript of *Jericho* leaves a much different impression, one that validates the more unflattering critiques cited above. The title character Jericho is a "physically huge—and very black"[10] son of a Southern pastor. When a dance hall opens in their town, the Pastor sends Jericho to deliver a message to the Northerners who run it: "Let em know dat dis communiteh doan want none uh dem! Run dose sinnuhs back to hell" (I, i, 8). Jericho enters the dance hall to denounce it to its owners as an un-Christian enterprise but allows himself to be seduced by a temptress named Delilah, earning his father's angry curses. The dance hall's manager conspires with Delilah to bring the muscular Jericho to New York, to exploit his size and strength as a prize fighter. The action resumes "some years later" (II, i, 1) in New York, in an apartment shared by Jericho and Delilah. At the peak of Jericho's successful boxing career, Delilah (whose interest in Jericho is purely financial) falls for the notorious Harlem gambler Randall Johnson. On the eve of a big bout, Randall convinces Delilah to try to persuade the heavily favored Jericho to throw the fight. She prevails on Jericho temporarily, but a surprise visit from an old friend reminds the boxer of his small-town roots, his religious upbringing, and his estranged father and inspires him to fight to win. After his victory, Delilah confronts Jericho as a "double crossin' bastard," (III, i, 4) and tells him, "Yuh don' think ah lived wid yuh 'cause ah loved yuh, did yuh? It was for bucks, money—all ah could git fum yuh" (III, i, 5). Delilah confesses her affair with Randall, who has meanwhile crept into the apartment with a pistol. They attempt to rob Jericho of his fight winnings, and a scuffle ensues in which Jericho seizes the gun and shoots Randall. Jericho flees home to hide, until the Pastor convinces his son to surrender to authorities and repent for his sins. Though Delilah finds him and threatens to blackmail him unless he returns to the ring to throw another fight, in a final revelation, Jericho declares: "Jesus, mah paws right. Ah sees dat now. Ah got to do like he say—an try to get right." As he exits with his father to surrender for murder, Delilah "looks after them incredulously," ending the play by exclaiming, "Well, I'll be damned" (III, ii, 17).

Caricatures, stilted Negro dialect, and racial tropes of the era abound in *Jericho*. The play is replete with racist clichés: a raucous revivalist church meeting, a smoky dance hall, smooth-talking criminals, a promiscuous Jezebel, a credulous Black brute, and an assortment of one-dimensional supporting characters. Even so, in line with some of the FTP's own positive evaluations, one reviewer found *Jericho* in its 1937 production at the Walnut Street Theater to be a work of "Slow-Moving Sincerity . . . impressive and deeply sincere . . . an exciting drama with many amusing touches."[11] Others were more skeptical. The *Evening Public Ledger* bemoaned the play's "much-too-naive thesis" that "the Negro peasant is better off in the Cotton Belt" and scoffed at its stilted portrayal of "gangsters, fight-fixers, and hotcha mammas." Amid these differing responses to the play, Philadelphia's critics consistently celebrated the performances of *Jericho*'s ensemble cast. "Casco Alston, in his interpretation of the title role, is worth the effort of the entire production," notes the *Daily News*, predicting future stardom for "an actor who, with the return of prosperity to the show business, will find his name in lights. . . . The only thing lacking toward a successful evening was a good play."[12] Pearl Gaines as Delilah and John Butler as the pastor also received frequent mention and commendation from reviewers.

Perhaps the most telling response to *Jericho* is the verdict of the *Philadelphia Tribune*, the city's largest African American daily newspaper. The review (credited to "T. A. S.") is the only response from an African American critic I found in my research, and it offers a window into the complexity of the moment for Philadelphia's Black artists and audiences. In one sense, this reviewer (aligning with other critics and a few of the FTP's own play readers) is dismissive of the play as a drama built on "weak theme" and a simplistic moral about "the evils of the 'flesh and the devil' and the pitfalls of big-city life." And yet, curiously, this same review draws real encouragement from this production as one that "justifies the dream of Mr. William Haggerty's [*sic*] for the innovation of an authentic Negro theatre in this city." The critic's cynicism and resignation about the play give way to a curious note of optimism about what the production achieved: "The somewhat weak theme of 'Jericho' is totally lifted out of the borderlands of triteness by the excellent performances of its players and the capable production of the play. Here is another instance where stellar acting on the part of the whole cast transmutes a slightly insignificant theme into a memorable occasion."

African American critics and audiences of the era often looked to Black actors not to embody their material faithfully but rather to *transmute* it: to infuse their roles with a dignity and complexity conspicuously lacking from an author's original vision. That the FTP had shifted its Philadelphia activities toward material that enabled such transmutation, supported those efforts with experienced direction, and placed the results on a prestigious Center City stage represented "a highly recognizable advance from the position of its former efforts" in low-brow buffoonery.[13] This was a vital (though conspicuously imperfect) step toward a more vibrant future for Black theatre in Philadelphia.

And while all published reviews of *Jericho* include praise for the cast, this review's particular language offers a different kind of emphasis on the company's efforts to elevate their characters beyond stereotypes. Casco Alston was "inimitable in the role of the hick prizefighter"; Pearl Gaines was "particularly convincing in the guise of the night club siren. . . . She was dynamic"; John Thomas Butler was "distinguished . . . stately . . . at all times authentic" in his interpretation of the southern pastor; Norman Johnson (as dance hall owner Horace Williams) showed "calm assurance and ease indicative of the mature actor."[14] This review's focus on the artistry of *Jericho*'s actors puts into relief what is missing from the historical record (at least, as I could unearth it). Were these professional performers? Were they experienced amateurs or neophytes? What past credits did they bring to their roles? What training did they have? There are no biographies in the printed program, and I could find no other information about these artists in the FTP's files nor in other archives or databases. How did they build their roles, in collaboration (and perhaps in tension) with Light's direction? The incomplete evidence of performance praxis strongly suggests that Philadelphia had the necessary talent to support the serious dramatic African American theatre that Light, Hagerty, and Flanagan were hoping to foster. However, *Jericho* turned out to be the only play written for a Black cast performed by the FTP in the city, though Light's work with local African American performers would continue.

One-Third of a Nation in Philadelphia

"Living Newspaper" plays were a signature achievement for the FTP. Blending realistic and nonrealistic narrative theatrical techniques, these inventive dramas used the stage to dramatize pressing social concerns and provoke civic debate. As Hallie Flanagan summarizes: "The Living Newspapers seek to dramatize a new struggle—the search of the average American today for knowledge about his country and his world; to dramatize his struggle to turn the great natural and economic and social forces of our time toward a better life for more people."[15] Flanagan's lofty, universalizing rhetoric captures the ambitions behind the genre but masks a blind spot in how Living Newspapers documented the life of the nation. According to Paul Nadler, "One issue . . . that was pointedly *not* addressed publicly by the living newspaper was the status of African Americans."[16]

Yet there was one *partial* exception to this pattern: *One-Third of a Nation*, by Arthur Arent. Unlike others developed and staged by the FTP, this Living Newspaper play takes a small step toward addressing social and economic struggles that uniquely impacted African Americans during the Great Depression. *One-Third of a Nation* debuted in New York City in January 1938 and became "probably the best known and most memorable production of the Federal Theatre."[17] The sprawling drama documents housing conditions in New York and explores the roots of those conditions within more than a century of land speculation and housing laws. The play sparked criticisms from the US Congress over its critiques of government policies and its promotion of redistributive measures to address injustices in the housing sector. The drama includes one scene depicting African American characters, set in a Harlem "hot bed" rooming house. As two tenants argue over whose turn it is to sleep in the bed they share, they give voice to grievances arising out of their situation: "What kind of thing I gotta put up with anyhow? In the bed, outa the bed! First me, then you, then that other fellow. What kind of thing is this anyhow! . . . Landlady tell me white folks live here by thirty dollars for this flat. Black ones move in—forty-five!"[18] The two men soon resolve to unite with other tenants and act collectively for the betterment of all: "Like this. . . . You go to the landlord and say: If you don't stop gougin' us . . . you know what we're goin' to do? YOU KNOW WHAT? We ain't gonna pay no rent!" (2–2C-4). The depiction (and implicit endorsement) of organized civil defiance by African American tenants against property owners fit within the overriding left-wing sensibility of *One-Third of a Nation*: a political perspective that inspired a backlash against the FTP by Congress. That this play included a brief vision of working-class African American resistance against capitalist exploitation inflicted by wealthy white residents as part of a larger critique of housing conditions raised the stakes even higher.

The popularity of the New York production of *One-Third of a Nation* inspired other regional FTP units to create their own adaptations of the script based on local histories and conditions. In March 1938, Pennsylvania's regional director Herbert Humphreys commissioned writer Edward Malle to revise the drama for presentation in Philadelphia. Malle "worked unceasingly for approximately three months obtaining the research needed for the adaptation of the play for Philadelphia." Collaborating with Ben Russak and Harold Berman of the FTP's National Play Bureau, Malle stuck as carefully as possible to Arent's original script: "We took the original New York script scene by scene and selected the best Philadelphia parallel, verbatim when possible and creating when necessary."[19] The new adaptation ranges from the earliest history of settlement and land apportionment of Philadelphia (starting with William Penn's original plan for the city) through contemporary discussions about overcrowding, the spread of diseases, fire hazards, and greedy slumlords. In keeping with the sprawling nature of the genre and the employment goals of the FTP as a relief program, this new version of *One-Third of a Nation* was massive in scale:

encompassing a cast of 67 performers enacting more than 160 distinct speaking roles over 21 different scenes and spanning more than 250 years of the city's history.

Arent's original drama uses a fatal 1924 fire at a Brooklyn tenement building as the inciting incident that sparks its investigation of housing problems. "What started this fire? Why did it spread so quickly? Why was the death toll so high?"[20] The search for answers leads the play's events through more than a century of New York history. The Philadelphia equivalent that Malle found for this incident was a building collapse on South Fifteenth Street, occurring on December 19, 1936, that killed seven and injured dozens more. The deadly incident had dominated local news coverage just two years earlier. According to Marcus Anthony Hunter, this collapse "became the catalyst for an unprecedented period of housing reform and construction in Philadelphia."[21] Thus it made for an ideal hook for the adaptation—its circumstances and impact still strong in the city's memory. The incident (which had occurred less than a mile from the Walnut Street Theatre) also created the opportunity to begin the production with a spectacular scenic effect: the orchestrated onstage collapse of replicas of two bandbox tenement buildings. This moment of stage magic, which was much remarked upon during the Philadelphia run of *One-Third of a Nation*, did not initially go as planned on the production's opening night of October 17, 1938. At the last instant, engineers discovered that the aging stage at the Walnut Street Theatre lacked sufficient support for the impact of falling scenic debris. For the first showing, the building collapse was "indicated by rumbles, screams, and alarms," with the opening curtain revealing the damage already having taken place.[22] The stage was reinforced that night for subsequent performances.

That this particular housing catastrophe had unfolded in the Seventh Ward —the historic epicenter of Black life in the city—did not scare Malle and his partners away from mining its dramatic value. This was the historic neighborhood famously chronicled by W. E. B. Du Bois in *The Philadelphia Negro* at the end of the nineteenth century. But conditions had deteriorated dramatically in the decades following Du Bois's study of the Seventh Ward as a middle-class African American community, due to an influx of poor migrants, severe overcrowding fueled by residential segregation, and a massive under-resourcing of local housing and infrastructure. The neighborhood had become a slum, nicknamed "Hell's Half Acre." Malle's script sets the scene: "As the curtain rises, a SMALL NEGRO GIRL is seen,"[23] followed soon by several more African Americans in a tableau of quotidian neighborhood life in the Seventh Ward. A disembodied Loudspeaker voice (which serves as a narrator of sorts for the entire play) announces, "December 1936. This might be 517 South Fifteenth Street,

Philadelphia. It might be the 1200 block on South Harmony Street, or the 1800 block on Shamokin Street." Soon "there is a crash," and a crowd that "is largely colored" (1-1-2) finds itself engulfed in loud rumbling noises, rubble, and dust, and then screams, sirens, and policemen. After a blackout, the Loudspeaker returns to announce, "Six persons lost their lives, fourteen injured when those houses on South Fifteenth Street collapsed.... What caused these houses to fall? Why did they collapse like a house of cards?" (1-1-3).[24]

The play continues with an on-site investigation in progress by a Solicitor—who first interviews a woman pulled uninjured from the rubble named Mrs. Brown, before also questioning a Building Inspector, a Fire Engineer, the Mayor, a Housing and Sanitation Officer, the Landlord of the property, a Lessee, the Realty Broker, and the President of the Trust Company in a search for root causes. The Mayor vows to punish those responsible; a Judge sentences the Landlord to two years in prison and orders the Trust Company to compensate injured victims. "What about me?" Mrs. Brown pleads. "My two children are dead." The president of the Trust Company responds: "You cannot blame us.... You'll have to go back into history and blame whatever it was that made Philadelphia real-estate sound and profitable speculation" (1-2-10). The action soon whisks back to the year 1681, to a scene between King Charles II of England and William Penn. With that leap back in time, the play sidesteps direct engagement with the present realities of life in the Seventh District, and its subsequent action leaves the grieving Black mother unrequited for her loss. Though Malle found a convenient dramatic hook, his adaptation of *One-Third of a Nation* never reckons directly with the role that systemic economic racism (past or present) played in the Thirteenth Street disaster.

Once that first scene is complete, no other African American characters occupy the stage for the rest of the first act, thus erasing Black Philadelphians from a survey of centuries of local housing problems. One brief scene in act 2 returns to "Hell's Half Acre"—an episode with two boarders in a rooming house that mirrors almost exactly the Harlem tenement scene from the original play described above. As the two men, who share a boardinghouse bed, resolve together to withhold their rent and press for better living conditions, the play leaps next to a dramatization of several rent strikes unfolding throughout Philadelphia in 1937. None of these brief scenes are set in the Seventh Ward, and none (according to the script) include African American characters. After an announcement by the Loudspeaker voice that some of the city's tenant strikes resulted in rent reductions and improvements to living conditions, the action transports us once more—in the fluid, episodic manner that typified the Living Newspaper dramas—to a separate discussion of zoning policy and housing supplies. Thus, once again, the realities of Black residential life in Philadelphia vanish quickly from view. Nowhere does Malle's version of *One-Third of a Nation* consider how historic political and economic injustice created the specific local conditions against which the two African American boardinghouse residents vow to protest.

Following Arent's original, Malle's adaptation of *One-Third of a Nation* concludes with its protagonist (an everyman-type hero called "Little Man") and his wife, Mrs. Buttonkooper, exhorting an angry chorus of residents to join together and "holler. And we're going to keep on hollering. . . . They'll hear us all right if we do it together." The stage fills with angry Philadelphians, who join Mrs. Buttonkooper's anguished cries: "CAN YOU HEAR ME—YOU IN WASHINGTON OR HARRISBURG OR WHEREVER YOU ARE! GIVE ME A DECENT PLACE TO LIVE IN! GIVE ME A HOME!" (2-5-8-9). Stage directions describe how "*all the inhabitants of the band-box houses who have appeared in the play*" converge in a hymn-singing chorus, including "*The Negroes [who] chant the song which mounts to a crescendo*" (2-5-10). This final image that audiences beheld—an integrated coalition, united for economic justice—makes for a potent ending for *One-Third of a Nation*. While theatrically impactful as a call to social action, and hopeful as a vision of interracial unity, such a conclusion is out-of-joint with the more scattershot treatment of racial conditions in Philadelphia that the rest of the play offers.

Jarvis notes a similar paradox in public reception of the performance. While the FTP's staging of *One-Third of a Nation* "marked a breakthrough in integrating Philadelphia's stage," in all published accounts of the production, "the integrated effort was not mentioned by the press."[25] Reviewers failed to acknowledge the contributions, or even the presence, of African American company members—Lottie White as Mrs. Brown, Norman Johnson and Clarence Basil as the two boardinghouse tenants, and the crowd of others portraying residents of the Seventh Ward. As with *Jericho*, the FTP's records are largely silent about the praxis of these artists. In his director's report, Light reflects on how "many of the actors lived under the very conditions portrayed on the stage [which] helped a great deal in keeping up the morale and enthusiasm of the cast." Does this reflection include the African American members of the cast? If so, rehearsals offered a meaningful opportunity for Philadelphia artists to form class-based social bonds with one another across racial boundaries. Yet in this same report, Light describes the challenge of orchestrating "so large a production . . . with an available cast of 40 in the White Dramatic Company, 15 people in the Colored Dramatic Company."[26] In describing the cast as two segregated companies, rather than a diverse and interconnected community, Light's rhetoric mirrors the larger civic vision of Philadelphia that *One-Third of a Nation* projected to that city's audiences—as a metropole whose racial groups are copresent and sometimes aligned in certain concerns but not equitably and ineluctably united as one community.

Prelude to Swing

In contrast to *Jericho* (which showcased African American actors in service of a hackneyed white vision of Negro life), the third and final production mounted under Light's leadership followed an opposite path. The dance-drama *Prelude to Swing* was conceived as an ambitious and historically grounded examination of Black culture, one crafted in collaboration with a prominent African American writer; at the same time, the staging of the work banished African American bodies from the stage. The FTP advertised *Prelude to Swing* as "A Modern Dance Production based on the Development of Negro Music." The project brought together several local WPA initiatives in an ambitious collaborative arrangement. Malvena Fried, director of Philadelphia's Modern Dance Unit of the WPA, directed and choreographed. A troupe of dancers under Fried's direction joined a swing band of musicians and a gospel chorus of singers from the Federal Music Project. FTP designers and technicians provided costumes, lighting, and a minimalist, multilevel set design for the Walnut Street Theatre stage. Carleton Moss, eminent African American playwright and codirector of the New York Negro Unit, composed the text for *Prelude to Swing*. Through this collaboration, as FTP publicity agents described it, *Prelude to Swing* traced "the evolution and development of Negro music from its African jungle source to the present-day syncopated rhythms of swing through the medium of modern interpretive dance." The project aspired to be, beyond a musical retrospective, a lesson about history—narrating a chronicle "of the Negro in the freedom of his original jungle home, his submission to slavery, his work and play songs, and, as his cultural development progressed, the influence of his music on the entire nation."[27] Another FTP summary of the project declared: "The history and development of the music of the American Negro from its source in the African Jungles down to the present day is depicted, beginning with the Barbaric chants and grotesque girations [*sic*] of the primitive savage."[28]

Such marketing copy for *Prelude to Swing* drips with racial condescension, and mirrors the primitivism and exoticism that propelled several other high-profile FTP Negro Unit projects (particularly New York's "voodoo *Macbeth*" and Chicago's "swing *Mikado*"). Evidence strongly suggests that the sensationalized language of publicity materials does not reflect the true nature of the script. No manuscript of Moss's text of *Prelude to Swing* survives in the FTP archives, however. A proposal for the project that Moss composed for Fried speaks not of jungles, savages, nor grotesque gyrations but of "the native source" of "ritual music . . . festive music . . . [and] warriors' drums." The proposal lists various musical modes deriving from periods of slavery and the Jim Crow South to be explored: "the work-songs of the fields," "the gay songs of recreation hours," and the spiritual soundtrack "of revivals, baptizings, and camp meetings." Sections dedicated to these phases of musical history constitute the first part of the playwright's vision for *Prelude to Swing*, connected by "a narrative emphasizing in dramatic language the actual source of these particular songs." This initial proposal is far less detailed in envisioning the second half of *Prelude to Swing*, which the writer conjectured "will have to do with Blues, Rag-time, Jazz and Swing."[29]

In a subsequent letter to Fried, Moss fills in more detail of his vision. The playwright offers suggestions for the quality of movements and the contextual information that would accompany each section of the first half of the performance. He envisions "lyric" dancing for "Swing Low, Sweet Chariot," imagines gestures with "a folkish quality" for "Rase a Ruckus Tonight," and describes spirituals as songs requiring "a feeling of joy expressed in the realistic way by hand shaking, clapping, short jumps (up) as the sisters and brothers shout—and they sort of half-shuffle as they go around in circles [with] a delightful little toss of the head indicating how proud they are that they have religion." For a baptismal scene, Moss describes how "most of the brothers and sisters go to the pool somewhat frightened. . . . Of course, there's always the one or two who go with their heads high in the air—almost a strut." A fuller description of act 2 outlines a journey from ragtime through blues and swing (the popular contemporary style of the 1930s). In the playwright's articulation, the entire production would "knit itself together, clearly making the point of our thesis [about] 'one continuous sequence of Negro music,' and that Swing is a new interpretation of this music."[30] In launching his collaboration with Fried, even as he enters into a milieu of modern dance, Moss clearly sought to ground *Prelude to Swing* in a realistic idiom of African American social and cultural history. A faithful embodiment of Southern Negro folklife onstage was for Moss a component of celebrating the continuity, perseverance, and adaptability of African diasporic culture in the modern world, despite historic disruptions and threats of erasure. It is unfortunate, and pointedly ironic, that a copy of Moss's finished script—the key vehicle through which an African American voice articulated the story of insuppressible Black cultural transmission—is missing from the archive.

It is unclear what effect Moss's concerns for the movement patterns of African American communal life had on Fried's work on the project. However, in the first half of its survey of Black musical history, *Prelude to Swing* did not call upon Black dance history. Fried's abstract choreography was not inspired by the juba, the ring shout, the cakewalk, or other African American vernacular traditions. Rather, movements were exclusively in the Euro-American idiom of modern dance. "Since spirituals and swing are truly American folk music," wrote Fried, "and since the modern dance in America is a purely American art form, the choreographer felt that modern dance was better equipped than any other dance form to utilize this music as thematic material."[31] Such sentiments align Fried's work with some of her contemporaries working within the FTP's Dance project in other cities. As Margaret Savalonis notes, in response to prejudices against modern dance as overly intellectual, politically radical, and even communist in its orientation, American choreographers interested in the form sought strategies for "carving out a space in which modern dance could provide a vocabulary for articulating American experience."[32] Along with Helen Tamaris (in New York) and Myra Kinch (in Los Angeles), Fried was part of a larger project pursued by FTP artists to Americanize modern dance in the public imagination. The final staging of *Prelude to Swing* intermixed group choreography with solo dance numbers performed by Fried and several choral selections. As one reviewer noted, dance numbers were "executed in the modern manner, [with] stark and angular movements" in the first half; the choreography included "a nice stylization of the elements of popular dance in the later portions."[33]

The grafting of African American music and history onto the formalist style of modern dance is, in one sense, a pluralistic gesture that brings Black and white aesthetic traditions into conversation with one another. However, clearly captured in production photographs—and which no newspaper reviewers cared to note in print—is that *none* of the fifteen dancers in Fried's company were African American. While Black singers and musicians performed accompaniments and interludes from the orchestra pit, a troupe of white dancers embodied African American musical history under the spotlight of center stage. The casting of *Prelude to Swing* fulfills Susan Manning's definition of "metaphorical minstrelsy, a convention whereby white dancers' bodies made reference to nonwhite subjects . . . not [to] mimic others but [to] present an abstraction or personification of others."[34] In that sense, the final stage picture mirrored the existing cultural hegemony in the United States, even as it explored an influential strain of African diasporic cultural history. In Jarvis's estimation, despite aspirations toward interracial artistic collaboration, *Prelude to Swing* nonetheless "demonstrated the underlying racism that existed in the late thirties."[35]

One week before *Prelude to Swing*'s scheduled opening in May 1939, Hallie

Flanagan observed a rehearsal while visiting Philadelphia. Deeming the production not ready for an audience, Flanagan announced that its opening would be delayed. According to the *Philadelphia Record*, what followed was "a series of postponements that lasted several weeks,"[36] which moved the production's official start (in the un-air-conditioned Walnut Street Theatre) into the warmer weeks of the summer. "Applause mingled with perspiration last night when the Federal theater's 'Prelude to Swing' opened," wrote the *Philadelphia Daily News* in its opening night review. "Despite the sultry, humid weather, the audience applauded and swung into the groove with an enthusiasm that defied discomfort."[37] The *Philadelphia Inquirer* similarly noted that "the sultry atmosphere outside and inside the theatre could not inhibit the enthusiasm of an audience that puffed and perspired as it applauded."[38] Neither the delay nor the temperature discouraged ticket buyers. *Variety*'s report speaks of *Prelude to Swing* as "attracting the largest audience an FTP show has ever had in Philly" and of the chorus "being forced into innumerable encores, for which it was unprepared when caught."[39]

As with *Jericho*, the virtuosity of African American performers became a specific focus for critical praise. Reviews of *Prelude to Swing* consistently applaud the chorus but are more equivocal about the production's content and the work of the dance troupe. The *Philadelphia Inquirer*'s critic writes, "The dance doings of the performance, colorful and captivating as they were, were wholly overshadowed by the freshness and fervor with which Negro spirituals were sung by a Negro choral group of 30 singers occupying the musicians' pit. . . . [who] 'stole the show' from the orchestra pit."[40] The *Philadelphia Record*'s critic thrilled in a "delightful spontaneity and camp-meeting gusto" shown by the singers while finding the dancers "at times a trifle too earnestly artistic to match the uninhibited voices rising from the pit."[41] Such critical praise shows a clear imprint of prevailing white racial attitudes of the era, which juxtapose a restrained, regulated, and civilized Euro-American temperament against an interpretation of African American sensibilities as particularly appealing when "uninhibited" and animated by "freshness and fervor." Performances of *Prelude to Swing* ended with audiences invited onstage for "a jitterbug contest . . . thus bringing our history right up to the living moment."[42] There is no surviving data on the racial composition of *Prelude to Swing*'s audiences, nor any indication of who danced with whom in these onstage dance parties.[43]

Positive reviews and enthusiastic local buzz led to two weeks of well-attended performances and discussions about a possible tour of the production when its open-ended Philadelphia engagement was finished. But circumstances abruptly changed when word came from Washington of the defunding of the FTP on

June 30, 1939. The House Committee on Un-American Activities, under chairman Congressman Martin Dies, had been investigating the FTP and its political leanings for more than a year. As happened in many FTP centers, sudden word of the defunding sparked confusion in Philadelphia as to how local productions and other operations would conclude. Initial reports published the following morning portended that "all scenery and costumes belonging to the theatre were required to be in the hands of the United States Marshal by midnight" and that all employees of the FTP (including performers from out of state) would no longer be housed.[44] The cast of *Prelude to Swing* defied these mandates and continued performing, without pay, for one more week "in an effort to evidence to Congress the interest and need . . . for continued existence" of the FTP.[45] Congress was not persuaded. The end of *Prelude to Swing* marked the end of the FTP in Philadelphia (and everywhere else, too).

Conclusion

Reflecting on the legacy and impact of the Negro Units nationwide, James V. Hatch writes, "The FTP's idealism continued to flow into the black theatres of the 1940s and 1950s."[46] Such an assessment pertains to New York or Chicago but is more difficult to apply to Philadelphia's local Black theatre history. If the FTP's ambition in bringing Light to Philadelphia was to establish an African American theatre that would outlast the federal government's opportunity to finance it, that ambition did not come true. Flanagan and Hagerty's dreams of incubating a locally grounded, sustainable, ambitious, and creative African American theatre in Philadelphia never took root in a serious way and seem to have evaporated with the cessation of the FTP. My research into the city's Black theatre history has not yet located any lasting activities in the city in the years that followed the Great Depression and the New Deal. With its lofty ambitions and some noteworthy (if compromised) progress over what preceded it, Philadelphia's Negro Unit seems to have served as a temporary foothold for the city's African American artists, rather than a solid and enduring foundation for future growth.

Notes

1. Arthur R. Jarvis, "Opportunity, Experience, and Recognition: Black Participation in Philadelphia's New Deal Arts Projects, 1936–1942," *Journal of Negro History* 85, no. 4 (Autumn 2000): 241. *JSTOR*.
2. John Houseman shared directorship on the New York Negro Unit with accomplished Af-

rican American actress Rose McClendon when the Unit was created in 1935. However, McClendon's poor health impeded her direct involvement in the group's administration. McClendon died in July 1936, and Houseman left his post soon after.

3. Cheryl Black, "After the Emperor: Interracial Collaborations between Provincetown Alumni and Black Theatre Artists, c. 1924–1946," *Journal of American Drama and Theatre* 20, no. 1 (Winter 2008): 26.
4. Matthew Countryman, *Up South: Civil Rights and Black Power in Philadelphia* (Philadelphia: University of Pennsylvania Press, 2007), 27.
5. Stanley Keith Arnold, *Building the Beloved Community: Philadelphia's Interracial Civil Rights Organizations and Race Relations, 1930–1970* (Jackson: University Press of Mississippi, 2014), 8.
6. Rena Fraden, *Blueprints for a Black Federal Theatre* (Cambridge: Cambridge University Press, 1996), 19.
7. W. J. Hagerty, quoted in "Local Actors Secure Roles in 'Jericho,'" *Philadelphia Tribune*, October 28, 1937, 3. Proquest Historical Newspapers. Hagerty was the FTP's regional director for Pennsylvania.
8. Playreader Reports File, 1935–1939: *Jericho*, Federal Theatre Project Collection, Music Division, Library of Congress, Washington, DC, Box 231.
9. "Production Bulletin: *Jericho*," Federal Theatre Project Collection, Music Division, Library of Congress, Washington, DC, Box 1026.
10. H. L. Fishel, *Jericho*, Federal Theatre Project Materials Collection, Special Collections Research Center, George Mason University Libraries, scanned TS. http://mars.gmu.edu/handle/1920/4492. Page I, i, 7. Parenthetical citations that follow refer to this manuscript.
11. A. B., "*Jericho* Presented By W.P.A. Players," review of *Jericho* by H. L. Fishel at the Walnut Street Theatre, *Philadelphia Record*, November 2, 1937.
12. "Acting Glorifies Federal Theatre Effort at Walnut," *Philadelphia Daily News*, November 2, 1937.
13. T. A. S., "'Jericho' Opens, First Play to Be Presented by W.P.A.," review of *Jericho* by H. L. Fishel at the Walnut Street Theatre, *Philadelphia Tribune*, November 4, 1937. Proquest Historical Newspapers.
14. T. A. S., "'Jericho' Opens, First Play to Be Presented by W.P.A."
15. Hallie Flanagan, quoted in Jane DeHart Matthews, *Federal Theatre, 1935–1939: Plays, Relief, Politics* (Princeton, NJ: Princeton University Press, 2015), 143. Proquest eBook Central. http://ebookcentral.proquest.com/
16. Paul Nadler, "Liberty Censored: Black Living Newspapers of the Federal Theatre Project," *African American Review* 29, no. 4 (Winter 1995): 615. Nadler identifies and analyzes three Living Newspaper scripts focused on racial issues written for the FTP but never staged. Two were by white playwrights: *The South*, by Elmer Rice, and *Stars and Bars*, by Ward Courtney. A third, titled *Liberty Deferred*, was by Black writers Abram Hill and John D. Silvera.
17. See *Free, Adult, Uncensored: The Living History of the Federal Theatre*, ed. John O'Connor and Lorraine Brown (Washington, DC: New Republic, 1978), 160.
18. Arthur Arent, *One-Third of a Nation*, Federal Theatre Project Materials Collection, Special Collections Research Center, George Mason University Libraries, scanned TS. http://mars.gmu.edu/handle/1920/4496. Page 2-2C-2. Parenthetical citations that follow refer to this manuscript.

19. "Production Bulletin: *One-Third of a Nation*," Federal Theatre Project Collection, Music Division, Library of Congress, Washington, DC, Box 1052.
20. Arent, *One-Third of a Nation*, 1-2-1.
21. Marcus Anthony Hunter, "Black Philly after *The Philadelphia Negro*," *Contexts* 13, no. 1 (Winter 2014): 30.
22. "Houses Creak, but Don't Fall; . . . 'One-third' Stage too Weak," *Philadelphia Record*, October 18, 1938. "Production Bulletin: *One-Third of a Nation*," Federal Theatre Project Collection, Music Division, Library of Congress, Washington, DC, Box 1052.
23. Arthur Arent, *One-Third of a Nation*, Philadelphia version adapted by Edward Malle, Playscripts File, Federal Theatre Project Collection, Music Division, Library of Congress, Washington, DC, Box 862. Page 1-1-1. Parenthetical citations that follow refer to this manuscript.
24. Historians have since revised the casualty statistics: "All told, seven people were killed, and more than two dozen were injured" (Hunter, "Black Philly after *The Philadelphia Negro*," 30).
25. Jarvis, "Opportunity, Experience, and Recognition," 243.
26. James Light, "Director's Report on Production," "Production Bulletin: *One-Third of a Nation*," Federal Theatre Project Collection, Music Division, Library of Congress, Washington, DC, Box 1052.
27. Playbill for *Prelude to Swing* at the Walnut Street Theatre, Philadelphia, Pennsylvania. Federal Theatre Project collection, Library of Congress, https://www.loc.gov/item/musftpplaybills.200221375/.
28. "Production Bulletin: *Prelude to Swing*," Federal Theatre Project Collection, Music Division, Library of Congress, Washington, DC, Box 1058.
29. Carleton Moss, Draft proposal for *Prelude to Swing*, Malvena Fried Taiz papers relating to Federal Theatre Project, 1938–1940, Archives of American Art, Smithsonian Institute, microfilm.
30. Carleton Moss, letter to Malvena Fried, May 3, 1939, Malvena Fried Taiz papers.
31. Malvena Fried, "Choreographer's Report," Production Bulletin: *Prelude to Swing*.
32. Margaret Savilonis, "Choreographing Diversity and American Experience: Myra Kinch and Group, Federal Theatre Project (1937–39)," in *Experiments in Democracy: Interracial and Cross-Cultural Exchange in American Theater, 1912–1954* (Carbondale: Southern Illinois University Press, 2016), 119. Savilonis notes, "Modern dance in the 1930s included many adaptations of Native American, African American, and non-Western dance vocabularies" (120).
33. J. L. B., "'Prelude to Swing' Federal Theatre Units Trace Development of Negro Music," *Philadelphia Evening Bulletin*, June 13, 1939. "Production Bulletin: *Prelude to Swing*," Federal Theatre Project Collection, Music Division, Library of Congress, Washington, DC. Box 1058.
34. Susan Manning, quoted in Savilonis, "Choreographing Diversity and the American Experience," 125. My discussion of *Prelude to Swing* is particularly indebted to Margaret Savilonis's entire essay (which I had the pleasure to edit) on the work of modern dance choreographer Myra Kinch in the Federal Theatre Project's Los Angeles Dance Unit.
35. Jarvis, "Opportunity, Experience, and Recognition," 245.
36. Edwin H. Schloss, "'Prelude to Swing' Unveiled at Walnut St. Theater," *Philadelphia Rec-*

ord, June 13, 1939. "Production Bulletin: *Prelude to Swing*," Federal Theatre Project Collection, Music Division, Library of Congress, Washington, DC. Box 1058.

37. "Federal Theater's 'Prelude to Swing' Hailed at Walnut," *Philadelphia Daily News*, 13 June 1939. "Production Bulletin: *Prelude to Swing*," Federal Theatre Project Collection, Music Division, Library of Congress, Washington, DC. Box 1058.
38. L. M., "'Prelude to Swing' Opens at Walnut St. Theater," *Philadelphia Inquirer*, June 13, 1939, "Production Bulletin: *Prelude to Swing*," Federal Theatre Project Collection, Music Division, Library of Congress, Washington, DC. Box 1058.
39. Herb., "WPA Plays: *Prelude to Swing*," *Variety*, June 28, 1939, 50–51.
40. L. M. "'Prelude to Swing' Opens at Walnut St. Theatre," *Philadelphia Inquirer*, June 13, 1939. "Production Bulletin: *Prelude to Swing*," Federal Theatre Project Collection, Music Division, Library of Congress, Washington, DC. Box 1058.
41. Edwin H. Schloss, "'Prelude to Swing' Unveiled at Walnut St. Theater," *Philadelphia Record*, June 13, 1939. "Production Bulletin: *Prelude to Swing*," Federal Theatre Project Collection, Music Division, Library of Congress, Washington, DC. Box 1058.
42. *Variety*, June 28, 1939, 50–51.
43. African American critical response to *Prelude to Swing* would surely have been different than that of the white reviewers working for the Philadelphia's mainstream daily newspapers. Unfortunately, I was unable to obtain and analyze a review from the *Philadelphia Tribune*, the city's major African American newspaper, for discussion in this essay. The Proquest Historical Newspapers database (where I found the newspaper's review of *Jericho* cited earlier) is missing all editions of the *Tribune* published between December 1938 and November 1939. Library closures due to coronavirus in the summer of 2020 prevented me from searching for a copy of the review on microform.
44. "WPA Closes Theatre Here," *Philadelphia Inquirer*, July 1, 1939, 24.
45. David W. Kellum, "Backstage with the Scribe," *Chicago Defender*, July 8, 1939, Proquest Historical Newspapers.
46. James V. Hatch and Errol Hill, *A History of African American Theatre* (Cambridge: Cambridge University Press, 2003), 334.

Stop Your Sobbing

White Fragility, Slippery Empathy, and Historical Consciousness in Branden Jacobs-Jenkins's *Appropriate*

—SCOTT PROUDFIT

When Brett Kavanaugh had an emotional breakdown during his 2018 Supreme Court hearings, the televised event became a prominent example of that rare contemporary social phenomenon "white men's tears." This particular type of public grief closes down any discussion of inequality and privilege and brings to a halt any social movement to address these issues, as resources that should be channeled to those being oppressed are instead redirected to those complicit, or even active, in the oppression. The suffering of the powerful supplants the suffering of the disempowered. This specific emotional indulgence is reflected in Branden Jacobs-Jenkins's 2014 play *Appropriate*, which culminates in the teary breakdown of the newly appointed patriarch of an Arkansas family struggling to come to terms with its inherited legacy of racial violence. Moreover, "white men's tears" appear in other recent commercial theatre productions written by playwrights of color (e.g., Young Jean Lee and Larissa FastHorse)[1] and featuring exclusively white characters, in what might be a mini-trend on Broadway and Off Broadway prior to and immediately following the election of Donald Trump. These scenes of emotional manipulation specifically employed by white men suggest that the rise of our national leader has inspired some theatremakers to try to come to terms with "whiteness" and how, though it remains largely invisible, the white identity continues to define culture and politics in the United States.

"White men's tears" is a subset of what writers on contemporary race relations term "white tears," a common reaction by white people when experiencing racial tension. Moreover, the phenomenon of "white tears" is only one expression of the larger social phenomenon of "white fragility" in modern US culture. In her 2018 book *White Fragility*, Robin DiAngelo defines "white tears" as "all the ways, both literally and metaphorically, that white fragility manifests itself through white people's laments over how hard racism is on *us*."[2] While these tears may seem to stem from pity, they are instead a form of self-pity. Race theorists such as DiAngelo have described "white tears" as the latest iteration in a long tradition of white women's displays of grief over racial injustice, recognizable in the United States since at least pre–Civil War Abolitionism. Historically, white women—especially socially progressive white women—when faced with racial conflict or racial violence, have presented themselves as suffering along with, or in place of, the victims of racism, drawing attention away from those actually suffering under this institutionalized system. Cultural historian Saidiya Hartman has described this problematic reaction to others' pain as the "slipperiness of empathy."[3]

Less common than the tears of white women, "white men's tears" are a particularly perverse example of white fragility in that they are shed by those most privileged within, and most benefiting from, the system of inequalities that supposedly prompts their emotions. For example, Kavanaugh's tears in his confirmation hearings put his own suffering center stage, displacing the grief of his accuser and of female survivors of sexual violence in general. The Kavanaugh hearings were, of course, more indicative of institutionalized gender bias and hatred than racial bias and hatred. However, they centered around a public display of self-pitying white male grief that offers a productive way into an analysis of *Appropriate*, a play that captures the significant dilemma facing race theorists and educators who have examined the twin phenomena of white fragility and white rage at the heart of contemporary US political culture. This dilemma is the fact that, when addressing white audiences through the arts, empathy (the supposedly altruistic motivation behind "white tears") historically has been considered the first step toward promoting social change, yet for some years empathy has also been understood to inhibit rather than promote such change.

Jacobs-Jenkins won the 2014 Obie Award for Best Play for two productions: *Appropriate* at the Signature Theatre and *An Octoroon* at Soho Rep. The more overtly avant-garde *An Octoroon* has received more critical attention than *Appropriate*.[4] This is no doubt partly due to the fact that its postmodern-pastiche approach to Dion Boucicault's 1859 racial melodrama *The Octoroon* is a theatre historian's dream. Unfortunately, though, this means that the equally provocative and profound *Appropriate*, a play that operates primarily in the traditional commercial-theatre mode of psychological realism, has been largely overlooked. *Appropriate*, however, may prove the more enduring of the two plays because of the way it carefully explores and exemplifies the phenomenon of white fragility by intervening in the long-standing debate over the political efficacy of empathy. *Appropriate* ultimately theatricalizes the argument detailed in Susan Sontag's 2003 book, *Regarding the Pain of Others*: Feeling empathy (or merely sympathy) and experiencing powerful emotions in general are not necessarily bad reactions when confronted with images or narratives of others' pain, but such emotions can serve as a dangerous detour away from actual political change. Moreover, such detours are so pervasive, that, according to Sontag and, I contend, Jacobs-Jenkins, the ability of any art to lead directly to social change, whether it specifically tries to evoke empathy or not, is limited at best.

As my argument here makes a distinction between "empathy" and "sympathy," I would like to preface the following analysis with a brief definition of terms. "Sympathy" means feeling compassion or pity for someone or something other than oneself. One can feel sympathy for another's suffering while still being cognizant of the specific history and identity that distinguishes the sufferer from the sympathizer. "Empathy" moves beyond sympathy and means imagining oneself in someone else's situation and believing one actually feels the emotions the sufferer is feeling. The empathizer identifies with the sufferer and indeed, on some level, replaces the sufferer with themself. Both sympathy and empathy are feelings created by acts of the imagination, but sympathy allows "the other" to remain distinct. Indeed, as the ending of *Appropriate* suggests, it may be that developing a historical consciousness is the key to preventing white audiences from crossing the line from informed sympathy into unthinking empathy. Moreover, this awareness of history is central to confronting and dismantling the privilege of white fragility.

The Tears of Kavanaugh and the Tears of *Appropriate* in Context

While entertainment journalists claim we are "having a moment for male tears"[5] in the last year or so, the trend they are identifying is solely in the arena of the arts. On TV programs such as *Queer Eye* or *This Is Us*, it may be increasingly common to find men crying without being treated comically, but among male political figures in the twenty-first century, tears are still rare. It is the rarity of such displays of emotion that partly accounts for the media attention paid to former Speaker of the House John Boehner's occasional displays of emotion, the extended discussion of President Barack Obama's tears in the wake of the 2012

Sandy Hook school shootings, and, more recently, the coverage of the Kavanaugh hearings.

The immediate reaction in the press to Kavanaugh's testimony before the Senate Judiciary Committee in October 2018 focused on Kavanaugh's tears more than on the content of his statements. Conservative columnists such as the Raleigh *News and Observer*'s A. C. Snow felt it important to defend the nominee's masculinity from perceived mockery by the mainstream media, noting "the Bible tells us that Jesus wept publicly at least twice."[6] Liberal columnists, such as the *Sacramento Bee*'s Erika D. Smith, on the other hand, underlined the "privilege" Kavanagh enjoyed in his hearings, as opposed to his accuser, Christine Blasey Ford, and his fragility in the face of criticism. She emphasized that two distinct audiences in the United States perceived Kavanaugh's testimony in very different ways. "To the loyal, populist supporters of President Donald Trump, Kavanaugh succeeded in looking like a victim of elitist politicians," Smith writes. "But to the rest of us, he just looked like an entitled, privileged white male, whining because he's unaccustomed to losing anything."[7] Columnist Damon Young of *The Root* put it more bluntly, explaining that Kavanaugh's performance reminded him of others he had witnessed from white male colleagues over the years: "When privileged white men fall, they somehow fall *up* as if gravity doesn't apply. And so you wonder, 'Why the fuck are you fucking crying?' And then it hits you: *Oh yeah. He's never felt this before. . . . This thing he's experiencing now—this disappointment, this fear, this shame, this doubt—is new to him.*"[8] In other words, Smith and Young recognized Kavanaugh's performance as self-pitying "white men's tears," and his performance, therefore, drew no tears from them.

So noteworthy was Kavanaugh's weepy testimony that the *New Yorker*'s Michael Lista dedicated an entire column to contextualizing the candidate's emotional breakdown in an article aptly named "The Tears of Brett Kavanaugh." Few reporters at the time were actually challenging Kavanaugh's right to weep, claims Lista. Indeed, unemotional masculinity has long been passé, there being a general consensus "that crying is good for a man, that his tears are the outward sign of his inward progress, the evidence and end result of his 'being in touch with his feelings.'"[9] Furthermore, Lista writes, the association of public tears with weakness and femininity was cultivated only in a relatively short period in the West, during the Victorian era: "For most of Western history, men cried incessantly." He cites the tearful Odysseus in Homer's *The Odyssey* as a prime precedent of the emotional masculine archetype.

Lista's exemplification of the commonness of white male tears in Western literature is correct.[10] More apt instances—in terms of contextualizing a play such as *Appropriate*, at least—might be found in Western theatre since the Ancient Greeks, which likewise, but more consistently, demonstrates that even throughout the Victorian era men wept openly onstage while retaining their perceived masculinity. After all, the nineteenth-century English melodrama was built upon pathetic heroes constructed to elicit tears from their audience members. The characters in Boucicault's *The Octoroon*, Jacobs-Jenkins's source for his 2014 adaptation, are no exception. Boucicault's character Pete tells his fellow enslaved people that their master George wept over the fact that he would lose the plantation and that Pete and the other enslaved people would be sold. Recalling his white master George's tears moves Pete to tears himself. This prime example of white fragility is re-presented in Jacobs-Jenkins's *An Octoroon*—as attention onstage (and perhaps in the audience) goes to the crying master as opposed to the enslaved people. Says Pete: "Mas'r George—You shoulda seen dem big tears in his eyes . . . (*Getting emotional.*) Yes, for you, for me, dem white folks cried. Dey cried! Fo' us! Fo' us sorry, no good nothing n___s."[11]

While political figures crying in public are different from actors crying onstage, Lista contends that the justification for such white male tears has long been a part of US political culture—and not just something found in the Western literary tradition. Lista points to the example of Thomas Jefferson's famous constitutional characterization of free existence as defined by "Life, Liberty, and the pursuit of Happiness." "Written into America's founding document," Lista claims, "is the franchise for a man like Kavanaugh to weep when he isn't fulfilled." Indeed, justified public grief over not receiving one's due historically has been a white man's franchise, not extended to women or people of color. This distinction is reflected in the press coverage of the Kavanaugh hearings. For example, columnists such as CNN's Michael D'Antonio argued that Ford's more stoic attitude in her testimony was necessary because, unlike a man, a woman crying before the Senate committee "would likely be dismissed as overwrought, even hysterical."[12]

Oddly, then, it seems that Kavanaugh's unassailable masculinity made it permissible to cry in this context while Ford's femininity prevented her from doing so, lest she be dismissed as unstable—further evidence that when it comes to public grief and empathy, identity matters deeply. Likewise, the aforementioned tears of President Obama after the Sandy Hook shootings, though clearly not stemming in any way from self-pity, were received dismissively by great sections of the public due to the fact that the "emotionality" of Black subjects in public spaces is assumed. Obama's emotionality, like a woman's "hysteria," is the Other against which reasonable, white discourse has supposedly defined itself. As E. Patrick Johnson points out in *Appropriating Blackness* (2003), women and people of color are expected to "perform" their emotion in public. Skepticism toward Obama's, or any person of color's, public tears corresponds with a tradition of antitheatrical prejudice in the West. Since at least Plato's *Republic*, Western ideology has relied on a binary of emotional expression (found in drama and poetry) on the one side and reasonable discourse (found in philosophy) on the other. Johnson argues that this binary is inseparable from a racial binary that has historically determined the reception of Black public speaking in the modern age. Black speakers are expected to express emotion, not to make reasonable arguments. As Johnson notes, "the devaluation of performance in Western intellectual traditions simultaneously coincides with the devaluation of black people as subjects of inquiry in the academy and in society as a whole."[13]

Despite his historical franchise, Kavanaugh's "white men's tears" were of course mocked by many, as the earlier mentioned newspaper articles attest. Indeed, whether his tears induced sympathy or not often depended on the identity of his audience member. As Susan Sontag writes in *Regarding Other People's Pain*, when contemplating images of pain and grief, "identity is everything. And all photographs wait to be explained or falsified by their captions."[14] An image of a soldier suffering on the battlefield might bring a tear to the eye until, that is, it is revealed that the soldier is actually the enemy. In terms of the importance of identity to reception, it is clear that even a decade ago members of the mainstream press would not have called out Kavanaugh's white male privilege the way they did in 2018. Today more writers of color—such as the above-quoted Smith and Young—are employed by news outlets, the result of which is that the opportunity to identify "whiteness," and thus to no longer automatically sympathize with a white man's tears, is acted upon in the contemporary media in ways it had not been before, even in the late twentieth century. Likewise, in recent years, new POC voices on and Off Broadway (Jacobs-Jenkins, Lee, FastHorse) have similarly begun to offer critical depictions of white men's privilege and their public tears, exposing this particular type of white fragility.

White Fragility in *Appropriate*

In the contemporary United States, white people react in two primary ways when pressured to acknowledge institutionalized sexism and racism and their own participation in this oppression. They react with anger and denial or with tears and self-pity. Such reactions fall under the umbrella term "white fragility," as described in such recent books as Robin DiAngelo's *White Fragility* (2018) and Michael Eric Dyson's *Tears We Cannot Stop: A Sermon to White America* (2017). Jacobs-Jenkins's play offers textbook examples of white fragility, not only in the culminating moment of grief but throughout the text. This play tells the story of the grown white children of a recently deceased white DC politician, who return to their crumbling homestead in Arkansas, a former plantation, to organize and sell off their father's effects. During the course of their preparation for a public auction and in the midst of typical dysfunctional-family squabbles, the Lafayette siblings discover among their patriarch's possessions lynching photographs and souvenirs. For much of the remainder of the play, the siblings insist that their father could not have had any relationship to this history of racial violence or the festishizing documentation of these lynching events.

In her book, DiAngelo contends that white fragility is exhibited by white people whenever the possibility of racial prejudice or racism is raised in a public context or even when the mere identification of "whiteness" as a cultural marker is made. The prevalence of white fragility, claims DiAngelo, means that "white progressives [as opposed to conservatives such as Kavanaugh] cause the most daily damage to people of color," because they see themselves as outside of the institutions of racism. They fall back on white tears when confronted with their own racist attitudes and actions.[15] She writes, "If we need to cry so that all the resources rush back to us and attention is diverted away from a discussion of our racism, then we will cry (a strategy most commonly employed by white middle-class women)."[16] "White tears," according to DiAngelo, are actually "a powerful form of white racial control":[17] "Our tears function as impotent reflexes that don't lead to constructive action."[18]

In *Tears We Cannot Stop*, Michael Eric Dyson, who also wrote the preface to DiAngelo's book, defines white fragility as "a will to innocence that serves to bury the violence it sits on top of."[19] This metaphor is an apt description of the setting and dynamics of Jacobs-Jenkins's *Appropriate*, as the Lafayette siblings continually deny their inheritance of their father's history of racial violence. Dyson outlines five stages of what he terms "white racial grief."[20] Each is clearly exhibited by the Lafayettes in *Appropriate*. The first stage of white racial grief is "amnesia": "to plead ignorance about black life and culture" and claim that neither has "played a role in your world or made a difference in your existence."[21] Accordingly, the Lafayette siblings do not acknowledge that their Arkansas family estate was a plantation, that a separate graveyard for enslaved people exists on their property, and that a system of violence is represented by the anonymous plots that fill this graveyard. For example, midway through the play, Bo, the eldest Lafayette son, who is struggling to reconcile his father's messy finances, laments that there is no possibility of selling the property since it contains the Lafayette family graveyard, a potential legal nightmare. He fails to mention the second graveyard the property contains, the resting place of the plantation's slaves. River, the girlfriend of Bo's younger brother Franz, attempts to correct Bo's apparent oversight: "Aren't there two/ graveyards—?" to which Bo immediately replies, even overlapping her question: "I don't even want to know."[22]

The second stage of white racial grief, Dyson says, is "denial," which he claims "is more sinister than amnesia" because it allows white people to concede that racism was once a reality in the United States but simultaneously to reject the possibility that it exists here anymore.[23] Addressing white people, Dyson writes, "You acknowledge that bigotry exists" but claim that you can't "find too many current examples" of it.[24] In line with such denial, not only does the Lafayette family willfully erase the slave graveyard from their minds, but for much of the play they insist that the lynching photographs must not be their father's property; they've somehow just got mixed in with his effects. When sister Toni and brother Bo reveal the photos to Franz, they hope that the items might be attributed to their brother's deviance. (Franz has a history with drug abuse and underage sexual relations.) Bo says to Franz, "Toni thought they might have been yours,"[25] to which Toni adds, "We have no idea where these came from,"[26] trying to exempt her father from any culpability.

As Dyson articulates, a common aspect of denial in this context is to admit that prejudice was part of the American past but to claim that it was simply the reality of the culture at the time, not something to condemn people for and certainly not something that has any bearing on current culture. As Toni says of her father, "Maybe he used the wrong word for somebody from time to time but that's just his generation—and it was never the—the—the N-word or anything like that!"[27] Even when Bo provides a clear example of his father's racist attitudes, citing an instance when his father dropped him off at college, saw that he would share housing with a Black student, and warned him to keep an eye on his possessions, Toni defends him, "Bo, it was a different time. These things were still so new!"[28]

"Appropriation," the third stage of white racial grief, is obviously highlighted by the title of the play. As Dyson explains, to "appropriate" is to "defer to black culture even as [white culture] displaces it" and to "claim an outsider status without actually having to be outsiders."[29] While the play relates to white appropriation of POC culture and history, critics have often cited the fact that Jacobs-Jenkins's play ironically and intentionally "appropriates" a number of canonical plays by white writers, including Sam Shepard's *Buried Child* and Anton Chekhov's *The Cherry Orchard*.[30] Indeed, a particularly "appropriate" Lopakhin line appropriated from *The Cherry Orchard* serves as one of the play's two epigraphs in print: "If only my father and grandfather could rise up out of their graves, and see all that's happened. . . . I've bought the land on which my father and grandfather were slaves, where they weren't even allowed in the kitchen."[31]

However, in terms of Dyson's definition of "appropriation," what is more significant in analyzing *Appropriate* through the lens of white fragility is the way the white characters claim other identities without actually experiencing the social barriers imposed on these identities. Appropriation is particularly prominent among white progressives, Dyson argues. This is exemplified by the most "progressive" character in *Appropriate,* Franz's New Age girlfriend, River, who, for example, humorously makes "quinoaffles" for the Lafayettes for breakfast[32] and parrots politically correct self-help mantras inspired by the twelve-step program she is helping Franz complete. Disturbingly, River seems to suggest that reparations for the violent history of the Lafayette plantation can be made fairly simply, in the same way she believes the family should simply move beyond Franz's past crimes. She says to Toni: "We can't go back and change the past . . . but we ease the pain of the present by enacting the eternal rites. . . . We acknowledge the reality of each other's suffering and, by the extension, the universality of suffering. We give our suffering up to the collective and we move on."[33] Her suggestion that Franz's history with his siblings can be reconciled so easily is problematic; even worse are her claims of "the universality of suffering" within the context of the family's uncovered lynching photos. River implies that the pain the enslaved people endured on the Lafayette plantation is a pain that she and all others share and a pain that might be expiated through some simple rituals.

For the fourth stage of white racial grief, "revision," or the rewriting of Black history, Dyson gives the example of "the flood of writing that tells us the Civil War wasn't really about slavery but about the effort to defend states' rights."[34] In terms of revising the past in *Appropriate,* the Lafayettes are mainly concerned with revising their family history—trying to blame each other for the problems they are now facing in their lives. Revision also plays a part in the ways the family revises father Ray's clear racism through subtle phrasing. Bo's wife, Rachael, for example, downplays her father-in-law's actions and beliefs through her careful wording to avoid offending her in-laws. When Toni notes that Rachael herself handed her son the lynching photos while they were cleaning up the house—not knowing what they were—and therefore shouldn't be blaming the Lafayettes for what he has seen, Rachael responds, "So whatever psychological damage my child has just incurred due to his grandfather's . . . *prejudice* is now *my* fault?"[35] Using the word "prejudice," Rachael avoids the term "racism," which, as DiAngelo notes, would be an immediate trigger for white fragility.

The fifth and final stage of white racial grief, "dilution," is directly related to the phenomenon of white tears. Dilution is the urge, Dyson writes, "to argue that bad stuff doesn't just plague black folks. . . . 'Bad stuff happens to everyone.'"[36] A common "diluting" response to racial tensions by white people, for example, is to say that, yes, racial discrimination still exists in the United States, but the *real* issue is economic inequality. In *Appropriate*, the tragedy of racial violence represented by the Lafayettes' inheritance of Ray's photos is largely forgotten in the course of the play as each sibling tries to outdo the others in arguing how bad they have it. Franz blames his addiction and sexual misconduct on being abandoned by his siblings to live with his "mentally ill" father. Toni upstages him, however, claiming that she also is a victim of circumstance. Toni has been fired from her job as vice principal of her son Rhys's high school after Rhys was caught with drugs and the pills were traced back to Toni. Toni blames her son's problems on the fact that she constantly had to keep an eye on her younger brother Franz while he was living with their father. "I should have been raising my own child when I was raising someone else's," she says.[37] Even Bo gets in on the competition of who has it worst, saying that his idyllic suburban family life in DC with Rachael and his two children is a veneer: "I'm about to lose my job, Toni," he claims, explaining that his corporation is shutting down his division.[38]

"White tears" are the extreme version of white racial grief's "dilution." Not only do "white tears" suggest that "everybody suffers," but, more to the point, they attest, "I am suffering *more* at this particular moment." Two parallel iconic moments in *Appropriate* present examples of "white tears." Each closes a scene in act 3, putting particular emphasis on the moment. At the end of act 3, scene 1, Ainsley, Bo and Rachael's younger child, who has no lines in the play, has been upstairs sorting through his grandfather's materials with his sister and his cousin. In a moment reminiscent of the final images of Shepard's *Buried Child* in which Tilden descends the stairs with the corpse of the baby, Ainsley "*comes slowly down the stairs, wailing. Over his head is a pointed white hood—an old pillow case with two eyeholes. Everyone watches him cry and cry.*"[39] The symbolism of this moment is layered. On the one hand, Ainsley in the Ku Klux Klan hood represents how the Lafayette siblings' perspective on the world has been determined by the racism of their ancestors, whether they are aware of it or not—a perspective they are passing on to their children. On the other hand, the white-hooded Ainsley embodies the "ghost" of racial violence that haunts the Lafayette home. Throughout the play, River insists that she feels the weight and sadness of "spirits" on the plantation. The Lafayettes, even the typically indulgent Franz, dismiss her. "It's an old cemetery and an old house that creaks. There are no spirits here," he says.[40] Yet when the ghostly Ainsley appears on the stairs, the violence that haunts the family is made corporeal.

Moreover, for the purposes of this argument, what makes Ainsley's appearance in the KKK hood particularly significant is that this white child weeping immediately focuses the attention of the adults on helping him to ensure he is not damaged by this trauma. At the same time, the trauma of the violence father Ray, or whomever wore this costume, perpetrated in the past is set aside. Ainsley's tears are not truly "white men's tears" because, as a child, he does not wield the same power as his father (or grandfather). Nevertheless, similar to "white men's tears," his grief displaces that of the true victims. It should be noted that the flip side to white fragility's tears—anger—is also represented in *Appropriate* in a knock-down, drag-out fight between all members of the family immediately prior to Ainsley coming down the stairs, a reminder to audiences that white fragility can express itself in different forms.

Bo, the new patriarch of the Lafayette family following his father's death, reenacts this moment of Ainsley's breakdown, to some degree, at the end of the play's penultimate scene. At this point in the plot, Bo has experienced the hope that he might profit off the cache of lynching memorabilia, as a way to restore some financial health to his father's estate. He has then seen those hopes dashed when Franz destroys the photos by submerging them in the property's lake. At the close of the play, therefore, the Lafayettes have abandoned the idea of selling off Ray's remaining effects, and Rachael and the children await Bo in the car, eager to get back to DC. Left alone in the house, Bo "*crosses to the door to exit but, before he knows it, he is sobbing. He sobs and sobs and sobs with his hand on the door, unable to open it.*"[41]

Are Bo's "white men's tears" the same as, for example, Brett Kavanaugh's? In one sense, no. Bo's grief is (technically) "private," while Kavanaugh's is public.[42] Kavanaugh's "white men's tears," whether purely calculated or not, more directly appeal to a public to comfort him rather than address the issues that supposedly prompted his grief. Bo, on the other hand, at least seems not merely to be crying in self-pity but in some sort of acknowledgment of the horrors of his family history and the victims that suffered on the Lafayette plantation. After all, when Rachael comes to get him and asks what he is crying about, Bo says, "I don't know . . . Why don't I know?"[43] In this moment, Bo seems aware of his amnesia and his denial. However (and Dyson and DiAngelo would argue this is key), this modicum of racial awareness seems to disappear once his tears have dried. Bo's self-knowledge is limited at best. He does not seem to fully grasp that, in attempting to sell off the lynching souvenirs, some of which are actual body parts of lynching victims, Bo has become a contemporary surrogate for his father and inheritor of the legacy of white people who owned and sold Black people. With his attempt to sell these items at an internet auction, Bo has become slave owner and auctioneer. As Harvey Young characterizes the power of lynching souvenirs in his book *Embodying Black Experience*: "Lynching souvenirs embody the past in the present. They not only fix the black body within a historical moment, but also transform it into a captive object to be owned, displayed, and, quite possibly, traded."[44]

Bo may grieve for his family's crimes. However, his grief and the audience's empathy for his tears are an insufficient response to this plantation's history. Even if the audience member "feels bad" for Bo in this moment, there is no suggestion that Bo is going to take his grief and *do* something with it—as Dyson exhorts white readers to do—through reparation, education, participation, and speaking up.[45] All of these are options Dyson describes at the end of *Tears We Cannot Stop* as ways white people can move beyond white racial grief to actually improve the situation of Black people. DiAngelo concurs that "grief must lead to sustained and transformative action."[46] Nor is there an impetus for the mostly white audience members of *Appropriate* to "act" on the grief they may be feeling in their empathy with Bo or with the slaves whose lives and suffering will once again be as forgotten as the dissolving refuse from the lake. Feeling empathy for these slaves (or, more problematically, for Bo) is simply not enough. This is the reason DiAngelo counsels that anyone engaging in conversations about race should try to avoid emotion. It can get in the way of action. She intentionally avoids prescribing what traditionally has been the advice to white Americans hoping to improve race relations in the United States: empathize with Black Americans.

Yet, because empathy historically has been accepted as the appropriate response when engaging with the Other, DiAngelo's warning is one rarely heeded in contemporary race relations. Indeed, empathy is precisely what Dyson, in his book, argues is the culmination of all the concrete work white people might do instead of succumbing to guilt and grief: "All of what I have said should lead you to *empathy*. It sounds simple, but its benefits are profound . . . walk a mile or two in the boots of blackness. The siege of hate will not end until white folk imagine themselves as black folk—vulnerable despite our virtues."[47]

The problem with empathy is that expressing empathy across racial lines seems very similar to "white tears." In these moments of racial tension, the question is always whether white people are crying for themselves or others—or perhaps crying for others only because they imagine others as themselves. No book more aptly describes the dangers of empathy than Saidiya Hartman's *Scenes of Subjection* (1997). Though Hartman specifically examines white audiences' reception of Black bodies onstage, her analysis also applies to the performance of *Appropriate* in which white audiences are held a mirror up to their "white tears," the ugly self-pity tied into the empathetic impulse. As Hartman explains in her book, abolitionist sentimental literature attempted to bring the suffering of Black people closer to white readers/audiences, "facilitating an identification" between characters and audiences and "establishing a common humanity."[48] In this way, abolitionist literature paralleled the methods of melodrama and, later, psychological realism onstage. Hartman further argues that the problems with abolitionist literature's employment of empathy to achieve its political ends carries over to the presentation of Black people onstage in modern theatre performance. Empathy is "slippery," Hartman notes, because empathy often erases the sufferer, and we feel only for ourselves.[49]

As a play clearly committed to portraying the many types of white fragility, *Appropriate* is undoubtedly skeptical about the possibility that empathy, whether on the part of the Lafayettes or on the part of the audiences witnessing the Lafayettes' family drama, will lead to social action. This does not mean that Jacobs-Jenkins, in the moment of Bo's crying or Ainsley's crying attempts to alienate his audience. The scenes play out as "real" in the realist vein. However, the play also makes it certain that, while audiences may pity Ainsley and Bo in these moments, Ainsley's tears are clearly in self-pity and Bo's are mostly in self-pity. This is why Jacobs-Jenkins sets up the action so that the image of the child in the KKK hood weeping haunts the subsequent image of Bo crying. The audience is meant to understand that Bo's tears are, like his son's, the tears of a child for himself, not the tears of a man fully coming to terms with the racial history of his family. As an audience member, you may feel bad for Bo as you feel bad for a child in pain, the play seems to allow, but be careful you don't credit this moment as more than "white men's tears."

Sontag and the Cicadas' Song

As mentioned earlier, there are two epigraphs to the script of *Appropriate*. The first is from *The Cherry Orchard*. The second is from Sontag's book *Regarding the Pain of Others*: "No 'we' should be taken for granted when the subject is looking at other people's pain."[50] Not only is this quotation a clear rejection of the possibility of empathy—to imagine that one could put oneself in someone else's shoes, the quotation suggests, is ludicrous—but Sontag's words also suggest the further critical work *Appropriate* achieves in performance. In addition to exemplifying white fragility and "white men's tears," the play parallels Sontag's final book of criticism in considering whether any artistic expression of pain, whether it relies on the receiver's empathy or not, can realistically hope to inspire social action. This connection to Sontag's book can be traced through Jacobs-Jenkins's device of the cicadas' song.

A close reading of the lengthy stage directions that frame the action of *Appropriate* reveals the central importance of the metaphoric cicadas' song in its relationship to the play's intertwined themes of empathy and white fragility. In the "Prologue" to *Appropriate*, the stage directions read, in part:

> *Light abandons us and a darkness replaces it.*
>
> *Instantly, a billion cicadas begin trilling in the dense, velvety void—loudly, insistently, without pause—before hopefully, at some point, becoming the void.*
>
> *The insect song fills and sweeps the theatre in pulsing pitch-black waves, over and beyond the stage—washing itself over the walls and the floors, baptizing the aisles and the seats, forcing itself into every inch of space, every nook, every pocket, hiding place, and pore until this incessant chatter is touching you.*
>
> *It is touching you.*[51]

The most striking aspect of this passage is the connection between the cicadas' song and Blackness. The traditional extinguishing of the house lights prior to lights-up onstage is here characterized by Jacobs-Jenkins as an audience being confronted with Blackness—a largely "white" audience, it should again be noted, especially in the 2014 Off-Broadway production. The cicadas are part of the "dense, velvety void" of the darkened theatre. Their song fills the playing space and viewing space "in pulsing pitch-black waves . . . forcing itself into every inch of space." The cicadas' "insistent" song demands that the white audience members recognize the Blackness around them not as the absence of light but rather as a living presence.

By the end of the play, the connection between the cicadas and Blackness is yet clearer. As mentioned earlier, when the Lafayettes discover their father's lynching photos buried in his effects, they wish them to remain buried and forgotten. Likewise, there are slaves buried on the family's land, and the Lafayettes wish them to remain buried and forgotten as well. In the first lines of the play, this willful amnesia of racial history is directly connected to the cicadas' song. Upon arriving at the homestead in the middle of the night, River, who has never heard the loud, incessant hum of cicadas, asks Franz what the noise is. "Cicadas. . . . They're bugs," he explains. "Every thirteen years they come out of the ground and make all this noise together. I forgot all about them."[52] Franz's lines here clarify the relationship between Blackness and the cicadas. Cicadas seem to be dead and buried, but they reemerge every thirteen years. Likewise, the racial history of the United States has been whitewashed and buried over and over again by revisionists and deniers, yet it continues to reemerge in the work of racial educators and activists and, unfortunately, also in ongoing acts of racial hatred. As the play progresses, then, what was mere metaphor in the initial immersive soundscape—whiteness confronting Blackness—becomes a social and historical confrontation of race, for the audience members as well as the characters.

Not only is the cicadas' song representative of the racial history of Black Americans that refuses to remain buried, but these creatures' miraculous reemergence also seems to hold the promise of new life, of life from apparent death. The song of the cicadas in the initial stage directions, particularly, seems to offer the potential for rebirth in the audience, as Jacobs-Jenkins describes the song "*washing itself over the walls and the floors, baptizing the aisles and the seats*." This desire for new life through the promise of baptism is played out in Franz's character arc in *Appropriate*. Franz is the "prodigal son" of the Lafayette family. His scandalous history of drug use and underage sexual relations has stained the family name. Franz hopes to exorcise his dark past through his return home and reconciliation with his siblings. In a final bid for expiation toward the end of the play, Franz takes the lynching photos and submerges them in the family lake, along with his own body. "I think I might have baptized myself!" he exclaims proudly upon returning home.[53] He goes on to describe what he considers a renewing experience: "I took everything—all my pain, all Daddy's pain, this family's pain, the pictures—and I left it there. I washed it away."[54]

However, Franz's sins, much less the sins of the Lafayettes or the sins of the system of slavery from which the United States has benefited for years, cannot be washed away so easily. Like a white man's tears in contemporary political culture, baptism in the water of the lake falsely suggests that the penance of tears can somehow erase social crimes. This is revealed by the fact that Franz actually seems to have made things worse by carrying the lynching artifacts into the lake. After facing his siblings' disapproval of what he considered a righteous act, Franz tries to retrieve the photos from the lake in order to make amends. He returns carrying "*a pile of wet paper pulp*."[55] His supposed act of renewal is shown as a further act of destruction, not only for the Lafayettes but also for the history of the lynching victims whose images in these photos have now been permanently erased.

The arrogance of this perceived easy expiation is tied to a faith in empathy. Fittingly, the last two lines of the initial stage directions describing the cicadas' song bring up the possibility that, when confronted with Blackness, empathy is the starting point for reparation between Blackness and whiteness. It sets up

Jacobs-Jenkins's later rejection of, or at least ambivalence toward, empathy as a social tool. Jacobs-Jenkins writes that the cicadas' song fills up the entire space of the theatre, "*forcing itself into every inch of space, every nook, every pocket, hiding place, and pore until this incessant chatter is touching you. It is touching you.*" The emphatic declaration that the song is "touching" the audience member seems to suggest that, whether or not the audience member wants to ignore the song—or, like the Lafayettes, wants to ignore the racial history of the United States encapsulated in the microcosm of the Lafayette family drama—the song *will* nonetheless make a connection. The audience member will be "touched."

Jacobs-Jenkins's interest in the political efficacy of empathy is paralleled in *An Octoroon*. The printed script of this play, for example, begins with a quotation from playwright Boucicault, Jacobs-Jenkins's source for his adaptation: "If such an imitation of human beings, suffering from their fate, be well contrived and executed in all its parts, the spectator is led to feel a particular sympathy with the artificial joys and sorrows of which he is the witness."[56] The manufactured emotions of the actor create "real" emotions in the spectator, and these emotions, through the pathways of a socially conscious plot, can be guided toward specific political ends. Boucicault's theory of empathy is put to the test later in *An Octoroon* when, in a moment that mirrors the Lafayette family's discoveries in *Appropriate*, the Assistant projects a lynching photograph onto the back wall of the stage, then describes the spectacular steamship fire in act 5 of Boucicault's play—which financial considerations prohibit the current production from recreating, he explains. The Assistant hopes his description, and perhaps the projected image of violence that lingers in the minds of the audience, will suffice to fulfill Boucicault's goal of evoking emotion from the audience. "The point of this whole thing was to make you feel something," the Assistant says.[57] In this instance, Jacobs-Jenkins, as he does throughout his adaptation of Boucicault's play, is working in the mode of pastiche rather than parody. He credits Boucicault's belief in the potential of emotion to inspire change and attempts to use emotion as a tool himself.

At the same time, it is a projected image of a lynching in *An Octoroon* and the Assistant's description of Boucicault's spectacle that are supposed to create the artificial sorrow that will then be experienced by the sympathetic audience member as real sorrow. Interestingly, *An Octoroon*'s use of projected image and description-after-the-event are employed to make the audience "feel something," not to think. Jacobs-Jenkins, then, shows that what have been used in the modern theatre as alienating devices often stir emotional reactions. Likewise, the cicadas' song in *Appropriate* seems designed to alienate the audience to some extent. As Jacobs-Jenkins writes in his initial stage direction, "[The song] *goes on and on and on and on and on until the same thought occurs in every head: "Is this it?" "Is this the whole show?"* Yet the song also "touches" the audience. Feeling is not a bad thing, and it is unavoidable. It is specifically the sense of empathy about which Jacobs-Jenkins seems more concerned.

In terms of the role empathy plays in art, Sontag's book *Regarding the Pain of Others*, which mainly addresses the popular reception of war photography, helps make sense of Jacobs-Jenkins's conflicted use of the cicada song. Reflecting Jacobs-Jenkins's faith in empathy in his first lines describing the song, Sontag starts by admitting that, earlier in her career, she felt images that captured others' suffering could create sympathy that, in turn, could translate into social action. Later in her life, though, she is not as certain. "Compassion is an unstable emotion," she writes. "It needs to be translated into action, or it withers."[58] Moreover, sympathy for others' suffering may seem a healthy reaction but can be politically problematic. "So far as we feel sympathy, we feel we are not accomplices to what caused the suffering," Sontag explains. "Our sympathy proclaims our innocence as well as our impotence. To that extent, it can be (for all our good intentions) an impertinent—if not an inappropriate—response."[59] It is important to note that Sontag uses the term "sympathy" (feeling compassion for others' suffering) here rather than "empathy" (imagining oneself in someone else's situation). However, by the end of her book, like Saidiya Hartman, Sontag makes it clear that it is the possibilities of *empathy* she wants to dismiss all together. Presented with others' suffering, she claims: "We don't get it. We truly can't imagine what it was like. . . . Can't understand, can't imagine. That's what every soldier, and every journalist and aid worker and independent observer who has put in time under fire, and had the luck to elude the death that struck down others nearby, stubbornly feels. And they are right."[60] No one can really put themselves in another's place, feel their pain, know their mind: "No 'we' should be taken for granted when the subject is looking at other people's pain."[61]

However, Sontag, like Jacobs-Jenkins, allows that feeling *sympathy* is not necessarily a bad thing, as long as it is not accepted as a full response. Ultimately, Sontag argues that confronting others' suffering is useful: "Let the atrocious images haunt us. Even if they are only tokens, and cannot possibly encompass most of the reality to which they refer, they still perform a vital function. The images say: This is what human beings are capable of doing—may volunteer to do, enthusiastically, self-righteously. Don't forget."[62] It is important, then, Sontag would argue, for the Assistant in *An Octoroon* to display the lynching photo, even if the political result of this action is immeasurable or slight.

Empathy may be a dead end, even an impossibility, but feeling sympathy, for Jacobs-Jenkins, can be a useful first step, if it is accepted as only a first step.

As DiAngelo and Dyson exhort in their descriptions of white fragility, the next and more important step after emotion is education and reflection. Or, as Sontag puts it, photographs of war horrors alone cannot "repair our ignorance about the history and causes of the suffering," but they can serve as "an invitation to pay attention, to reflect, to learn, to examine the rationalizations for mass suffering offered by established powers."[63]

The cicadas' song, which returns at the end of *Appropriate*, suggests just this progression from feeling to historical consciousness. In an even longer stage direction than his first, Jacobs-Jenkins clarifies that white audiences should not presume they can walk in a Black man's shoes. This is the lie of empathy and the ugliest expression of this lie is the indulgent self-pity of "white men's tears" presented in the play. Nevertheless, he has hope for what a sympathetic listener to the cicadas' song might do next: reflect on history. His second description of the song begins: "*The cicadas? They just go on singing—singing loudly, singing incessantly—a long, enormously complicated, deeply-layered, entirely improvised ancient song, which is mostly about the morning, but also about the evening and the day but also the night and the sun but also the moon.*"[64] The form of the stage directions seems intentional here, a way of signaling the otherness of the cicadas in relation to the human drama of the play that the song frames. Written as stream-of-conscious in one long sentence, Jacobs-Jenkins's stage direction pays homage to the end of James Joyce's *Ulysses*: Molly Bloom's chapter-length single-sentence stream-of-consciousness that genders the rest of the Joyce's novel as "male" in opposition to the "female" writing that gets the last word. In *Appropriate*'s case, the stage direction's formal difference "others" the whiteness of the realist dialogue that precedes it.

Moreover, how the description ends is particularly important, as it reverses the earlier suggestion that the song "touching" the audience was actual communication, that it expressed any content beyond emotion. After the long description of the song, Jacobs-Jenkins writes, "*And we can't understand a word of it.*"[65] And of course the audience literally cannot understand the song of the cicadas that would be piped through the sound system in performance. Furthermore, the irony of Jacobs-Jenkins's script compared to the theatrical performance of *Appropriate* emphasizes this impossibility of understanding, the impossibility of empathy, the impossibility that an audience can put itself in the place of the cicada. After all, what sound designer could convey all that Jacobs-Jenkins insists the cicadas' song expresses in his long stage direction: the evening, the day, the night, and so on? The playwright emphasizes the impossibility of empathy through his impossible-to-realize stage direction.

Like Sontag, though, Jacobs-Jenkins still wants his audience to feel something—as long as they do not deceive themselves into a false sense of empathy—because feeling can lead to reflection. He manufactures this space for audience reflection in the final stage direction of the script. This scene begins as the script began, paying homage to Chekhov's *The Cherry Orchard*. Like Chekhov's final image of the servant Firs lying down onstage, forgotten, as the sound of the orchard being chopped down is heard in the distance, Jacobs-Jenkins's progression of images of the empty Lafayette home asks his audience to reflect on what has been forgotten and what will be forgotten in this space: "*lights immediately come up on the living room, some day—any day. A knocking is heard at the front door. Someone says, 'Hello?' Beat. Then more knocking. But no one answers.*"[66] The playwright, however, then moves beyond the bleakness found in Chekhov's final moment to ask the audience to take a different journey. In a series of moments divided by blackouts, the audience witnesses the Lafayette home crumble into disrepair:

> "*a part of the floor collapses beneath the sofa and one of the display tables . . .*
>
> *A rock comes flying through the window and shatters it . . .*
>
> *There is a thunderstorm. Lightning flashes. Wind howls. A tree branch is seen crashing through another window . . .*
>
> *A part of the ceiling collapses, bringing the dead chandelier down with it, but just before it can crash to the floor, the chandelier is caught by some sort of cord and swings like a pendulum.*[67]

Jacobs-Jenkins does not allow the audience to wallow in grief in parallel with Bo's final tears nor merely to experience some vague emotional response to the "otherness" of the cicada song. Rather, he asks audiences to consider the Lafayette plantation through time. He turns them into historians, as they reflect from a distance on the themes of the play without characters onstage to whom the audience can empathetically attach themselves. When experiencing art, true objectivity may be an unachievable ideal. As Sontag claims, for example, identity will always determine how suffering is read. Nevertheless, *Appropriate* offers some sort of objectivity by giving the audience the long view of an object disintegrating, not the close-up of a subject suffering. The audience members move from feeling to thinking in these final moments of *Appropriate*. Will it inspire them to social action? Jacobs-Jenkins seems as skeptical as Sontag about this possibility. However, also like Sontag, he seems to hope that at least his art can haunt the audience and serve as "an invitation to pay attention, to reflect, to learn," as Sontag put it, and as DiAngelo and Dyson would no doubt approve of.

Finally, it is not coincidental that Jacobs-Jenkins describes the leaps in time through these series of snapshots as "*—thirteen years from now—twenty-six years from now.*"[68] The thirteen-year increments suggest that we are on cicada time in this final scene. It is an "other" perspective we are offered at the end of the play, the same kind of "other" perspective that Jacobs-Jenkins used to help his audience recognize whiteness, the same distanced otherness that allows Smith and Young to identify the bogusness of Kavanaugh's white tears. The ending of *Appropriate*, then, seems hopeful with the political promise of such perspectives, and this is only tempered by the reminder that Jacobs-Jenkins's vision for this ending seems as unstageable as his description of the cicada song. It is a wish for a theatre that might move the audience from emotion to reflection to political action.

Notes

1. "White men's tears," following the definition of "white tears" by Robin DiAngelo, can be found in Lee's *Straight White Men*, which played Off Broadway at the Public Theater in 2014 and on Broadway in 2018, and FastHorse's *The Thanksgiving Play*, which played Off Broadway in 2018.
2. Robin DiAngelo, *White Fragility: Why It's So Hard for White People to Talk about Racism* (Boston: Beacon, 2018), 131.
3. Saidiya Hartman, *Scenes of Subjection* (Oxford: Oxford University Press, 1997), 18.
4. The playwright pronounces his play's title as you would the adjective "appropriate" but wants readers/audiences to acknowledge that the verb form of "appropriate" also makes sense as a title. Eliza Bent, "Branden Jacobs-Jenkins: Feel That Thought," *American Theatre*, May 15, 2014, https://www.americantheatre.org/2014/05/15/brandenjacobsjenkins_appropriate_octoroon-2/.
5. Elahe Izadi, "Men Crying on TV as Never Before," *Washington Post*, Arts and Entertainment—Perspective, March 30, 2018, https://www.washingtonpost.com/news/arts-and-entertainment/wp/2018/03/30/men-are-crying-on-tv-like-never-before/?utm_term=.5717739479b8.
6. A. C. Snow, "When Is It OK for Men to Cry in Public? After Kavanaugh Hearing, Debate Continues," *Raleigh News and Observer*, October 21, 2018, https://www.newsobserver.com/living/liv-columns-blogs/article220194020.html.
7. Erika D. Smith, "A Crying Brett Kavanaugh: This Is What White Male Privilege Looks Like," *Sacramento Bee*, September 27, 2018, https://www.sacbee.com/opinion/opn-columns-blogs/erika-d-smith/article219146885.html.
8. Damon Young, "The Delicious Salt of Brett Kavanaugh's White Tears," TheRoot.com, September 27, 2018, https://verysmartbrothas.theroot.com/the-delicious-salt-of-brett-kavanaughs-white-tears-1829374238.
9. Michael Lista, "The Tears of Brett Kavanaugh," Culture Desk, *New Yorker*, October 4, 2018, https://www.newyorker.com/culture/culture-desk/the-tears-of-brett-kavanaugh.

10. In contextualizing Kavanaugh's testimony, Lista is generally describing the literary history of male grief. The white male tears he describes should be distinguished from the specific contemporary phenomenon "white men's tears," my proposed extension of the commonly described reaction to racial conflict "white tears," articulated by theorists of white fragility.
11. Branden Jacobs-Jenkins, *An Octoroon* (New York: Dramatists Play Service, 2015), 46.
12. Michael D'Antonio, "When Men Cry in Public," CNN.com, September 28, 2018, https://www.cnn.com/2018/09/27/opinions/kavanaugh-and-crying-men-dantonio/index.html. D'Antonio's use of the word "hysterical" is not arbitrary. It is a reminder that interest in the believability of (and the motivation behind) emotions in public speech can be traced to the movement of realism in the theatre. As Elin Diamond elaborates in her 1990 essay "Realism and Hysteria" and her subsequent book *Unmaking Mimesis* (1997), in early European Realist drama the influence of Freud and Breuer's "talking cure" meant that spectators for the first time were "put in the position of analyst/discoverer," almost exclusively for female characters such as Nora Helmer or Miss Julie. ("Realism and Hysteria: Toward a Feminist Mimesis," in *Discourse* 13, no. 1 [1990], 68). Realism turned the audience member into the amateur psychoanalyst. Some critics have read *Appropriate* (and similar plays) as examples of playwrights of color both following and challenging theatrical realism. (See Kee-Yoon Nahm's "Visibly White: Realism and Race in *Appropriate* and *Straight White Men* in *The Journal of American Drama and Theatre* 27, no. 2 [2015].) This essay, however, is specifically concerned with one aspect of realism that has been part of the theatre experience and has been debated by theatre critics in the West since at least Aristotle: the inducement and effect of empathy on the audience member.
13. E. Patrick Johnson, *Appropriating Blackness: Performance and the Politics of Authenticity* (Durham, NC: Duke University Press, 2003), 7. The flip side to the way Black journalists characterized Kavanaugh's tears can be found in Johnson's discussion of the way white queer theorist John Champagne challenged Black gay writer and activist Essex Hemphill's presentation at the 1990 OUTWRITE Conference. Hemphill's tears while presenting on Robert Mapplethorpe's use of Black men's bodies in his photography were perceived by Champagne as "an attempt to shame the audience into refusing to interrogate the terms of his address." Champagne, therefore, participates in the long tradition of contrasting emotion (and the Black performance of emotion) with reasonable discourse. Johnson, building on bell hooks's work on Black culture aesthetics in *Yearning* (1990), defends Hemphill, arguing that his "tears, as a performance of black style that draws on emotionality, may be read as more than simply a willful act of manipulation to substantiate the black gay 'experience' of subjugation and objectification"; rather they may offer resistance to the authoritative Other of white authority that controls public space. See Johnson, "'Quare' Studies, or (Almost) Everything I Know about Queer Studies I Learned from My Grandma," in *Black Queer Studies*, ed. Johnson and Mae. G. Henderson (Durham, NC: Duke University Press, 2005), 131–33; John Champagne, *The Ethics of Marginality: A New Approach to Gay Studies* (Minneapolis: University of Minneapolis Press, 1995), 58–59; and hooks, *Yearning* (Boston: South End, 1990), 22.
14. Susan Sontag, *Regarding the Pain of Others* (New York: Farrar, Straus and Giroux, 2003), 10.
15. DiAngelo, *White Fragility*, 5.
16. DiAngelo, *White Fragility*, 112.

17. DiAngelo, *White Fragility*, 112.
18. DiAngelo, *White Fragility*, 135.
19. Michael Eric Dyson, *Tears We Cannot Stop: A Sermon to White America* (New York: St. Martin's Press, 2017), 103.
20. Dyson, *Tears We Cannot Stop*, 73.
21. Dyson, *Tears We Cannot Stop*, 74.
22. Branden Jacobs-Jenkins, *Appropriate* (New York: Dramatists Play Service, 2016), 39. The slash is Jacobs-Jenkins's indication that Bo interrupts and overlaps River's line.
23. Dyson, *Tears We Cannot Stop*, 78.
24. Dyson, *Tears We Cannot Stop*, 78.
25. Jacobs-Jenkins, *Appropriate*, 27.
26. Jacobs-Jenkins, *Appropriate*, 28.
27. Jacobs-Jenkins, *Appropriate*, 34.
28. Jacobs-Jenkins, *Appropriate*, 52.
29. Dyson, *Tears We Cannot Stop*, 82.
30. See, for example, Ben Brantley, "A Squabbling Family Kept in the Dark," review of *Appropriate*, *New York Times*, March 17, 2014: C1.
31. Jacobs-Jenkins, *Appropriate*, 9.
32. Jacobs-Jenkins, *Appropriate*, 25.
33. Jacobs-Jenkins, *Appropriate*, 46.
34. Dyson, *Tears We Cannot Stop*, 87.
35. Jacobs-Jenkins, *Appropriate*, 28.
36. Dyson, *Tears We Cannot Stop*, 88.
37. Jacobs-Jenkins, *Appropriate*, 50.
38. Jacobs-Jenkins, *Appropriate*, 50.
39. Jacobs-Jenkins, *Appropriate*, 71.
40. Jacobs-Jenkins, *Appropriate*, 14.
41. Jacobs-Jenkins, *Appropriate*, 76.
42. Bo's tears are private in the sense that he has no onstage audience. He is alone in the family home at this point in the play. However, as a piece of theatre, *Appropriate* stages Bo's emotional moment as a repeated public performance for multiple audiences. In this sense, Bo's breakdown is a clear example of "white men's tears." It invites a public, composed mainly of white audience members—in the 2014 Off-Broadway production, at least—to pity, and desire to come to the aid of, this white man in his grief. As stated before, the danger is that Bo's grief supplants and even erases from the audience's mind the true suffering that has occurred on the Lafayette plantation. Hearts break for this white patriarch while the Black slaves who haunt the play are forgotten.
43. Jacobs-Jenkins, *Appropriate*, 76.
44. Harvey Young, *Embodying Black Experience: Stillness, Critical Memory, and the Black Body* (Ann Arbor: University of Michigan Press, 2010), 176.
45. Dyson, *Tears We Cannot Stop*, 197–212.
46. DiAngelo, *White Fragility*, 137.
47. Dyson, *Tears We Cannot Stop*, 211.
48. Hartman, *Scenes of Subjection*, 18.
49. Hartman, *Scenes of Subjection*, 19.
50. Jacobs-Jenkins, *Appropriate*, 9.

51. Jacobs-Jenkins, *Appropriate*, 11.
52. Jacobs-Jenkins, *Appropriate*, 13.
53. Jacobs-Jenkins, *Appropriate*, 65.
54. Jacobs-Jenkins, *Appropriate*, 67.
55. Jacobs-Jenkins, *Appropriate*, 74.
56. Jacobs-Jenkins, *An Octoroon*, 5.
57. Jacobs-Jenkins, *An Octoroon*, 64. By displaying this photo in *An Octoroon*, Jacobs-Jenkins turns Boucicault's play into a kind of lynching play. As Koritha Mitchell's *Living with Lynching: African American Lynching Plays, Performance, and Citizenship, 1890–1930* (Urbana: University of Illinois Press, 2011) argues, lynching plays, though seldom produced on US stages, were circulated and discussed in Black communities at the turn of the century and indeed cultivated an audience for serious Black drama. It is unlikely that the Off-Broadway production of *An Octoroon* for a majority white audience in 2014, like these earlier lynching plays, created an alternative space for Black audiences to look beyond the violence of lynching spectacles to see Black families and communities continuing to struggle with racial violence. Nevertheless, Jacobs-Jenkins's "modernization" of the scenes between the enslaved people in his adaptation of Boucicault's drama likewise emphasizes the ongoing struggle of Black people living with racism and provides a greater context to the tragic depiction of lynching victims.
58. Sontag, *Regarding the Pain of Others*, 101.
59. Sontag, *Regarding the Pain of Others*, 102.
60. Sontag, *Regarding the Pain of Others*, 125.
61. Sontag, *Regarding the Pain of Others*, 7.
62. Sontag, *Regarding the Pain of Others*, 115.
63. Sontag, *Regarding the Pain of Others*, 117.
64. Jacobs-Jenkins, *Appropriate*, 77.
65. Jacobs-Jenkins, *Appropriate*, 77.
66. Jacobs-Jenkins, *Appropriate*, 77.
67. Jacobs-Jenkins, *Appropriate*, 78.
68. Jacobs-Jenkins, *Appropriate*, 78.

Asia and Alwin Nikolais

Interdisciplinarity, Orientalist Tendencies, and Midcentury American Dance

—ANGELA K. AHLGREN

The dancers in Alwin Nikolais's *Kaleidoscope* (1953 and 1956) appear in full-body leotards that bisect their bodies in blocks of black and white.[1] Makeup covers one half of their faces in white and the other half in black. At one moment, a group of these harlequin-esque dancers wield large oar-like paddles painted with rough, bold strokes, evoking indigenous patterns of the South Pacific. At another, two dancers balance a long pole between them, sometimes on the tops of their flexed feet and at other times on their shoulders, as they balance in a yoga-style boat pose on the ground. To music listed simply as "ethnic" in the program, they move in a slow unison so as to keep the pole balanced between them, evoking the slow and flex-limbed precision of Southeast Asian dance styles. Dance historian Rebekah Kowal has written that they "resemble Thai court dancers," while dance critic Anna Kisselgoff likens them to "Javanese dancers."[2] *Kaleidoscope*'s flashes of Asian dance and movement styles, coupled with so-called ethnic music sources, foreshadow the Asian aesthetics Nikolais developed further in *Totem* (1960) and *Imago* (1963). Alwin Nikolais (1910–1993) was a twentieth-century American choreographer, designer, musician, and theatremaker whose choreographic works blurred lines between dance and theatre. He began choreographing in 1936 and premiered his final and 118th work in 1992, the year preceding his death. Between 1948 and 1970, Nikolais taught dance classes and formed a dance company at the Henry Street Playhouse in the Lower East Side of New York City. He stated that he favored motion over emotion in choreography and often extended his dancers' bodies through props and objects. He began these body-extending experiments in the early 1950s, around the time he began to conceptualize his art-making as "total theatre" and to experiment with electronic music composed in the style of *music concrete*, a Bauhaus-inspired genre in which the composer uses and manipulates "found sounds."[3] Because Nikolais often masked the provenance of his inspirations, musical or otherwise, Asian influences like those in *Kaleidoscope* can become "invisible-ized" and difficult to trace.[4]

Like his modernist predecessors, Nikolais used many sounds and gestures that came from Asian performance, African music, and other so-called ethnic sources, especially in his 1950s and 1960s choreographies. While the dancers seldom directly imitated particular forms, a focused eye and sensitive ear can detect Japanese drumming, gamelan music, and Kabuki-influenced makeup (and more) in pieces such as *Kaleidoscope*, *Totem*, and *Imago*. Nikolais's work departs from earlier character-driven, Orientalist costume dramas by choreographers like Ruth St. Denis and José Limón, yet it continues the practice of appropriating Asian performance. In what follows, I contextualize the Orientalist tendencies of midcentury white American choreographers such as Nikolais within the global circulation of Asian performance in the Cold War era. Japanese theatre and music ensembles toured extensively in New York in the 1950s, and the Southeast Asian ensemble music tradition of gamelan also influenced modernist Western composers both before and after the introduction of gamelan ensembles in the United States during this period. That Nikolais incorporates these influences into his work during the 1950s and 1960s is both an aesthetic and a historical phenomenon. I show how the Asian aesthetics within these dances belong to a historical moment in which the meanings produced by "Asia" in the arts were shifting. Thinking through this issue together with insights from musicology, dance, and theatre complicates and broadens conversations about the circulation of Asian aesthetics in American modern dance while resisting the urge to "reify a binary divide between passive victims and Western thieves."[5] As Michelle Liu Carriger argues, binaristic thinking between appropriation-as-bad and appreciation-as-good can simplify complicated historical connections and erase any agency the non-Western Other may have had in circulating their own artistry. Here, I hope to demonstrate that Nikolais's use of Asian aesthetics added a layer to an already sedimented field of appropriation that cannot be discounted and that his borrowing also depended on the presence of Japanese, Chinese, Indian, Cambodian, and other artists in New York, as well as the circulation of instruments and other objects that could be purchased and experimented with for relatively little money.

Furthermore, these performances present an opportunity to think through what I am calling "Orientalist tendencies" across performance disciplines, since these influences emerge not only visually—through choreography, costumes, and scenography—but also aurally, through electronic music and soundscapes. Thus, a broader aim of this essay is to argue for the value of interdisciplinary analysis, investigating dance, music, and theatre histories together. Nikolais is best known in dance history, and to a lesser degree, in music history, since he choreographed dancers and composed music and sound for these performances. But he also designed the lights, costumes, and scenic elements for these performances and often referred to himself as an artist invested in making "total theatre." His early career also places him in theatre history: in the 1930s, he directed a marionette theatre and provided choreography for Federal Theatre Project productions, and later, at the Henry Street Playhouse, he created a number of dance-plays for children.[6] Writing about *Totem* in 1960, critic John Martin characterized Nikolais's creations as "avant-garde" work "with dancing scarcely more than the taking-off point for a theatre synthesis of light, sound, and 'props.'"[7] It can be tempting, as Kate Elswit notes in *Theatre and Dance*, to simply categorize work like Nikolais's as "performance" and elide disciplinary divides between dance and theatre, but this elision undermines the "mechanics of nomenclature," or the ways these terms have produced meaning in specific contexts.[8] Given how much value Nikolais placed on creating sound for his works (he even released an LP of his electronic music in 1959), relatively little scholarship deals with the sonic aspects of his repertoire.[9] Listening to, in addition to looking at, Nikolais's work opens up insights about Asianist elements that are only minimally or sporadically available through movement, costumes, and makeup. Similarly, attending to nuanced details of movement, particularly in the absence of narrative, is a dance studies strategy that can be deployed in theatre history scholarship, as well. Thus, this essay models a way to examine music, dance, and theatrical elements of a given work—in this case, two works that might reasonably be considered as theatre—without collapsing them into a catchall category of performance.

Focusing on two evening-length works, *Totem* (1960) and *Imago* (1963), I show how Nikolais's modernist borrowing of Asian theatre, dance, and music is tied to the conventions of modern dance in New York City and the global circulation of Japanese, South Asian, and Southeast Asian performing arts in the Cold War era. While these early works clearly evoke Asian aesthetics, Nikolais deflected questions about the provenance of specific elements, preferring to "invisible-ize" the sources of his inspiration, which also makes identifying the sources difficult. Archival materials from the Alwin Nikolais and Murray Louis Dance Collection at Ohio University—including programs, video and audio recordings, unpublished manuscript pages, and other ephemera—as well as other newspaper sources and circulating video recordings, support my analyses of the sonic, choreographic, and visual elements of *Totem* and *Imago*. I argue that these two works signal shifts not in *whether* but *how* midcentury choreographers incorporated non-Western elements into their works and raise questions about the national racial politics of these choreographic and compositional strategies.

Performing Asia in Cold War America: Global Circulations and Embodied Histories

Totem and *Imago* emerged in the midst of a Cold War period during which the United States' economic, military, and diplomatic relations with Asia intensified. Representations of Asia proliferated in US cultural productions from the 1940s to the 1960s in the form of plays, musicals, books, and other forms; and while Americans' fascination with Asia was not new, these representations shaped ideas about Asia in what Christina Klein terms the "middlebrow imagination" of Americans.[10] But it was not just Western representations of Asia that circulated in the Cold War; Asian artists from Japan, India, Cambodia, Indonesia, and other Asian nations represented themselves in the United States through theatre, dance, and music tours, and also took to stages and classrooms on the East and West Coasts in the mid- to late 1950s.

As I explore later, Barbara E. Thornbury documents how cultural critics who wrote about Japanese theatre influenced discourse about Japan and helped introduce Kabuki to New York audiences. Throughout the 1950s, tours of Kabuki artists from Japan (as well as practitioners of other Japanese arts) helped shape discourse about Japan and Japanese aesthetics. A plethora of coverage in major news outlets like the *New York Times* contributed to a discourse Thornbury calls "America's Kabuki Japan," in which Kabuki came to stand in for Japanese arts as a whole.[11] Additionally, the late 1950s marked the increased circulation within the United States of gamelan music from Southeast Asia. Andrew Clay McGraw writes that gamelan was introduced to American audiences in 1893 at the Chicago World's Fair, although it was only in the 1950s that it was again performed in the United States.[12] In 1958, ethnomusicologist Mantle Hood was the first to begin a gamelan ensemble in the United States as a teaching tool for graduate students at UCLA.[13] Thus, performing arts from various parts of Asia circulated on both coasts in the 1950s, adding to the layers of influence that had already existed.

One of the enduring problems of articulating the relationship between Asia and the United States from a US perspective is that Asia and Asians are typically figured as permanently outside of, rather than part of, the fabric of the United States.[14] This sentiment is evident even within influential dance studies texts like Brenda Dixon Gottschild's *Digging the Africanist Presence in American Performance*. She writes, "Africanisms are not a choice but an imperative that come to us through the culture. Unlike modern and postmodern decisions to appropriate imported elements from Zen Buddhism, yoga, T'ai Chi, Qi-Gong, or other Asian disciplines, the Africanist presence comes to Americans from home base, from the inside."[15] In this formulation, Africanisms are part of American culture "from the inside," but Asianist elements are "imported." I want to complicate Dixon Gottschild's division of how African and Asian elements make their way into American art: Do some artists not circumvent African American influences to borrow directly from African sources? And haven't some Asian performance forms been practiced in the United States for long enough to no longer be considered "imported"? Asadata Dafora, born in Sierra Leone, performed West African drumming and dancing to acclaim in New York starting in the 1930s.[16] Katherine Dunham is an example of a US artist whose ethnographic study of dance in Haiti and elsewhere in the Caribbean brought Africanist elements into her choreographies and enabled her to invite Caribbean artists to the United States. While this is one strand of a much deeper relationship to the African diaspora (and one centered in the Caribbean rather than the African continent), Dunham's Africanist influence was not solely "from the inside."[17] On the other hand, yoga, which has roots in South Asia, has been practiced in the United States since the nineteenth century.[18] While Dixon Gottschild's formulation emphasizes the ways Africanisms are tightly woven into US culture, her statement also reflects the enduring sense that, no matter how long Asians have been part of US culture, they are also perpetually outsiders. I want to complicate, rather than dispute, the idea that Asian elements are only ever from the outside. In my analyses below, I consider how Asian performance circulated in New York not only through tours but also through longtime practitioners and through the Asian aesthetics already embedded in modern dance and music histories.

While it is possible that Nikolais consciously "quoted" Asian designs, music, and movement in his choreographies because of what he perceived as their exotic (and therefore unrecognizable) qualities (at least to Western audiences), it is also equally likely that he had already absorbed Asianist aesthetics "from the inside," having been trained in an American modern dance tradition, which, as Yutian Wong writes, "is *already* Asian American."[19] Dance historians have detailed how the white women who pioneered American modern dance appropriated the aesthetics—and often the very choreographies—of the Asian dancers with whom they came into contact. For example, the successes of Ruth St. Denis and Loïe Fuller especially rested on costuming, choreography, and other performance effects from Indian dance.[20] Later, Martha Graham's long-standing interest in yoga principles and movement further embedded Asian aesthetics in modern dance technique.[21] Beyond these individuals, Nikolais names the German expressionist dances of Mary Wigman and the modernist designs of Edward Gordon Craig, themselves both influenced by Asian aesthetics, as influences.[22] Bob Gilmore writes that a thirty-something Nikolais attended a performance by Mary Wigman and was "impressed both by the qualities of the dance and by the fact that the performance made use of percussion music, a new sonority in 1930s America." Gilmore concludes that this early impression influenced Nikolais's later and widespread use of percussion in his choreographies.[23] The use of Japanese, Indian, and Southeast Asian dance and music was therefore not a strategy unique to Nikolais, nor was it a strategy that required him to work outside the norms of modern dance practice at midcentury.

Similarly, for composers in the middle of the twentieth century, it was commonplace to appropriate the styles and structures of Asian and other non-Western music into their compositions. According to musicologist Amy Bauer, eighteenth- and nineteenth-century composers employed certain musical devices (for example, the arabesque and Phrygian mode) to signal foreignness and exoticism, while in the early twentieth century, "orientalist elements often featured an explicit homage to particular locations." Modernist composers, she writes, "rejected the surface charm of chinoiserie in favor of less obvious structural appropriations."[24] Nikolais's borrowing was not new, but it happened in a historical moment in which the modernist practice of appropriating from Asia was undergoing a shift. Citing John Corbett's distinction between "conceptual" and "decorative" Orientalism, Bauer writes, "Paradoxically, the rise of [John] Cage's conceptual Orientalism coincided with the increasing ubiquity of the non-Western and its consequent loss of identification with the strange, the mysterious, and the sexually alluring" and "comes to serve a grander, more exalted function."[25] Cage is a good touchstone for a discussion of Nikolais, since Cage's compositional strategies, begun at least a decade earlier, certainly influenced Nikolais's musical composition. As early as the 1950s, Nikolais had incorporated elements he described as "primitive" or "ethnic" into his dance-theatre pieces. By 1960, Nikolais had already begun to incorporate sounds such as *koto*, gongs, and other instruments from well-established Asian genres, into the music for earlier works like *Kaleidoscope* (1956) and *Prism* (1958).[26] When Nikolais looked beyond Western aesthetic traditions for inspiration for his abstract, nonliteral style of dance, music, and design, he was partaking in a practice that was both relatively new in its specific strategies, yet centuries old in its use of "ethnic sources."

How and where did the "ethnic sources" in Nikolais's music and choreography circulate in the 1950s and 1960s? My aim in the following section is to better understand the historical circumstances that allowed such choreographic modes to flourish, even for an artist whose early-career Orientalist tendencies remained just a phase, never developing further into a career-long trajectory, as was the case for Martha Graham's engagement with yoga and Ruth St. Denis's career-long inhabiting of Oriental characters.

Gamelan and Southeast Asia in *Totem* (1960)

At its premiere at New York's Henry Street Playhouse in 1960, *Totem* comprised sixteen sections, mostly titled with roman numerals; by 1962, Nikolais had revised and condensed the piece and used a different set of titles to describe the subsections. This imprecision with titles is typical for Nikolais, who preferred not to impose narrative or thematic interpretations on his dances by providing too much information. As in other dances, here Nikolais experiments with what one critic calls a "sheer multiplication of surface elements,"[27] rather than crafting psychologically or politically motivated narratives, the modes associated with his predecessors in modern dance. Indeed, surfaces are important in *Totem*, from the dancers' full-body color-blocked leotards to the patterned lights that shine across them and the silhouettes the dancers' bodies make against a cyclorama lit in deep blue during the opening and closing segments. Gamelan provides a clear source of inspiration for the largely percussion-based sound design, with gongs featuring prominently in several sections. The title, *Totem*, gestures toward the primitivist themes of the dance, which, according to the film *The World of Alwin Nikolais*, "dealt with fetishes and mysticism, with dances both sacred and profane" and "provokes the mood of ceremonies and the foundation of rites."[28] South and Southeast Asian dance and gamelan surface within *Totem* choreographically and musically. My analysis below attends to how gamelan and Southeast Asian dance circulated in the United States during the mid-twentieth century, as well as to the primitivist racial politics that surround the work.

How do gamelan and Southeast Asian dance materialize in *Totem*? I look and listen to three key moments in the piece in which these influences become apparent: "The Shadow Opening" and "Finale," which bookend the piece; the duet sometimes called "Hoop"; and a three-person dance called "Reliquary."

"The Shadow Opening" and "Finale" (which recycles elements of "The Shadow Opening") showcase what appear as "graphic designs" formed by the dancers' bodies. In "The Shadow Opening," the dancers are visible only in silhouette against a triangle of deep blue light. They form two rows, one positioned closely in front of the other, and as each row alternates between kneeling and standing, the lines give the impression of stacked-ness, perhaps a reference to the stacked icons on totem poles. Against a score composed of bells, drums, and other metallic percussion, the dancers link hands, sometimes with the others in their row, sometimes with the person in front of or behind them. As the lines of arms wave and flow, they resolve momentarily into patterns: flattened hands reminiscent of Thai dance gestures or Indian mudras form a hexagonal pattern across the stage; when dancers grasp hands with the person in front of them, their arms and torsos become a series of large eyes; dancers lying on their backs in a line create fluted columns with their hands and feet. The patterns look as if they could line the hem of a garment; they repeat; they are motifs; limbs create embodied graphic design. The percussive and sometimes clangorous music that underscores the dance at times sounds like gamelan, with gongs forming the basis of parts of the score (figure 1).

The duet that is sometimes called "Rite IV," "Hoop," or "Circle" also features a score that is gamelan-inflected, along with choreography that quotes from Indian and Southeast Asian dance styles. A duet (danced in 1960 by Murray Louis and Gladys Bailin), "Hoop" is composed of the couple's movements within and around a golden ring the size of a hula hoop. Initially, they move in unison, her back to his front so they both face the audience. They rise up on their toes once, twice, three times before moving forward in shuffling steps. Perhaps more than in other sections, the score here is unmistakably gamelan-influenced, yet it is also slightly mechanized and distorted. Is a piano being played underwater? Are they cogs in a chiming grandfather clock? Their leotards, one blue and one green, suggest a watery theme, and at times the mudra-like movements of their hands and arms also look like swimming strokes. About halfway through the approximately four-minute duet, both dancers grasp the golden hoop, holding it upright in front of them like a window. Their forearms holding the hoop in place, they open out their hands, lotus-like. Then they each extend a bent leg to the side (one lifts her left and the other his right) and slowly extend both their arms, elbows bent slightly, forming a singular, multilimbed Shiva-like figure. They shift their arms and hold another, a similarly iconic pose. A moment later, the image of Hindu deity dissolves, and the dancers become mechanized parts again, moving in rhythm with the gong-tinged percussion.

Experimenting with Asian music and dance was certainly not new in 1960,

Figure 1. Dancers create patterns with their limbs in *Totem* (1960). Photograph by David S. Berlin. Alwin Nikolais and Murray Louis Dance Collection, Courtesy of Mahn Center for Archives and Special Collections, Ohio University Libraries and the Nikolais/Louis Foundation for Dance. Used with permission.

but both gamelan and Southeast Asian classical dance circulated in the United States in the years leading up to *Totem*'s premiere. As I noted in the introduction to this essay, gamelan ensembles did not begin to form in the United States until 1958, and that trend began in Los Angeles. But as ethnomusicologist Judith Becker writes, Western composers were studying gamelan and other music from Southeast Asia (whether through travel or recordings) and incorporating aspects of it into their own compositions as early as 1936. John Cage composed *Three Dances for Two Amplified Prepared Pianos* in 1945, a piece Becker describes as "clearly influenced by Balinese gamelan with its interlocking melodies and rhythmic patterns and its percussiveness."[29] Cage's *Three Dances* uses "prepared pianos," that is, pianos with screws or bolts stuck between strings to produce different tonalities, to emphasize the percussive aspects of a piano's sound. Cage first prepared pianos to evoke an African sensibility for dancer Syvilla Fort in the late 1930s, but in *Three Dances*, the sound of the prepared and amplified pianos resembles gamelan.[30] *Three Dances* was used as the music for Merce Cunningham's "Dromenon" in 1947.[31] Given that Cage, Cunningham, and Nikolais moved in similar circles, it is entirely possible that Cage's composition, if not *Three Dances* itself, influenced Nikolais's music for *Totem*.[32] Moreover, parts of earlier works like *Kaleidoscope* are danced to John Cage's music, so it is possible that Cage's gamelan-influenced music is quoted in the score for *Totem*. Listening to the two compositions side-by-side, the second movement of Cage's *Three Dances* in particular creates a slow, underwater effect similar to Nikolais's music for the "Hoop" section of *Totem*.

It is clear that Nikolais did not need to see Asian dance to borrow from musical sources, but might the choreographic references to Cambodian or Thai dance have come from something he saw live? Magazine and newspaper reviews from the 1950s and early 1960s indicate that various forms of Southeast Asian dance were being regularly performed in New York. *New York Times* articles spanning from 1952 to 1962 indicate that Balinese dancers were performing in New York somewhat regularly during that decade.[33] While it is true that Nikolais's gestures could have been a way of borrowing the choreographies of Ruth St. Denis, who copied Indian and Cambodian dance in more directly imitative ways, it is also possible that Nikolais or his dancers, who were known to improvise as part of the choreographic process, could have learned them elsewhere, from Indian, Cambodian, and other Asian dancers practicing in New York.

Each of the two sections described above pairs a gamelan-like soundscape with choreography reminiscent of Southeast Asian dance (alongside, potentially, Indian dance or yoga), whether in the form of a visual pattern or iconic poses. Some of these poses, shapes, and sounds appear in other sections of the work, as well, suggesting a choreographic tendency to borrow from the dance traditions of Southeast Asia and, in some moments, from Hindu mythology. Doris Hering references the gods Sita and Rama in one review, which not only supports a reading of these poses as having South or Southeast Asian influence but also suggests that Hering saw such dances in New York.[34] The last scene I want to examine, sometimes titled "Reliquary," moves beyond pattern and posture and into a rare suggestion of narrative. This foray into narrative, relatively unusual for Nikolais, opens up the possibility of interpreting the piece as either indulging in or critiquing modernist primitivism.

"Reliquary" begins when two white male dancers with erect posture enter the stage carrying a pole horizontally between their shoulders. Hanging from it is a jester-like figure struggling against the chain that keeps him attached to the pole. Nikolais conceived of the jester figure as an "evil little fetish doll eager to escape his chains."[35] Accordingly, it is hard not to read a master-slave relationship in this dance, as the impassive and affectless guards reign in the restrained, yet much more physically animated, captive. A costume covered in multicolored fringe recalls both animal fur and the diamond-patterned harlequin costume, while the hood that exposes only the dancer's eyes and nose creates a distinctly monkey-like appearance. At times, the trickster figure leaps off the pole and swings the guards around by his chains, yet by the end, the guards carry him out as he hangs by his knees, upside down and limp, from the pole. The scene is a departure from others, which employ dancers' bodies as elements of a larger design or environment. Here, the scene suggests a colonial, monolithic whiteness keeping an emotionless hold over an exoticized Other with animalistic qualities whose struggles are entertaining, yet ineffectual. In this sense, the scene seems to indulge in, rather than critique, its primitivist, Orientalist narrative: not unlike blackface minstrelsy stage types, the harlequin may delight the audience in his relentless struggle, but he is ultimately, narratively subdued. Throughout, the driving beat of a gong and drum cement the scene as one that emphasizes Western notions of the primitive.

"Reliquary" is an anomaly that opens up questions about the Orientalist tendencies of *Totem* as a whole and calls into question Nikolais's claims that he sought to avoid human situations in his choreographies. While much of the piece incorporates non-Western elements as unnamed sources for Nikolais's more abstract designs and sound score, this scene references the title's primitivism in a more direct way. The dancers in this section are both more recognizably "human" than Nikolais's work generally allows, while at the same time the captive figure is de-humanized as a mere "fetish doll." Doris Hering, writing for *Dance Magazine* in 1960, claims that the dancers in *Totem* "were all rendered anonymous by white face-masks like the basic make-up of a Kathakali demon" and that the audience is "forced to forget that they are people."[36] What precisely, we might ask, qualifies a dancer to seem like a person in *Totem*? Hering equates Indian dance-drama with the nonhuman, and masks (or, at least, makeup that functions in some ways as mask) are assumed to take away the dancers' humanity. Hering's view is not unique in pointing to masks and makeup as the locus for Nikolais's "dehumanization" of his dancers. This view is, of course, deeply Eurocentric in its assumption that masked forms from Asia are inherently dehumanizing or alienating. It also displays a common mid-twentieth-century critical bias toward choreographers like Graham and Anna Sokolow, whose dances were rooted in human situations. I do concur with Hering that the scene is dehumanizing, but not because the characters wear masks or makeup. Rather, it is dehumanizing precisely because it dramatizes—without critique—a human situation of colonialism and domination. This scene highlights the very power dynamics embedded in cultural appropriation and inadvertently demonstrates that cultural borrowing rarely happens on an even playing field. The percussive scores and gamelan sensibility are meant, on some level, to invoke a sense of the Other-as-primitive in *Totem*.

Still, the way Nikolais deploys Asian elements in his choreography and music is not as simple as borrowing from "over there." By midcentury, Asian music had already been circulating in the United States and had been incorporated into modern choreography for several decades. In *Totem*, the musical Asianist aesthetics are more prominent, whereas the choreographic and scenographic elements appear, disappear, and reappear, giving them an elusive quality. Three years later, the premiere of *Imago* raised similar issues, and in the next section, I look to the Japanese influences that emerge in the work's choreographic, sonic, and visual designs.

America's Kabuki Japan in *Imago* (1963)

Nikolais called *Imago: The City Curious* one of his "most satisfying creations." The tubular arm extensions of "Mantis" and the vertical-striped tunics of "Dignitaries" are recognizable segments of this work that are most often featured in photos and clips. The piece premiered on February 24, 1963, in Hartford, Connecticut, with costumes, choreography, and lighting designed by Nikolais and a sound score Nikolais created with assistance from James Seawright.[37] It was subsequently scheduled for a six-week run at the Henry Street Playhouse in New York City and then an international tour. *Imago* was originally performed in twelve movements, though segments of the work are often excerpted and performed as stand-alone compositions. The work's subtitle, "The City Curious," matches the English translation of the title of a 1920 book by Belgian author and illustrator Jean de Bosschere, which features colorful, surrealist drawings of odd people and fantastical creatures somewhat reminiscent of Lewis Carroll's *Alice's Adventures in Wonderland*. The illustrations in de Bosschere's book have their own touch of Orientalism, with exotic-looking characters being carried in sedan chairs and coaches, against a backdrop of cities with mosque-like spires. Nikolais acknowledges that the book was an early inspiration, but on the whole, the city of curious characters in *Imago* is Nikolais's own invention. As I illustrate below, the whimsical costume and scenic designs, the electronic soundscape, and the choreography of *Imago* comprise a multilayered field out of which Asian performance elements sporadically emerge, both aurally and visually.

The *Imago* sound score is a more sophisticated composition than the scores from even a few years earlier. Nikolais's access to more advanced technology at the Columbia-Princeton Electronic Music Center likely allowed him significantly more possibilities for creating and manipulating sounds.[38] It is composed in the style of *music concrete*, a Bauhaus-inspired style of composition meant to disassociate sound from its source. As in *Totem*, as well as many other pieces, Nikolais costumed the *Imago* dancers in full-body leotards and face paint to downplay the importance of individual identities; in parallel, his soundscapes masked the sources of the sounds, so as to avoid identifying them with a particular type of music. While the gamelan influence in *Totem* seems fairly obvious, especially given other Western composers' borrowing from this form, the Asian music in *Imago* is more enigmatic. Nevertheless, I identify parts of the score as having Japanese influence.

The *Imago* soundscape brings together a range of sounds: those that evoke the synthetic and mechanical, as well as those that seem to originate in instrumental sources. These elements combine to produce different effects in each section. "Dignitaries," the opening group section of *Imago*, establishes a tone that is slightly eerie and foreboding, while the more lighthearted mechanical toy sounds of "Clique" support a trio of female dancers who move like flouncy windup toys. The horizontal lines and hurried cross-stage paths of the dancers in "Fence" suggest a busy and traffic-filled city, with sounds that resemble car horns and the clanging of train signals above a rapid, driving pulse. This continues until "Arcade," the last of twelve sections, which fuses sounds from each of the preceding sections in a vaudevillian, circus-like number. To understand *Imago*'s aesthetic and historical connection to Japanese and other Asian performance forms, I turn my eyes and ears to three sections of *Imago*: the opening segment, "Dignitaries"; a solo originated by Murray Louis called "Artisan"; and a section called "Logicians," which is notably absent in all but one recording.

"Dignitaries," the nine-minute opening section of *Imago*, builds on a percussive pattern that I contend is rooted in Japanese drumming. Percussion is layered with other "found" sounds and long silences to create a somewhat eerie atmosphere. There is never consistent rhythm or melody. The piece begins with about ninety seconds of what sounds like an orchestra tuning up before a concert and then layers percussion patterns with foreboding synthetic sounds that evoke an emergency testing signal, tuning in to a radio station, and an eerily amplified version of crumpling paper. The percussive pattern that repeats at various speeds and tones is what might be called an "acceleration pattern."[39] Such a pattern can be heard in Kabuki performance at moments of heightened emotion or during entrances and exits. In Kabuki, this acceleration pattern is played on *tsuke*, or wooden clappers. A version of this pattern called *oroshi* can also be heard in a range of Japanese drumming traditions; it is composed of a brief series of beats that increase in rapidity, sometimes leading into a drum roll. Sometimes when this pattern emerges in "Dignitaries," it sounds as if it is produced by strikes to a *shime-daiko*, a small rope-tensioned drum used in many traditional Japanese musical forms, as well as in contemporary taiko ensembles. At other times, the strikes sound more metallic, and at still others, more like the Kabuki clapper version. At still others, when the pattern is sped up, it sounds like a door creaking open. The variation in speed and sound is the result of Nikolais's ability to use a synthesizer to manipulate sound electronically. Partway through "Dignitaries," the acceleration pattern begins to repeat at various speeds and volumes, then overlaps and layers on top of itself. Layering the acceleration pattern at various speeds produces an off-kilter sensibility that I associate with certain traditional Japanese drumming styles. For example, the ideal in styles that accompany Noh, Kabuki, and festival traditions like Edo Kotobuki Jishi is not for drummers to play "as one," as might be desired in Western drum traditions. Rather, the desired sound is one in which each instrument can be heard, which produces the effect of sounding slightly off-kilter, if not offbeat.[40] As I watched a black-and-white VHS recording of the piece, my years of training as a taiko (Japanese drum) player identified the sounds of *shime-daiko*.

How much Japanese music might Nikolais have listened to? How much theatre and dance did he see? At minimum, Nikolais saw the Azuma Kabuki Dancers and Musicians perform in 1954. Producer Sol Hurok brought the troupe for a month-long engagement at the Century Theatre in 1954,[41] a playbill for which appears in Nikolais's archive.[42] The program provides the usual list of performers and acts, but it also performs an educational function: notes on the choreographic and musical aspects of Kabuki, information on related forms of Noh and Kyogen, and details about instruments used in the performance, including *taiko* (drums) and *samisen* (a three-stringed lute), instruct audiences in how to listen to and watch Kabuki. This was only the first of many performances of Japanese theatre (including more Kabuki, as well as gagaku, Noh and bunraku), to play in New York throughout the 1950s. Given the prevalence of Japanese performance presented in New York at this time and Nikolais's professed fondness for "Oriental" aesthetics, it seems highly likely he saw more than one troupe perform. Barbara Thornbury writes in *America's Japan and Japan's Performing Arts* that Kabuki enthusiasts and cultural critics Paul Green, James Michener, and Faubion Bowers wrote about Japanese theatre in widely read outlets like *Reader's Digest*, the *New York Times*, and others, as well as in books. Through their writings, they "promoted [Kabuki] as part of a larger, postwar project focusing on American-initiated international reciprocity and exchange." Moreover, these critics framed Kabuki as an "entry point for postwar American appreciation of

Japan."[43] While we don't know whether Nikolais regularly attended Japanese performances, it is unlikely he could have avoided reading about it.

Given the ubiquity of Japanese performance (to say nothing of recorded music, which Nikolais also likely accessed), it is entirely possible that Kabuki, Noh, or another form of Japanese music became part of the *Imago* score. Gilmore bolsters this assertion when he notes that the "ethnic" sources Nikolais mentions in his 1950s music drew from "primarily Japanese" sources.[44] Part of the difficulty of pinning such a thing down is that Nikolais intentionally obscured the sources of his sounds. In a 1963 essay for *Dance Perspectives*, Nikolais wrote about manipulating sound electronically: A "series of drum sounds, when speeded, filtered, and chopped up, lose their identity with their source—they become released sounds, freed of their actual physical derivation. This, to me, is one of the potent values of electronic tape. Divorced from its source, the sound becomes a free agent, emphasizing the imagination-provoking reactions that more conventional sound causes."[45] Nikolais has written and spoken extensively of his wish to reject literal associations in his dances and in his music. Many scholars have critiqued the ways Western musicians (and other artists) use non-Western music as "raw material" and achieve the status of artist while erasing the labor and artistry of those who created the so-called raw material.[46] I write from a position of alignment with these arguments. My purpose, here, is to point to how the slipperiness of identifying what is Asian is part of Nikolais's compositional strategy. Furthermore, working against this slipperiness by attempting to identify and historicize non-Western sources highlights how "freeing" sounds from their sources is its own contrivance, in this case, a contrivance based on the assumption of whiteness. Rebekah Kowal writes that Nikolais's work asks audiences to adopt "social blinders, so to speak, so as not to see (or to pretend not to see) any information that would contradict Nikolais' illusion of objectivity."[47] The Asian elements in *Imago*, as in *Totem*, are inevitably shaped by the historical and political context in which they were deployed.

How do Japanese and other Asian elements emerge in choreographic and scenographic aspects of *Imago*, in concert with its score? How might the makeup, costume, and movement materialize ideas about Asia? While the music and costumes shift between each section of the evening-length work, the makeup design and white conical headdresses for *Imago* remain constant throughout the piece, providing continuity to sections that variously use poles, tubes, kites, and ballooning costumes to create distinct environments and moods. The dancers' faces are covered in white makeup, and their hair is contained within a tight white hood, reminiscent of a swim cap. Atop the hood sits a white cylindrical cap, a few inches in diameter and about five or six inches high. The effect is that dancers with long and short hair look similar, as the cap seems to contain any dancers' longer locks within it. It also makes the dancers look somewhat otherworldly in that it changes their silhouette from human to humanlike. It is also possible to read the white cylinders as a variation on the spire-like headdresses worn by Thai dancers. Performers' lips are painted bright red, and their eyebrows are darkened in heavy black lines. In some photos, the women's eyebrow lines are more delicate than the men's, but they all extend in a black upward stroke, tapered toward the hairline. The space between eyebrow and lashes is painted in blue. Because the makeup works in tandem with a number of different design, musical, and lighting effects, its appearance and effects inevitably shift throughout the piece. At times, the dancers look like Kabuki actors and at others, Barnum and Bailey circus clowns, or "armless white-faced Pierrots," as one reviewer noted.[48]

Dance critics writing about *Imago* note the shifting effects of the show's visual elements and influences. About a 1968 performance of *Imago* in Paris, John Percival writes in the *New York Times*, "Jean Cotte in France-Soir, claiming to trace influences from the Far East, Egypt, and ancient Greece in Mr. Nikolais's two-hour theater piece 'Imago,' declared that 'the resulting cocktail of civilizations is completely original and delicious.'"[49] While this American reporter commenting on a French critic's words did not specify which elements corresponded to the "Far East," it is clear that the piece signaled to the critic a sense of its Asian—and, indeed, global—aesthetics. In a review of a 1993 remounting of the evening-length version of *Imago*, *New York Times* dance critic Anna Kisselgoff writes, "The first act begins with 'Dignitaries.' Part Mikado, part Conehead, each dancer wears a robe with vertical stripes and a pyramidlike form on the head. Rigid, set in their ways, the dignitaries tilt in various directions until the choreography becomes more complex and signals an emotional release."[50] For Kisselgoff, who had been covering Nikolais's work for decades, the opening section of the piece called to mind the Gilbert and Sullivan operetta, *The Mikado*. This reference is telling because, as Josephine Lee argues, *The Mikado* notoriously slips out from under its own relationship to Japaneseness. Its enormous popularity relied on notions of authenticity in training white actors to embody Japanese etiquette and bodily comportment, and at the same time, producers deflected accusations of Orientalism by citing its lighthearted humor and denying any connection between the play and the "real" Japan.[51] The term "Conehead" refers to a *Saturday Night Live* sketch from the 1970s that was later made into a film (1993) about a group of cone-headed aliens making their way on Earth. Thus, Kisselgoff's claim that these dancers were both *Mikado*-esque and Conehead-like point to the ways their off-kilter bumbling is at odds with their

Figure 2. Dancers in "Dignitaries," the opening section of *Imago* (1963). Photograph by Robert Sosenko. Alwin Nikolais and Murray Louis Dance Collection, Courtesy of Mahn Center for Archives and Special Collections, Ohio University Libraries and the Nikolais/Louis Foundation for Dance. Used with permission.

self-seriousness. It is hard to know whether it is the mood, the choreography, or the costuming that makes the "Dignitaries" dancers seem *Mikado*-esque, or if, as I find likely, it is the combination of all three that creates the sense that these characters are not "us" exactly but bumbling aliens, with all the ambiguity the word "alien" implies.

In "Dignitaries," the dancers are dressed in pencil-straight (though not tight) vertical-striped tunics that constrain their movement (figure 2). Together with the music sources I noted above, the white makeup, the heavy eyebrow lines, and the tunics, whose verticality is reminiscent of Japanese garments like kimono and *yukata*, the dance suggests a loose idea of Japanese performance. The dancers hold themselves stiff and tilt from one leg to the other, rocking back just as they seem about to fall. They bend at the knee and waist, halfway between a stiff-backed formal bow and a yoga "chair pose," before they pop back to a rigid upright posture and continue tilting from foot to foot. Yvonne Hardt writes, "The initial appearance of stiff, puppet-like beings is created by movements provoked by long tubular costumes that prevent wide steps, bends, or the lifting of legs."[52] The costumes prevent dancers from spreading their legs much beyond shoulder-width, and the dignitaries often scurry across the stage in short, shuffling steps. The robotic or "puppet-like" movements signal that they are "rigid,

Figure 3. Murray Louis (foreground) in *Imago* (1963). Photograph by Robert Sosenko. Alwin Nikolais and Murray Louis Dance Collection, Courtesy of Mahn Center for Archives and Special Collections, Ohio University Libraries and the Nikolais/Louis Foundation for Dance. Used with permission.

set in their ways," in Kisselgoff's words; they are busy and officious, responding not to each other's presence but to cues in the music.

The makeup and costume for the solo, "Artisan," also suggests Kabuki, or at least the "Kabuki-Japan" that Barbara Thornbury argues circulated so widely in Cold War America. Here, soloist Murray Louis is dressed in a leotard that covers his arms and legs (figure 3). Bright red and yellow color blocks, divided with wide white lines, run up and down his legs, arms, and torso. In one sense, the colorful costume can be seen as simply abstract (Rebekah Kowal calls them "Mondrian-like"),[53] but together with Louis's white face and severe, drawn-in eyebrows, the leotard's design is also reminiscent of strength lines painted on the limbs of Kabuki's *aragoto* performers. Each of these sections seems to hint at, but never fully reference, Asian art forms of Kabuki, Japanese drumming, and Southeast Asian dance. Any of these choreographic, visual, and sonic elements alone might be insignificant. But taken together, these disparate features of *Imago* create if not a constant and overarching approach, then at least a strong motif of Asian influence.

The white face makeup and conical headdresses the dancers wear throughout the piece recall Kabuki makeup and Thai dance. While theatrical makeup manuals from the early twentieth century provide instructions for making up a number of racial types, the approach Nikolais used in his works was not geared toward the realistic imitation of ethnic or racial Others, nor, I believe, toward staging recognizable theatrical types such as in blackface minstrelsy or yellow-face theatrical productions.[54] These approaches would have been readily available to Nikolais, and certainly in his theatre work before the war, he would have come into contact with practices of racial stereotyping for the stage. But because Nikolais avoided creating individualized characters and dances that emphasized human relationships and identities, being more interested in the relationship between humans ("man," in his words) and the environment, or "man" and the universe, it seems more likely that the makeup design for *Imago* was inspired not by melodrama stage types, but by other performance styles, such as Kabuki and Jingju. While makeup manuals describing techniques for applying Asian theatre makeup were not in wide circulation until after *Imago* premiered, postcards of Kabuki performers, for example, would have been widely available.[55] In addition to Japanese performances, noted above, that toured in New York throughout the 1950s and early 1960s, well-known film performances by Mei Lanfang and a range of other New York–based practitioners of Asian performance forms would have been available to Nikolais. Inspiration for the *Imago* makeup, in other words, could have come from any number of sources yet does not correspond directly to any particular genre or performance event.

A section of *Imago* called "Logicians" further showcases Asian aesthetics through costume. This part of *Imago*, however, seems to have been cut early in the work's development. It appears on the program for the 1963 Henry Street Playhouse recording in the Nikolais and Murray Dance Collection, as well as in photographs from that year, but does not appear on subsequent programs. Moreover, when I interviewed dancer Phyllis Lamhut, she had no recollection of the piece, despite her near-encyclopedic memory of other dances we discussed.[56] Nonetheless, its archival traces suggest another deployment of Asianness within the work. "Logicians" is a trio for three dancers in leotards who wear bulbous paper lanterns on their heads, making them look eggheaded. In the archival recording of a 1963 performance of *Imago*, "Logicians" happens in total silence until the last few seconds. Whether this section was intentionally performed in silence or whether the sound on the recording was lost, I cannot determine, especially given the prolonged silences featured in other parts of the *Imago* score. The dancers in this section reprise some of the vocabulary from "Dignitaries," shuffling their feet while bending at the waist, giving an impression of top-heaviness. At other moments, they balance on one leg and execute mudra-like gestures with their arms and hands. Toward the end, they line up one in front of the other, facing into the stage right wings, spooning each other as their large, oval bulb-heads fan out just beyond their bodies (figure 4). Certainly, there is some suggestion of Indian gesture in the choreography, but moreover, Nikolais deploys a concrete, material artifact of commodity Orientalism—paper lanterns, likely cheap and widely available in Chinatown—in service of an abstract dance. The title, "Logicians," of course, suggests that the dancers' eggheads signal their intellect; and like the shuffling, self-seriousness of the dancers in "Dignitaries," this dance draws attention to the humor in how these serious and top-heavy logicians move in the world.

Outside the world of the dance, though, the lantern props of "Logicians" are artifacts of chinoiserie or japonaiserie, pointing to the long-standing desire on the part of Americans to incorporate Asian objects into their homes.[57] Japanese American artists like Isamu Noguchi and Ruth Asawa were making their high-art sculptures with light, paper, and wire famous at midcentury, but simple paper lanterns like these likely remained cheap and widely available. In a lecture at Ohio University, dancer Gladys Bailin reminisced that Nikolais was a great "junk hunter" and frequented shops on Canal Street, where he often acquired items with which dancers might improvise.[58] If he acquired these lanterns on Canal Street, they have not only an aesthetic, but also a material, connection to Asia, given Canal Street's location in Chinatown, a prime locale for acquiring inexpensive souvenir-like goods from China and other parts of Asia. The eggheads/lanterns, used here as costumes, call to mind what Sean Metzger articulates about the *qipao* (and wardrobe more generally) in *Chinese Looks*: that "individuals may be caught in transnational networks in ways that they might themselves not fully apprehend."[59] Nikolais may have been a "junk hunter," but what other layers of meaning might be found in these paper lanterns from Canal Street? In the nineteenth century, a paper lantern may have signaled a clear, intentional connection to an "exotic" Japan, as Lee argues Japanese objects did in *Mikado* merchandise,[60] but in the kind of mid-twentieth-century aesthetic Nikolais deployed, it is not possible to identify a clear intention or message. Neither is it possible to know with certainty where the lanterns originated; thus, they are neither Chinese lanterns nor Japanese lanterns but rather lanterns with an Asian aesthetic. Nonetheless, it is hard to ignore the Orientalist underpinnings of procuring "junk" from Canal Street for New York dancers to play with. As David Palumbo-Liu writes, "'Asia' and 'America' have merged and continue to merge . . . in real political, ideological, and economic arenas."[61] Yet Chinatown itself—here metonymically referred to as Canal Street—points to the uneasy relation between Asians in/and the United States, particularly in the mid-twentieth century. The lanterns, then, might align with how other mid-

Figure 4. Dancers in a section of *Imago* (1963) called "Logicians." Photograph by Susan Schiff Faludi. Alwin Nikolais and Murray Louis Dance Collection, Courtesy of Mahn Center for Archives and Special Collections, Ohio University Libraries and the Nikolais/Louis Foundation for Dance. Used with permission.

century artists were deploying Asian aesthetics—that is, not to signal exoticism but as part of a larger field of experimentation—while also serving as a potent reminder of the uneven terrain upon which such experiments take place.

Taken together, the musical, choreographic, and design elements in *Imago* that either originate in, recall, or evoke Japanese, South Asian, and Southeast Asian aesthetics may point to a number of different phenomena. First, they are part of a pattern in Nikolais's oeuvre that was well established by 1963. *Kaleidoscope* and *Totem*, as well as *Prism* (1959), and perhaps other works, all incorporated Asian music, choreography, or design. Moreover, his use of Asian aesthetics is also part of a much larger phenomenon, in music, dance, and theatre, an Orientalist tendency that stretches across genres and artists. Finally, it is significant to note that, without the circulation of Asian choreographies, music, and goods in New York, some of what Nikolais does in *Imago* would not have been possible. Kabuki tours, gamelan recordings, and paper lanterns from Canal Street form a basis for experimentation that was far from unusual for white modernist choreographers in New York. These Orientalist tendencies are not merely aesthetic but also material and historical. What ramifications might these tendencies have had for racial and other identity politics in the mid-twentieth century?

Racial Politics of Objectivity

Nikolais characterized his choreography as emphasizing association over interpretation and of de-centralizing the spectator; that is, rather than "open channels of communication between audiences" and his choreography, Nikolais left out cues that would invite an audience to interpret the work.[62] What are the implications of choosing objectivity over subjectivity, environment over character, movement over narrative? Yvonne Hardt writes of Nikolais's work that "abstraction is not the denial of emotion or the literal, but a specific body concept that challenges notions of the 'natural' body that was paramount to the early modern dance."[63] Dance historian Rebekah Kowal suggests that Nikolais's insistence on removing cues that would allow spectators to apprehend dancers' gender, race, or age was a way of distancing his work from his own identity as a gay man: this "objectivity defied the dominant aesthetic mode in dance (i.e., expressionism), [and] it minimized the role of the choreographer (and his subjective impressions) in the creative process."[64] If the dancers were genderless and did not engage in libido-driven actions anyway, then the choreography could not be seen as an expression of Nikolais's own desires. Kowal writes that objectivity as such "protected him in that it frustrated the viewer's attempt to make a connection between the choreographer's life and his work."[65]

While Kowal focuses on the queer identity of the choreographer in her discussion of objectivity, it is also worth noting that the company of dancers working with Nikolais in the 1950s and 1960s was a racially integrated group, with white and Black dancers rehearsing, performing, and later touring together. Only a year before *Imago* premiered, for example, Arthur Mitchell and Allegra Kent's interracial pas de deux in George Balanchine's *Agon* caused a stir for the international audiences who saw the piece on US diplomatic tours.[66] In contrast, a duet from *Totem*, featuring white, European American Murray Louis and African American dancer Gladys Bailin, produced little, if any, critical notice of the dancers' racial identities, despite some critical attention to the formal aspects of the duet itself.[67] The minimalist aesthetics of *Agon*, performed in rehearsal clothes (skin-revealing leotards and tights), as well as its erotic, tangling choreography, highlighted the "iconic sexualized taboo of the black man and white woman," in an intimate duet inevitably overlaid by the widespread misapprehension by white Americans that Black men posed an inherent threat to white women.[68] The duet in *Imago*, on the other hand, perhaps due in part to the less-threatening dynamic of a white man and a Black woman, maintained a sense of the ordinary and pedestrian, receiving little critical notice. The full-body leotards, identical headdresses, and white makeup may have deflected attention from both the gender and the racial dynamics of the pairing. I am not claiming that these effects literally hid the dancers' identities, but that they did not call attention to the interracial partnering the way Balanchine's duet did.

Whitened faces, red lips, and darkened eyebrows produced a variety of effects in *Imago*. On the one hand, the makeup and headdresses serve to mask the racial identities (and, to some extent, the gender identities) of individual dancers, neutralizing aspects of their bodies that would differentiate them. On the other hand, in the ensemble section "Dignitaries," the effect of sameness produced by the makeup, when fused with the robotic movements and Japanese-derived percussive score, also signal a diffuse Asianness to some critics, if only fleetingly. In *Totem*, white-faced and color-blocked makeup and costume similarly de-emphasize dancers' identities, only to allow moments of modernist primitivism to bubble to the surface. If the musicologists are right, then the brand of Orientalism Nikolais uses is not about displaying the exotic, sexually available other, an approach more closely associated with Ruth St. Denis. The widespread availability of Asian music, choreography, and consumer goods, along with his position as a white male choreographer, meant that Nikolais was able to borrow freely from multiple genres and sites; and while the methods and meanings of appropriations from Asian forms and objects no longer solely signaled exoticism at midcentury, I contend that they performed another kind of work.

Inasmuch as Nikolais sought to decentralize humans in his work, that is, to understand humankind as one small part of a larger universe rather than its center, Nikolais's use of Asian aesthetics might be seen as a critique of Western attitudes and aligned with spiritual and philosophical traditions of yoga and Buddhism. At the same time that Asian or "Oriental" elements may lose their aesthetic significance as exotic, it is also important to keep in mind that, as Yutian Wong writes, this particular mode of borrowing reinforces how easily "the Asian or Asian American body can be voided of its physicality and abstracted into a collection of symbols."[69] The white-faced, long-robed, shuffling dignitaries and eggheaded logicians can be read as more than simply whimsical beings in an imaginary "City Curious." During the Cold War, Asians were propagandized as robotic and nonhuman. In this light, the *Mikado*-esque self-important buffoons of "Dignitaries," in their very ordinary and undifferentiated appearance, might align with other white American readings of Asians that serve to bolster American exceptionalism.

The long history of Western appropriation of Japanese, Indian, and Southeast Asian art and philosophy explains, but does not necessarily justify, Orientalist borrowing as an artistic strategy. That the Asian—for they are seldom concrete enough to be tied to specific national traditions—borrowings in Nikolais's work appear and disappear seemingly without a pattern makes them difficult to identify. His compositional and design strategies also confuse attempts to read these choices in a systematic way. Taken together, the sonic, scenographic, and choreographic flashes of Asian movement, sound, and design coalesce just enough to apprehend if not a pattern, then a tendency. This tendency to "junk hunt" for things—ideas, sounds, images—for dancers to play with is both Nikolais's own and also deeply embedded in American choreographic tradition and wider cultural commodity fetishism. This sedimented history of borrowing, as well as the histories of Japanese, Indian, and Southeast Asian artists performing in the United States, complicates the here/there, inside/outside binary that often attends discussions of Asian aesthetics in American performance.

Notes

1. *Kaleidoscope* premiered in 1953, but an expanded version, which has apparently become the standard, was staged in 1956. My observations about this piece are based on a VHS recording of a televised performance from 1960 that aired in France. (4.2b1, box 1, The Alwin Nikolais and Murray Louis Dance Collection, Robert E. and Jean R. Mahn Center for Archives and Special Collections, Ohio University, Athens, OH [hereafter, "Nikolais-Louis Dance Collection"]). A copy of the program is reprinted in Bob Gilmore, "The Music of Alwin Nikolais: A Provisional Study," in *The Returns of Alwin Nikolais: Bodies, Boundaries and the Dance Canon*, ed. Claudia Gitelman and Randy Martin (Middletown, CT: Wesleyan University Press, 2007), 137.
2. Rebekah Kowal, "Being Motion: Alwin Nikolais' Queer Objectivity," in *The Returns of Alwin Nikolais: Bodies, Boundaries and the Dance Canon*, ed. Claudia Gitelman and Randy Martin (Middletown, CT: Wesleyan University Press, 2007), 96; and Anna Kisselgoff, "Dance: Nikolais Troupe in 1953 'Kaleidoscope,'" *New York Times*, February 9, 1984.
3. That Nikolais purchased the first Moog synthesizer provides evidence of his longstanding interest in creating and experimenting with electronic music for his performances. See Randy Martin, "Nikolais Returns," in *The Returns of Alwin Nikolais: Bodies, Boundaries and the Dance Canon*, ed. Claudia Gitelman and Randy Martin (Middletown, CT: Wesleyan University Press, 2007), 1. For Nikolais's discussion of his "total theatre concept," see "Excerpts from Nik: A Documentary," in *The Vision of Modern Dance*,

ed. Jean Morrison Brown, Naomi Mindlin, and Charles H. Woodford (Hightown, NJ: Princeton Book Company, 1998), 2nd ed., 116–17; Nikolais's experiments with props and costumes inevitably drew comparisons to Oskar Schlemmer and other Bauhaus performers whose sculptural costumes explored the limits of the body and possibilities of new technology in the early twentieth century. While Nikolais denies that his works were directly inspired by Bauhaus, his experiments nonetheless exhibit similarities. Yvonne Hardt writes that Bauhaus experiments served a political vision of "overcom[ing] class differences and the separation between artist and craftsmen. This is a political vision that probably was not shared by Nikolais. However, his emphasis on the larger context in which humans move echoes some of that idealism." See Yvonne Hardt, "Alwin Nikolais—Dancing Across Borders," in *The Returns of Alwin Nikolais: Bodies, Boundaries and the Dance Canon*, ed. Claudia Gitelman and Randy Martin (Middletown, CT: Wesleyan University Press, 2007), 77.

4. I borrow the term "invisible-ize" from Brenda Dixon Gottschild, who argues that Africanist elements pervade American popular forms without their connections to African diasporic cultures being acknowledged. See Brenda Dixon Gottschild, *Digging the Africanist Presence in American Performance: Dance and Other Contexts* (Westport, CT: Praeger, 1996).
5. Michelle Liu Carriger, "No Thing to Wear: A Brief History of Kimonon and Inappropriation from Japonisme to Kimono Protests," *Theatre Research International* 43, no. 2 (2018): 169.
6. Special thanks to Tresa Randall for allowing me to cite two of her presentations on Alwin Nikolais's early career: Tresa Randall, "Alwin Nikolais' Performing Objects," Interdisciplinary Arts Performing Objects Seminar, School of Interdisciplinary Arts, Ohio University, September 21, 2016; and Tresa Randall, "Acts for Children: Dance, Play and Innovation at Midcentury," Society of Dance History Scholars/Nordic Forum for Dance Research Joint Conference, Trondheim, Norway, June 2014.
7. John Martin, "The Dance: Season Turns to Concert Artists," *New York Times*, February 7, 1960: X18.
8. Kate Elswit, *Theatre and Dance* (London: Palgrave, 2018), 7.
9. Gilmore, "The Music of Alwin Nikolais," 140.
10. Christina Klein, *Cold War Orientalism: Asia in the Middlebrow Imagination, 1945–1961* (Berkeley: University of California Press, 2003), 5.
11. See Barbara E. Thornbury, *America's Japan and Japan's Performing Arts: Cultural Mobility and Exchange in New York, 1952–2011* (Ann Arbor: University of Michigan Press, 2013).
12. Andrew Clay McGraw, "The Gamelan and Indonesian Music in America," OUP Blog, blog.oup.com, accessed November 7, 2018.
13. Judith Becker, "One Perspective on Gamelan in America," *Asian Music* 15, no. 1 (1983), 83. Becker also notes that along with acquiring gamelan instruments, UCLA also hired its first Javanese gamelan teacher, Hardja Susilo.
14. David Palumbo-Liu articulates issues of the incorporation of Asians in the United States in legal, historical, and cultural terms. See David Palumbo-Liu, *Asian/American: Historical Crossings of a Racial Frontier* (Stanford: Stanford University Press, 1999), 3.
15. Dixon Gottschild, *Digging the Africanist Presence in American Performance*, 23.
16. John Perpener, "Dance of the African Diaspora: Asadata Dafora," Jacob's Pillow Dance

Interactive, https://danceinteractive.jacobspillow.org/themes-essays/african-diaspora/asadata-dafora/. See also Susan Manning, *Modern Dance/Negro Dance: Race in Motion* (Minneapolis: University of Minnesota Press, 2004), 8–9.

17. See Joanna Dee Das, *Katherine Dunham: Dance and the African Diaspora* (New York: Oxford University Press, 2017), 7–8.
18. Andrea R. Jain, *Selling Yoga: From Counterculture to Pop Culture* (New York: Oxford University Press, 2015), 20–36.
19. Yutian Wong, *Choreographing Asian America* (Middletown, CT: Wesleyan University Press, 2010), 51.
20. For discussions of Loïe Fuller and her appropriations of Indian dance, see Anthea Kraut, "White Womanhood and Early Campaigns for Choreographic Copyright," in *Choreographing Copyright: Race, Gender and Intellectual Property Rights in American Dance* (New York: Oxford University Press, 2016), 55–63.
21. For a discussion of St. Denis and Graham, see Priya Srinivasan, *Sweating Saris: Indian Dance as Transnational Labor* (Philadelphia: Temple University Press, 2012), 104–9.
22. Joseph H. Mazo, *Prime Movers: The Makers of Modern Dance in America*, 2nd ed. (Hightstown, NJ: Princeton Book Company, 1977), 246.
23. Gilmore, "The Music of Alwin Nikolais," 134.
24. Amy Bauer, "The Other of the Exotic: Balinese Music as Grammatical Paradigm in Ligeti's 'Galamb Borong,'" *Music Analysis* 27, no. 2/3 (July–October 2008), 337–38.
25. Bauer, "The Other of the Exotic," 339.
26. Gilmore, "The Music of Alwin Nikolais," 138–39.
27. L. B., "Reviews of the Month," *Dance Observer* 1960, 40.
28. *The World of Alwin Nikolais* Program 5, ADF Video, 2002.
29. Becker, "One Perspective," 83–86.
30. John Cage, "How the Piano Came to Be Prepared" (1973), excerpted on the website johncage.org.
31. "Dromenon." Merce Cunningham Trust website. https://www.mercecunningham.org/the-work/choreography/dromenon/.
32. Among other sources, my interview with longtime Nikolais dancer Phyllis Lamhut indicates that Nikolais and Merce Cunningham, Cage's partner, were friends. Phyllis Lamhut, interview with author, October 15, 2016.
33. See "Dancers from Bali," *New York Times*, July 30, 1952, 22; Denis deMarney, "Bali Dancers Remain—Recital Programs," *New York Times*, October 27, 1957, X15; and John Martin, "Dance: Projects: City Ballet in Demonstration Series," *New York Times*, February 4, 1962, 110.
34. Doris Hering, *Dance Magazine*, March 1960. 7.5a, Box 1, Folder 2, Nikolais-Louis Manuscript Collection.
35. *The World of Alwin Nikolais*, Program 5.
36. Hering, *Dance Magazine*, Nikolais-Louis Manuscript Collection.
37. Nik Auto Part 2, 1963, 2.1D, Box 2, Folder 85, Nikolais-Louis Dance Collection.
38. Gilmore, "The Music of Alwin Nikolais," 142–43. Nikolais created the soundscape for *Imago* in collaboration with James Seawright, who would later become known for his kinetic and electronic sculpture work. At that time, Seawright had access to sophisticated sound equipment through the Columbia-Princeton Electronic Music Center, where he was employed. Gilmore writes, "The RCA II synthesizer had a frequency/tone generator,

with oscillators and white noise; a pitch glide and vibrato generator; a volume and envelope controller; a timbre (tone color) controller; and amplifiers and mixers" (143).

39. Thank you to Martin P. Regan for sharing his valuable insights into Japanese music performance, instrumentation, and composition and for listening to and discussing this piece with me. These insights were very helpful in shaping my analysis in the early stages of writing.
40. I base this analysis on my experience as a taiko player and specifically on my experience having taken master classes with teachers in Noh Bayashi and Edo Bayashi.
41. See Thornbury, *America's Japan and Japan's Performing Arts*, 42. Chapter 1 details the tours and the discourse created by them.
42. "The Azuma Kabuki Dancers and Musicians Program, 1954," 5.1, Box 1, folder 9, Nikolais and Murray Dance Collection.
43. Thornbury, *America's Japan and Japan's Performing Arts*, 33.
44. See Gilmore, "The Music of Alwin Nikolais," 138–39.
45. Alwin Nikolais, untitled essay, *Dance Perspectives* 16 (1963): 28–36.
46. See Timothy Taylor (1997) and Anthea Kraut (2008) for two of many examples.
47. Kowal, "Being Motion," 88.
48. Anna Kisselgoff, "Nikolais's 'Imago,' Forever Young," *New York Times*, July 28, 1993, C13.
49. John Percival, "Paris Dance Critics Welcome Nikolais," *New York Times*, November 7, 1968, 36.
50. Kisselgoff, "Nikolias's 'Imago,' Forever Young."
51. See Josephine Lee, *The Japan of Pure Invention: Gilbert and Sullivan's* The Mikado (Minneapolis: University of Minnesota Press, 2010).
52. Hardt, "Alwin Nikolais," 75
53. Kowal, "Being Motion," 95.
54. One example of many such makeup manuals is S. J. Adair Fitz-Gerald, *How to Make Up: A Practical Guide for Amateurs and Beginners* (London: Samuel French, 1901). For a discussion of makeup manuals and yellowface in the late nineteenth and early twentieth centuries, see "From Aversion to Fascination: New Lyrics and Voices 1880s-1920s" in *Yellowface: Creating the Chinese in American Popular Music and Performance, 1850s—1920s*, ed. Krystyn R. Moon (New Brunswick, NJ: Rutgers University Press, 2005).
55. Thank you to my colleague Bradford Clark for helping me identify when makeup manuals may have circulated. Ruth Shaver's *Kabuki Costume* would not have circulated in the United States until 1966, but museum artifacts and other popular images would have been widely available, if indeed they were ever consulted by Nikolais.
56. Lamhut, interview with author.
57. In a chapter titled "My Objects All Sublime" in *The Japan of Pure Invention,* Josephine Lee argues that part of the appeal of *The Mikado* rests on audience's familiarity with Japanese objects, which had become widely available to the middle class in Europe and the United States in the nineteenth century. See Lee, *The Japan of Pure Invention*, 3–38.
58. Gladys Bailin, "Exploring the Career of Gladys Bailin" event, Music and Dance Library, Glidden Hall, Ohio University, Athens, Ohio, October 11, 2019.
59. Sean Metzger, *Chinese Looks: Fashion, Performance, Race* (Bloomington: Indiana University Press, 2014), 5.
60. Lee, *The Japan of Pure Invention*, 7–11.
61. David Palumbo-Liu, *Asian/American*, 3.

62. Kowal, "Being Motion," 87–88.
63. Hardt, "Alwin Nikolais," 75.
64. Hardt, "Alwin Nikolais," 90.
65. Kowal, "Being Motion," 93.
66. See Clare Croft, *Dancers as Diplomats: American Choreography in Cultural Exchange* (New York: Oxford University Press, 2015), 75–83.
67. Hering, *Dance Magazine,* Nikolais-Louis Manuscript Collection.
68. Croft, *Dancers as Diplomats,* 80.
69. Wong, *Choreographing,* 44.

Part II

WITCH CHARACTERS AND WITCHY PERFORMANCE

Editor's Introduction to the Special Section

Shifting Shapes: Witch Characters and Witchy Performances

—CHRYSTYNA DAIL

"It's the witch from next door."
—STEPHEN SONDHEIM AND JAMES LAPINE, *INTO THE WOODS* (1986)

The Baker's line in *Into the Woods* introduces the character moments before we gaze upon her: aging and hunched, dressed in tattered rags, and maybe even drooling. In this brief interstitial space between aural and visual perception, the audience erupts in hesitant laughter. Perhaps this is the elicited reaction because many audience members assume the Baker's subtextual intention is that the visitor is actually the *bitch* from next door. In contemporary US culture, these words often conflate to vilify intelligent, assertive women. And that is precisely what the Witch is in *Into the Woods*. She is a decisive, hardworking, single mother much maligned by her neighbors' ancestors and populace. She is not lacking in empathy; she also doesn't value one person's loss over another's. The Witch contextualizes what ultimately separates her from the rest of the community in her pre-death song "Last Midnight," addressed to the remaining fairy-tale characters in the woods (The Baker, Cinderella, Little Red, and Jack):

> You're so nice.
> You're not good, you're not bad, you're just nice.
> I'm not good, I'm not nice, I'm just right.
> I'm the witch. You're the world.[1]

For the editors and authors of this special section, Sondheim's lyrics in this moment reinforce the trope of the witch as an outsider standing up to—often politically and ethically—her community. We see this trope replicated throughout theatre and performance history to various degrees: the witch-demons in *kyōgen*; the virgins in Hrotsvitha's *Dulcitius*; Adeola and several witch doctor characters in Amos Tutuola's plays; the weird (or "wyrd") sisters in Shakespeare's *Macbeth*; drag witch Jinkx Monsoon; the men creating Ufe and Wine in Carmen Boullosa's *Cocinar Hombres*; the "good/bad" witches in iterations of *The Wizard of Oz*. Onstage witch characters, depending on cultural context, vacillate between being scapegoats for the fears and superstitions of a community and operating as instruments of wisdom and healing. Occasionally feared, often respected, and almost universally marginalized, witch characters are notoriously powerful and sublimely fragile. This duality is perhaps best represented through the Japanese Hannya mask present in Noh and in Balinese performances including the Rangda mask. As performance ethnographer Margaret Coldiron explains, "Whether viewed as a projection of man's fear of woman as 'Other' or as a demonstration of the power of evil to transform that which is 'good,' positive, and nurturing into something wicked, negative, and deadly, there is perhaps no other image as universally fearsome. In both of these masks these contradictory qualities of fiendishness and goodness coincide."[2] Witch characters may levitate or curse a family, burn or melt, and in more than a few instances, claim no knowledge of magical arts at all. Many of the authors in this special section write about the prevalence of witch tropes or archetypes. But it is perhaps more appropriate to argue that no universal applies to the witch character—except their outsider status. Therefore, treatment of witch characters onstage mirrors what in their offstage communities may be perceived as an innate human desire to destroy or condemn what is feared, misunderstood, or undesired. Interrogating why witches are present in performance allows us to better understand the complex social constructs undergirding a cultural moment. For example, stage witches of Greek and Roman antiquity such as Circe and Medea are knowledgeable herb and root workers but were also described by poets and playwrights in various adaptations through their inviting or distasteful scents. This connection between magic and scent was then projected onto women in antiquity as a whole. As classics scholar Britta Ager argues, "While a variety of scenting agents were important in religious and magical rituals, witches use scented spells in classical poetry less because of the real practices of ancient magicians than because the evolving witch trope equated them first with root cutters, women with access to specialized and dangerous knowledge, and later with wearers of seductive perfumes, whose sexuality threatened men's self-control."[3] The connection between witchcraft and women's plant and root knowledge, along with associated bodily scents surrounding this wisdom, is present across literary cultures. Fernando de Rojas's famous witch, *Celestina* (1499), conjured perfumes used by prostitutes to entice customers as well as medicine for controlling menstruation.[4] Manuela López Ramírez explains how Toni Morrison hails the aforementioned ancient Greek witch, the crone in the fairy tale "Hansel and Gretel," as well as female elders in African cosmologies through the character Circe and her surrounding scents in *Song of Solomon* (1977).[5] In Morrison's novel, Milkman encounters "a sweet spicy perfume. Like ginger root—pleasant, clean seductive," upon entering the Butler mansion and embracing the aging servant.

Whereas plant magic and accompanying olfactory arousals are one way witches have drawn admiration—and sometimes animosity—from community members, more often than not it is a woman's transgressions against cultural norms that invite ire and social othering. Elizabethan and Jacobean England are notorious for accusing supposedly transgressive or outsider women with witchcraft. William Rowley, Thomas Dekker, and John Ford's *The Witch of Edmonton* (1621) "attacks conventional beliefs about the dangers of witches" through the put-upon character of Elizabeth Sawyer, an aged beggar woman living on the outskirts of town who befriends a stray dog she believes to be the devil.[6] But the play also leaves the door open in early modern English society to the potential harm and power of demonic influence. In 1890, US author and playwright Mary E. Wilkins co-opted the trial of elderly witchcraft-denier Martha Corey to highlight the unequal treatment facing rebellious nineteenth-century women in *Giles Corey, Yeoman*.[7] Hilda Kuper's *A Witch in My Heart* (1969), set in 1930s Swaziland and centering on Bigwapi, a young wife accused of witchcraft because she is barren, normalizes witchcraft belief while asserting that women aren't punished for the practice unless the community is "motivated by envy, hatred, and malice."[8] Throughout the majority of theatre history, alienating and marginalizing witches for their misfit status was the norm. Operating as outsiders in their community, most (though not all) face isolation, shunning, and even death due to their age, sex, marital status, race, reproductive abilities, or class. Furthermore, these pre-twenty-first-century witch characters are written absent any obvious magical power but also holding little agency in their lives to combat the oppression facing them.

Playwrights during the past decade have intervened on behalf of witch characters, restoring much of their agency while retaining their outsider status. This is especially true of witch characters created or adapted from "canonical" works. Jen Silverman's *Witch* (2018) draws heavily from *The Witch of Edmonton* in a play aimed at condemning gender roles and patriarchy. Likewise, playwrights Winsome Pinnock and Kimberly Belflower both use Arthur Miller's *The Crucible* as foundational material for reevaluating hegemonic ideas of race and sexism in their respective works *Tituba* (2016) and *John Proctor Is the Villain* (2019). These feminist playwrights are heeding Audre Lorde's call from thirty years ago that still resonates with many contemporary theatre artists and witches alike: "Those of us who stand outside the circle of this society's definition of acceptable women; those of us who have been forged in the crucibles of difference—those of us who are poor, who are lesbians, who are Black, who are older—know that *survival is not an academic skill.* It is learning how to stand alone, unpopular and sometimes reviled, and how to make common cause with those others identified as outside the structures in order to define and seek a world in which we can all flourish. It is learning how to take our differences and make them strengths."[9] Witch characters have survived the millennia and waves of religious and political backlash not in spite of their outsider status but because of it. Their difference is a reminder that "the edges of culture are exactly where new and beautiful meanings are generated. The edges help hold the center together."[10] Witches' onstage histories remind us that power is indeed located in difference.

All of the essays included in this special section focus in some way on the cultural connections between womanhood, outsider status, and witchcraft; however, only one author approaches the witch and her craft as actualities and not as superstition or fantasy. Jane Barnette, coeditor of this special section, in her essay, "To Wright the Witch: The Case of Joanna Baillie's *Witchcraft*," adopts the stance that witches exist, both historically and in our audiences today, and therefore contemporary directors and dramaturgs might consider their presence when staging witch characters. Barnette's essay, calling upon both Baillie's 1836 text and a 2011 Canadian production of the play as case study, invites comparison to the observations of Margot Adler, long-standing National Public Radio producer and journalist, who completed an extensive study on American pagans in 1979, updating it several times prior to her death. In *Drawing Down the Moon*, Adler asserts magic "is a convenient word for a whole collection of techniques, all of which involve the mind." These techniques include "mobilization of confidence, will, and emotion brought about by the recognition of necessity; the use of imaginative faculties, particularly the ability to visualize, in order to begin to understand how other beings function in nature so we can use this knowledge to achieve necessary ends."[11] Not only does Adler's definition of magic connect with the methodologies of many cultural historians, but it also functions as an approach to the art of acting and theatremaking, an assertion shared and expanded upon by Barnette.

Jessica Holt's essay "Nothing Wicked This Way Comes: Shakespeare's Subversion of Archetypal Witches in *The Winter's Tale*," provides readers with a historical foundation on early modern western European witchcraft views and their link to church-mandated misogyny. Holt critiques commonly held beliefs regarding witchcraft, magic, sexuality, and womanhood in early-seventeenth-century England through analysis of the three major female characters in *The Winter's Tale*: Hermione, Paulina, and Perdita. Holt pushes against the oft-asserted perspective that a female witch's magic, if one believes in it at all, is located outside of her and in the supernatural (meaning a force beyond the laws of nature, e.g., the devil), and therefore is not grounded in her own innate abilities nor ultimately under her control. This inability to control her magical powers, due to woman's perceived paucity of moral and intellectual fortitude, eventually led to a large body of anti-witchcraft treatises in western Europe and subsequent witch hunts unevenly targeting women.[12]

In Mamata Sengupta's essay, "Of Women and Witches: Performing the Female Body in Caryl Churchill's *Vinegar Tom*," readers are reminded of how well historical moments and events can be co-opted and adapted by playwrights to comment upon contemporary concerns (i.e., the concept of the usable past). Churchill famously wrote she "wanted to write a play about witches with no witches in it," and Sengupta supports this articulation in the essay by addressing how witchcraft accusations lodged against major characters in *Vinegar Tom* are the retaliatory actions of men and women fearing loss of power or status in their community.[13] Highlights of the essay include Sengupta's deconstruction of the song lyrics in *Vinegar Tom*, which focus on a host of women's topics including menstruation, ageism, patriarchal oppression, sexuality, heteronormative marriage practices, and hysteria. Additionally, the essay is bolstered by a wealth of feminist critical theory, ranging from cultural critics and poets to scientists. Ultimately arguing that witches are constructed through societal need, Sengupta reminds readers that they "are kept alive by the persistence of patriarchal oppression on women and by women's indomitable desire for freedom."

The musical *Wicked*, based on Gregory Maguire's novel (1995), opened on Broadway in 2003 and traces Elphaba's journey from awkward schoolgirl to powerful activist witch. Much like Sengupta's argument that witches are socially constructed, Rebecca K. Hammonds suggests in her essay, "(Un)limited: The Influence of Mentorship and Father-Daughter Relationships on Elphaba's Heroine Journey in *Wicked*," that Elphaba *becomes* a witch (referencing both Judith Butler and Simone de Beauvoir's theories of gender construction) not through generalized, repetitive social interactions but through direct and intentional mentorship. Grounded in literary and psychosocial theories arguing for the significance of a father figure in female development, Hammonds articulates that in Elphaba's journey, "male-identifying" mentors keenly shape her identity, aiding both in her eventual self-realization and her ability to mentor other young activist witches.

Although immersive performance experiences have existed for millennia, a string of high-cost, site-specific immersives emerged in New York City beginning in 2011. In "Immersive Witches: New York City under the Spell of *Sleep No More* and *Then She Fell*," David Bisaha contends that witches and witchy characters are essential to the productions' popularity and financial success. However, Bisaha cautions against an empowering feminist reading of the witches populating these productions, making the case that "antiestablishment, radical desire has been placed onto the figure of the witch across time, but in these productions, the figure of the witch and the environment of the occult commoditizes the supernatural." Bisaha offers a counterargument to the other essays in this special edition, suggesting that witches are the ultimate insiders in these specific immersive performances and operate as neoliberal "traffic-cops of experience economies."

Witches perpetually populate our stages and performances because societal need for them continues. Whether one conjures three hags in a forest, a masked creature with wild hair, a beautiful seductress, a green-skinned broom-riding being, or a local coven of Triple Goddess adherents, witches provide the corporeal figures onto which we may easily project our desires and fears. Still commonly used in Western parlance as an epithet for outsiders—those strong-willed and outspoken, perhaps even "nasty," women—an equal number embrace the moniker as representative of the magical wonderment and power to be found in nature and in an alternative to monotheist patriarchal spirituality. The editors hope this collection of essays, drawing from multitudinous theoretical and historical methodologies, awakens your curiosity about witches, shifts some of your perspectives or assumptions, and offers insightful ways of reading and viewing these characters and performances onstage.

Notes

Chapter epigraph. Stephen Sondheim and James Lapine, *Into the Woods* (New York: Theatre Comunications Group, 2017)

1. Sondheim and Lapine, *Into the Woods*, 121
2. Margaret Coldiron, "Lions, Witches, and Happy Old Men: Some Parallels between Balinese and Japanese Ritual Masks," *Asian Theatre Journal* 22, no. 2 (2005): 232.

3. Britta Ager, "Magic Perfumes and Deadly Herbs: The Scent of Witches' Magic in Classical Literature," *Preternature* 8, no. 1 (2019): 24.
4. Lesley K. Twomey, "Perfumes and Perfume-Making in the *Celestina*," *Bulletin of Hispanic Studies* 86, no. 1 (2009): 145–46.
5. Manuela López Ramírez, "The New Witch in Toni Morrison's *Song of Solomon* and *God Help the Child*," *African American Review* 53, no. 1 (2020): 46.
6. David Nicol, "Interrogating the Devil: Social and Demonic Pressure in *The Witch of Edmonton*," *Comparative Drama* 38, no. 4 (Winter 2004–2005): 427.
7. See Chrystyna Dail, "When for 'Witches' We Read 'Women': Advocacy and Ageism in Nineteenth Century Salem Witchcraft Plays," *Theatre History Studies* 2020 Vol. 39.
8. Hilda Kuper, *A Witch in My Heart* (London: Oxford University Press, 1970), xxvii.
9. Audre Lorde, *Sister Outsider: Essays and Speeches by Audre Lorde*, rev. ed. (New York: Crossing, 2007), 112.
10. Lidia Yuknavitch, *The Misfit's Manifesto* (New York: Simon and Schuster, 2017), 4.
11. Margot Adler, *Drawing Down the Moon: Witches, Druids, Goddess-Worshippers, and Other Pagans in America Today* (New York: Penguin, 1986), 8.
12. To be fair, there exists an expansive record of religious and legal actions taken against magical crimes and witchcraft prior to the fifteenth century, however the *Formicarius* (1435), by Johannes Nider, as well as the anonymously written *Errores Gazariorum* (ca. 1435–1440) are some of the earliest treatises treating witchcraft as a crime. See Wolfgang Behringer, *Witches and Witch-Hunts* (Cambridge: Polity, 2004), and Edward Peters, "The Literature of Demonology and Witchcraft," Accessed online http://ebooks.library.cornell.edu/w/witch/peters.html.
13. Caryl Churchill, *Plays: 1* (London: Methuen Drama, 1996), 130.

To Wright the Witch

The Case of Joanna Baillie's *Witchcraft*

—JANE BARNETTE

When contemporary playwrights imagine worlds that include witch characters, they frequently do so under the assumption that the accusation of witchcraft stems from ignorance, superstition, or discrimination. More often than not, their so-called witches are outspoken and powerful women who threaten the status quo but do not conjure spells or celebrate the cycles of the moon. The focus in these plays is rarely on literal witchcraft, then—rather, they are signaling the *idea* of the witch, usually in order to reveal injustice or misogyny. As one of today's most-cited experts on witch culture, Pam Grossman, puts it, "show me your witches, and I'll show you your feelings about women."[1]

The "craft" in "witchcraft" suggests the act of making something with one's hands, although it can also mean "a skillful contrivance, a device, artifice, or expedient."[2] Similarly, the "wright" in "playwright" refers to a kind of material construction: "one who works in wood; a carpenter, a joiner."[3] As I suggest with the title of this essay, I seek to "wright the witch" in the following pages—by that, I mean to move beyond *writing*, to include what Jon D. Rossini calls "a simultaneous process of correction, revision, and cultural repositioning in the act of creating a new conceptual framework."[4] This use of "wright" is meant to conjure the witch as spectator and/or reader who does indeed exist: while there is no singular doctrine of witchcraft, there are many individuals who cast spells and perform rituals, in keeping with their particular religious or spiritual tradition of witchcraft.[5] For those who identify as witches, this wrighting intervention is a necessary step that has the potential to reframe the way we read, see, and understand witchy women not only onstage but also in everyday life. In seeking to "wright the witch," I ask: How might practicing witches—both currently and historically—interpret the stage witch as a character?

The urgency for taking this approach stems from the historiography of witches. Frequently, those who write about witches focus on the Burning Times, in part because the legal records provide a (deeply flawed) kind of primary evidence.[6] In the wake of the thorough debunking of Egyptologist Margaret Murray's theory about pre-Christian goddess worship, the popular "notion that the witch trials . . . represented the persecution of an actual rival religion" fell entirely out of favor.[7] Instead, scholars have argued for decades that at the root of the witch-craze was misogyny and the overall desire to contain and control women's (and sometimes men's) behavior: to maintain the heteronormative patriarchy of white supremacy undergirding capitalism from its earliest expression onward. This perception is especially persuasive because of how Americans have come to understand the phrase "witch hunt" after the Red Scare of the 1950s, particularly after Arthur Miller's play *The Crucible*, followed by the revelations of Watergate and Richard Nixon's defensive claim of the "witch hunt" that ultimately led to his resignation. In recent years, especially in the wake of the #MeToo movement and the election of our "predator in chief," as provocateur Lindy West calls former president Trump, purveyors of social media have seen a resurgence of the phrase "witch hunt" used to deflect repeated (and ongoing) attempts to hold powerful men accountable for their corrupt behavior.[8]

While this take on the European and American purge of witches is not incorrect, it is misleading, insofar as it reinforces the monotheistic outlook of witchcraft as part of the uncivilized and premodern, polytheistic past: it contributes to colonial and missionary mindsets that read any religion that embraces the worship of more than one god as one followed by lost souls who need to be saved (converted). From this perspective, witchcraft is mere superstition, a practice rooted in folklore and ignorance, or—worse yet—it is child's play, mere make-believe. After all, magic is all sleight of hand hokum.

For those of us who make theatre regularly, making believe is our currency—we bank on the fact that we can convince spectators to willingly suspend their disbelief long enough to accept Elphaba or Mary Poppins taking flight or that the audience will believe that the magic wands onstage in *Harry Potter and the Cursed Child* are endowed with power. More crucially, the role of theatre from its earliest days was tied to ritual and religion—in Ancient Greece, tragedies were performed as part of the City Dionysia, to celebrate (that is, worship) the god of theatre, wine, and fertility, Dionysus.[9] In short, it is not a stretch to suggest that theatre itself is a kind of spellcasting, a rite of magic. Author and podcaster Pam Grossman explains it this way: "There are many ways to be a witch, and . . . witchcraft and magic are these fluid terms that to me are very highly interrelated to creativity."[10] Making, crafting, creating—these are ways of using intention and practice to sculpt reality: Is that not a form of magic?

Within the long history of theatrical characters that have become archetypes, however, the witch stands apart: Most audience members do not recognize the witch as a caricature in the same way that we do the stage Jew or the tragic mulatto or the dumb blonde. With any of these three examples of stage types, critics and scholars recognize the exaggeration and cultural, racial, or societal bias that sustains this stereotype, because we agree that offstage, these categories of human beings exist. We see the disconnect between the exaggerated type represented onstage and the people we know who are Jewish, or who pass as white, or who embody social expectations of young female beauty. Witches remain, for many spectators, fictional characters without human counterparts.

Indeed, the witch as a stage character type has a significantly longer history than the examples discussed above, because witchcraft is a polytheistic practice and several of the religions undergirding it predate monotheism.[11] References to witches abound in our earliest literature, suggesting that they were characters in oral culture predating written stories.[12] It was during the nineteenth century, Grossman suggests, that depictions of witches began to shift, in response to growing sympathy for the thousands of women (and men) who were falsely accused of witchcraft. In an attempt to romanticize the witch as a "powerful but misunderstood and maligned woman," writers and artists "started reframing powerful rebellious women as witches" in an attempt to reclaim the character type of the witch to serve these nascent feminist goals.[13]

Mostly, this reclamation has been a positive step, but it has also had unintended consequences. In coopting *witchiness* as a feminist identity, we risk the erasure of *actual* witches from the range of representable subjectivities. After all, if the stage witch is consistently a woman falsely accused, where does that leave those who *do* practice witchcraft? How can we "wright the witch" as she appears onstage? In what follows, I consider this question in light of a lesser-known but significant play written in the early nineteenth century by a woman whose unusual upbringing gave her in equal measure the influences of emergent anatomical science and those of the romantics' quest for the sublime.

As a youth, playwright Joanna Baillie (1762–1851) lived in the home her uncles William and John Hunter created to also serve as the Great Windmill Street School of Anatomy in London. There, her uncles (and later her brother) trained physicians in pathology and anatomy, employing their impressive collection of corpses and human body parts to aid their instruction. With the tools of drama rather than science, Baillie mirrored the process of instructional dissection she had learned in this curious upbringing to ferret out the inner workings of human passions, which were thought to have a physiognomic connection to disease, including mental illness.[14] Her *Plays on the Passions* (1784 to 1791) investigate different states of emotional excess (jealousy, fear, anger, etc.) in a carefully organized series, with the goal of serving as a source of both delight and edification.

Although she spent her formative years in England, Baillie was Scottish, and she based three of her plays and one musical play in Scotland.[15] Whereas much of the scholarship about the witch-craze centers on the zeal of the continent, Scotland was hardly immune to hunting witches. Quite the contrary, in Scotland three times as many individuals were tried for witchcraft as in England, although Scotland's population was only a quarter the size of England's.[16] William Shakespeare's *The Tragedy of Macbeth* took inspiration from Scottish king James VI's *Daemonologie*, published in 1597.[17] In the vein of the *Malleus Maleficarum* (1486), *Daemonologie* sought to define witchcraft as anti-Christian so that the threat of it might be contained and controlled. Witchcraft remained a capital crime in Scotland from 1563 until 1736, when the act against it was officially replaced with a new legal approach that made it a crime for those "who *claimed* to work magic," the maximum punishment for which was one-year imprisonment. This shift, from punishing what the law considered *actual* witches to individuals who *pretended* to conduct witchcraft, was solidified in the Vagrancy Act of 1824, around the time when Baillie was in the midst of writing *Witchcraft*.[18]

Reading *Witchcraft*

In 1836, Baillie published three volumes of plays, including the five-act tragedy *Witchcraft*. Never produced during her lifetime, this play has been rediscovered and produced a handful of times in the twenty-first century in Canada and the UK. Like other plays of its ilk (including *The Witch of Edmonton*), *Witchcraft* explores the potentially fatal consequences for already marginalized women of being condemned as a witch. Those who hunted witches believed witches made pacts with the devil and enacted his wishes upon others, with the ultimate goal of leading the faithful away from Christianity altogether. Their assault was, in other words, on the deviant behavior of the women accused as witches.

Frequently given the title of "the female Shakespeare" by her contemporaries, Baillie had few things in common with the bard. She was not a professional actor, nor did she write primarily for theatrical production. She wrote with the intention of publication.[19] Indeed, her relative lack of theatremaking credentials would typically disqualify her for serious study by many theatre historians, including myself, who insist the productions, architecture, and collaborative processes of theatre matter as much (if not more) than the text. However, as feminist historiographers have recovered Baillie's contributions, intrepid directors have staged some of her work, including one of the last plays she wrote, in her late sixties: *Witchcraft: A Tragedy in Prose, in Five Acts.*

The plot of this so-called tragedy is more akin to melodrama: at the center of the conflict is a love triangle of sorts, between Violet and Dungarren, who love each other, and the unrequited desire that Annabella has for Dungarren.[20] Violet is presumed to be an orphan because her father has been in hiding, pretending to be dead, since he killed a man in self-defense and his only witness to the deed is nowhere to be found. Dungarren's mother is preoccupied with her daughter (his younger sister), who is terribly sick without credible diagnosis. Lady Dungarren's maternal anxiety has more than a tinge of superstition, making her susceptible to the nurse's claims that the town witches are to blame for the child's mysterious illness. Seizing on this opening, Annabella plots to frame Violet as the witch who has cursed the child, by leaving a piece of Violet's dress in the child's bedroom.

So far, the setup for these events is entirely familiar: Annabella, a wealthy jealous woman, intends to frame Violet, a younger woman who is presumed to be an orphan, as a witch so that her courtship "rival" will no longer be of consequence. The mysterious illness of the youngest Dungarren provides a customary opportunity for such an accusation: Anytime human behavior cannot be fully understood by extant medical explanation, it is not uncommon to blame forces of evil. The detail of the dress fabric is an interesting touch, however, as it accomplishes both the task of tying Violet to the child as well as signifying a misunderstanding of how spells might work for a witch. To exert her will onto the child—that is, to curse (or bless) the daughter—a witch would need some personal item from her, such as a lock of her hair or (perhaps) a piece of her garment, especially if it was worn closest to the skin. Witches would use this swatch of fabric in their spell, and depending on the outcome they desired for the person from which it was taken, the fabric would be treated accordingly, usually starting at the witch's altar, and then either being buried, burned, or carried close to the witch's body. But here, Baillie has Annabella's minions place a piece of Violet's dress in the child's room, which can be seen as the inverse of how such a spell would actually be performed. Alternatively, in the act of retrieving cloth from her rival's frock, might not Annabella be performing the first part of a spell herself?[21]

While the plotting against Violet occurs, three "reputed witches" meet in the woods in an attempt to summon Satan, led by the inscrutable Grizeld Bane. These same woods just happen to be the secret spot where Violet has planned to meet her father, under the dark of night. Humorously, shortly after calling upon their "dark prince," Violet's father Murrey appears in the distance, and Grizeld Bane greets him as "mighty Satan!"—to which Murrey promptly answers "*in a deep strong feigned voice*, 'What is your will with me?'" After agreeing to grant the witches power in exchange for servitude "in the pit of fire and brimstone for ever [*sic*]," he convinces them to wait for him on the other side of the woods, so that he can talk with his daughter undisturbed.[22] When a local minister rides through these woods and sees Violet heading toward the moor and then witnesses a man everyone presumes to be dead, with witches nearby, he makes the same conclusion anyone in the midst of a witch hunt would: She's clearly one of them! Since Violet cannot answer these charges without betraying her father's secret, she is condemned to burn at the stake.

By this point in the plot, we can rightly ask ourselves what Baillie's purpose is in staging these "reputed witches" in the woods; by suggesting that they are summoning the devil, the playwright relies upon one of the key premises of the *Malleus Maleficarum*, the notion that witchcraft stems from Satan and is specifically anti-Christian. Does she agree with this characterization of witches, or is she inviting the audience to react to these women in much the same way the townspeople would? In her preface to the play, Baillie suggests her perspective: "The design of the play," she shares, is to imagine the rationale behind "some of those unhappy creatures" accused of witchcraft who confessed to their crimes, knowing they might be burned at the stake. Specifically, she zeroes in on accused women who "actually did believe themselves to have intercourse with the Evil One, [and] consequently to be witches."[23] Thus, the playwright accepts the premise of witches being agents of the devil but allows for the possibility that some of the individuals accused of witchcraft were indeed attempting to perform these magic rituals in a desperate attempt to change their lives.

The play culminates with a flurry of revelations that make poetic justice possible. At the moment that Violet is going off with the sheriff to meet her unhappy fate, her father appears, demanding that the execution be stopped. Once the shock of recognizing that he is alive wears off, the sheriff and his men begin to take Murrey to jail, and Violet proclaims that she will never marry, in protest of her father's wrongful conviction. Just then, however, an officer of the Crown interrupts the judgment with a repeal of the laws endorsing witch-burning, and whom should he have as a companion? Why, none other than the witness to the self-defense-based killing for which Violet's father has been accused—a man named Fatheringham! (Readers might wonder where Fatheringham has been, and why he couldn't testify for Murrey before now. They will be gratified, I'm sure, to learn he was captured by pirates.) While the arrests of Violet and her father were occurring in the town square, Grizeld Bane sneaks into Lady Annabella's tower and strangles her. As Grizeld is brought to justice for this act, Fatheringham recognizes her as a woman who lost her mind when her husband was executed for murder, offering a psychological rationale for her extreme behavior and "spell-casting." Finally, Grizeld is led off to "her keepers" who (we assume) manage her mental health, and with Murrey exonerated, Violet and Dungarren are reunited in their love.

The moment in the play when the officer of the Crown appears and delivers the repeal of the Witchcraft Act places the play's action in 1736, when the law against witches changed throughout the kingdom. "Henceforth," the sheriff reads to the gathered townspeople who have been clamoring to see an execution, "there shall be no person prosecuted at law as a wizard or a witch, throughout these realms."[24] By placing the action at this moment of transition, Baillie invites readers to consider this performative shift in the law: What did it mean for the townspeople to learn that witchy behavior would no longer be considered a capital offense? As discussed earlier, the adoption of this new Witchcraft Act ultimately led to what came to be called the Vagrancy Act in 1824, which made illegal "persons pretending or professing to tell fortunes, or using any subtle craft, means and device, by palmistry or otherwise, to deceive and impose."[25] In disallowing the persecution of individuals as *actual* witches, the new act codified the belief that witches were speculative figures of the imagination and that belief in magic was mere superstition. The performative turn that Baillie's play exposes, then, is one where the guilt of conjuring shifts from the accused witch figure (conjuring magic) to the accusers, whose conjectures are suspect.

Producing *Witchcraft*

As suggested above, the very act of making live performance is its own kind of magic, and the roots of theatre are inextricably tied to polytheistic religious rituals. The script is an extended spell of sorts, which theatremakers rehearse and perform with the hopes of creating a staged reality. While we recognize that the performance is fictional, we nevertheless cultivate the willing suspension of disbelief in our audiences, so that they might join us in the imaginary world we have conjured onstage. Likewise, production dramaturgy relies upon a similar kind of witchery—the dramaturg's research reveals the ancestral history of productions preceding the one they are currently producing and helps them navigate the conversations and sacred objects or images (for the lobby or playbill) that will best encourage the spectators' reception of the dramatic event, so that the audience might be transformed by it.

Because *Witchcraft* (unlike some of her other plays) was never produced in Baillie's lifetime, several of the questions or interpretations that I have raised thus far about the playwright's goals remain speculative. Despite its limited production history, however, there is one extremely well-documented example to consider. In 2011, Concordia University in Montreal concluded a three-year study of Baillie's *Witchcraft*, culminating in a full production of the play.[26] Now that we have looked closely at the script and plot on the page, I turn to examining how they imagined and presented the witches, especially Grizeld Bane, on the stage. As part of a longer project that considers the design of witch characters onstage, the remainder of this essay contextualizes the particular designs of Concordia's *Witchcraft* within the overall framework of iconic witches performed onstage in the twenty-first century. In it, I ask: How do we know a witch when we see one? How do stage costume, makeup, and wig designers signify that a character is a witch? Do they design with the assumption that witches might be in the audience (or part of the production itself)? What does that shorthand tell us about the assumptions we make about women on the margins of society?

During the years leading up to the show itself, the team studying *Witchcraft* created a number of "resonant responses" in addition to conducting traditional research—from what I gather online, the resonant responses appear to have been short performances inspired by aspects of or scenes from the play, performed publicly in year one. Although I will not consider all of the responses here, one remained a source of inspiration for the costume designer, Danielle Laurin: the resonance of nineteenth-century movement training and an in-depth study of the passions.[27] In Laurin's sketch for Grizeld Bane's costume (figure 1), she emphasizes the flow of her movement and the liminality of her character between earthly reality and the supernatural or the numinous. In contrast, her design imagery for the Nurse (who looks after the sick child) is more directly representational of the character, integrating the addition of props designed by Hannah Gorham-Smith: the knotting bag and a candelabra that Gorham-Smith meant to resemble deer antlers (and the cross), in reference to the hunt.

For Lady Annabella, the villain of this story, Laurin found inspiration in the phrase "like a moth to a flame," referencing Annabella's troubled relationship with witchcraft—she is both fascinated by it and terrified of its power. From

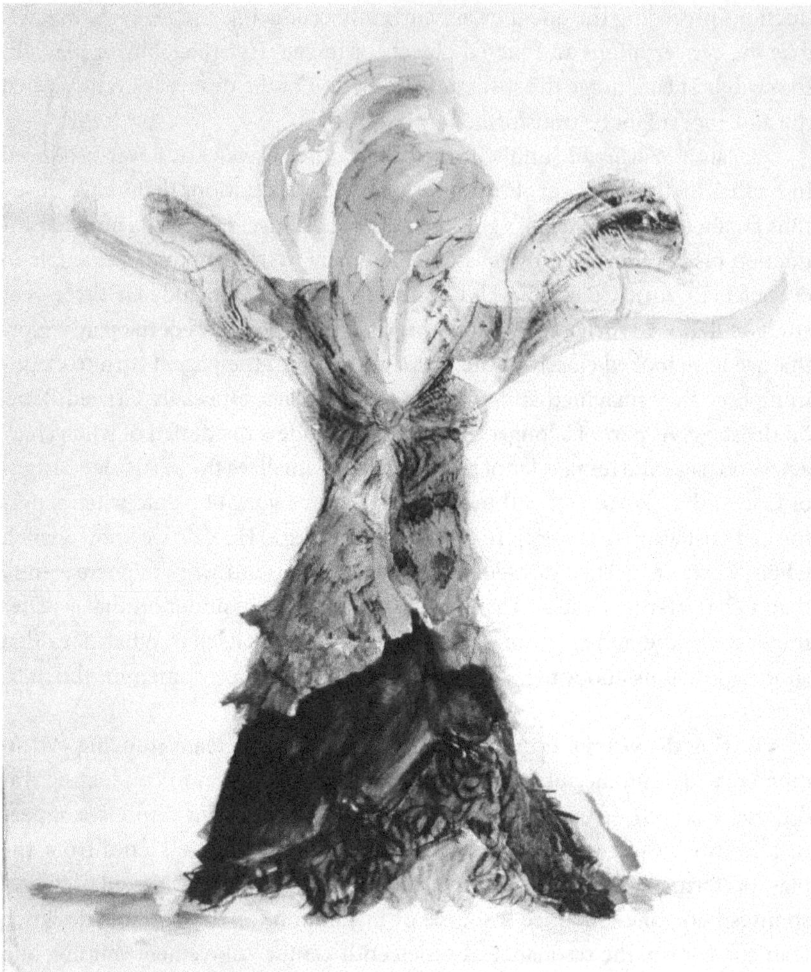

Figure 1. Initial sketch for costume designs: Grizeld Bane, *Witchcraft*, Concordia University, Montreal. Designs and illustrations by Danielle Laurin. Copyright Resonance Lab and Concordia University, 2011.

what I can glean from imagery and short video clips online, in one of the confrontation scenes between Annabella and Grizeld Bane, the actors stood on either side of a looking glass, further emphasizing both Annabella's vanity and the ways her wickedness reflected Grizeld's reputed witchcraft.

Ultimately, however, my primary interest in this research zeroes in on the character that comparative literature scholar Dorothy McMillan calls "a most unusual witch." It is Grizeld Bane "in the end who is the agent of justice," McMillan notes, through her strangling of the villain Lady Annabella.[28] In the final year of the Concordia project, Miriam Cummings played this role, imbuing the character with bodily presence, assisted by the makeup design of Kyle Purves. Purves signals the "otherness" of Grizeld (and the other witches on the moor in their initial scene of dalliance with "the devil") by extending the bridge of her nose upward to the center of her forehead, in a nonhuman look (that recalls the Romulans of *Star Trek*). At the very least, it signals those "unhappy creatures" whom Baillie references in her preface to the play and in a contemporary context reads as a kind of alienness.

In addition to changing the profile and bone structure of the actors' faces, Purves emphasized Cummings's eyes with heavy black eyeliner in a nod to the Egyptian style of kohl-winged eyes, originally meant to enhance beauty while also providing protection from the sun. American popular culture references to Ancient Egypt rarely extend beyond Cleopatra (or Elizabeth Taylor onscreen), but hieroglyphs and other extant sources suggest the mathematical specificity of eye makeup design, especially in the Eye of Horus.[29] While the cultural appropriation of using Egyptian-based makeup on white bodies is certainly troubling, there are intriguing historical data to support a possible dramaturgical rationale for this graphic eyeliner. Primary sources for cosmetic chemical history credit Cleopatra with authorship for several aspects of early facial makeup and hair care and for alchemical recipes for love spells, as well as those to counter curses or conjuring. Jennifer Park notes, "The figure of Cleopatra . . . was closely associated with medicine, cosmetics, gynecology, and alchemy, and the construction of her medical authority is comprised of not one but three significant traditions of medical thought."[30] Although the general public likely would not know these details about Cleopatra, those who study and practice witchcraft might be aware that the queen of Egypt was reputedly one of the most powerful workers of magic and therefore interpret this exaggerated kohl cosmetic as a gesture to her. Moreover, since Grizeld is the only one of the three women with this Egyptian style of eyeliner, Purves's design also helps the audience recognize her immediately as the self-appointed leader.

In Grizeld's case, not only does the kohl wing extend the outer edge of her eye, but it also extends into the tear duct, emphasizing the power of her gaze. Her eyebrows also feature a winged flick on the outer edge, and the points of contact between the tear duct extension and the inner limit of the eyebrow with the forehead prosthesis further emphasize the unusual appearance that she and the other witches, to a lesser degree, feature. Together, these details draw the onlooker's attention to her eyes, an important source of power for a witch who wants to exert her will, especially when using a spell of glamour. To "glamour" in

Figure 2. Miriam Cummings as Grizeld Bane. Concordia University production of *Witchcraft* directed by Louis Patrick Leroux and Cristina Iovita, 2011. Copyright Resonance Lab and Concordia University.

witch parlance is to be seen (or to have another be seen) not as one is but as the witch wills the self (or other) to be seen. As Grossman shares, "the word *glamour* is related to [both] the word *Grimoire* and *grammar*. And both of these are about language that can transform."[31] Thus, although today we might consider glamour simply a noun rather than a spellcasting verb, etymologically the word remains linked to magic and witchcraft.

Thus far, the design for Grizeld's makeup has relied upon fairly well-known stereotypes of othering—her face shape has been altered to seem somewhat nonhuman, and her eyes have been dramatically transformed in a way that suggests both an exotic Orientalism in sharp contrast with Cummings's white body and the witchy history of Queen Cleopatra. In contrast with these expected choices of signaling witch-ness, her cheeks and lips are cherry red, a youthful, vibrant color associated with both beauty and promiscuity (or prostitution). As a widow and an outcast, we would expect Grizeld to be, well, grizzled, and thus to appear more like a hag or a postmenopausal woman. As the sheriff asks Annabella in the play, "Are not witches always old and poor?"[32] In keeping with Baillie's vision of Grizeld, who is neither poor nor elderly, Cummings's vivid makeup emphasizes her sexual power and zeal for life (figure 2).

Of course, on a practical level, considering the undergraduate age range of the students in the cast, this was a wise choice to emphasize the actors' features rather than cover them in age makeup. But it is also unusual, from my research thus far. Typically, when college productions feature witches—especially "hags" or "spinster" types—they cast actors of size for the role and either omit evident makeup altogether or use contour and highlight to create the illusion of wrinkles and sagging skin. While practicality is always a consideration for theatre production, in this case I suspect that the choice was also dramaturgically in keeping with Baillie's conception of Grizeld: that she would be an agent and subject, rather than an object or victim in the play. Indeed, Grizeld is the only character who speaks in verse (when casting spells), although several of the major figures (Violet and her father, the Dungarren family, and Lady Annabella) are all wealthy members of the elite. Dialect is reserved for the servant characters, epitomized by Bawdy, the Dungarren family's herdboy, and the other two witches in the woods.

Opening the Circle

While *Witchcraft* is not "the Scottish play" we reference in our theatre language of superstition, it is also not *not Macbeth*: It is not mere coincidence that Baillie chose to feature three witches in Scotland as well as a jealous noblewoman consumed with murderous plans. In Baillie's witch play, however, the women are the changemakers, and one witch might even be the heroine. Beyond merely revising the past or representing the history of her homeland, Baillie sets the stage for nearly two centuries of witchy plays that will follow—from Arthur Miller's *The Crucible* to Susan Gayle Todd's *Sycorax* and Jen Silverman's *Witch*. There are traces of Grizeld Bane in all of these stage witches.

And how do we recognize a witch when we see one? Typically, something about her dress, her hair, her skin, or her makeup indicates her otherness. In the case of *Witchcraft*, although the "rational" explanation for Grizeld Bane's odd behaviors is given (that she's gone mad because her husband has been executed), there is also room for doubt: After all, she never renounces her actions. To the contrary, her last words are defiant and threatening: "Lay hands on me who dare! I defy you: my master is stronger than you all, since you sent him to his kingdom of darkness. Ye cannot stop the breath of a spirit, though you had a score of executioners at your beck. Lay hands on me who dare!"[33] For witches watching or reading the play, the fact that Fatheringham claims Grizeld "became distracted" after losing her spouse and then escaped her "keepers" only adds to her credibility as a witch, especially after she responds as forcefully as above.[34] For the spectator witch, the lasting impression of Grizeld Bane is not a madwoman. Instead, spectator (and reader) witches remember Grizeld as the one who saved Violet from wrongful persecution and who punished the vengeful Annabella. As McMillan recognizes, "we have also been allowed to glimpse Griseld's [*sic*] power, to feel ourselves in the grip of something other, certainly dark, but paradoxically a force for good."[35] This paradox is entirely familiar to witches watching and reading, for it is on the threshold of this world and the spirit world that witchcraft resides—witches, like Bane and Baillie herself, are liminal creatures.

Like all magic rituals, after casting the circle, Baillie must open it, and she does so by turning to the patriarch of the play, Dungarren.[36] His final words of the play echo the theme of all Baillie's plays, when he argues against the suggestion of a "grand funeral" spectacle for the fallen Annabella: "She shall be interred with decent privacy; and those who have felt the tyranny of uncontrolled passions will think, with conscious awe, of her end."[37] Amending his proclamation, I would add: May we have equal respect for the witch who made such decency possible. So mote it be.

Notes

1. Pam Grossman, "Are Witches Real?" *Time Magazine*, May 30, 2019, https://time.com/5597693/real-women-witches/.
2. "craft," *Oxford English Dictionary*: 3a.
3. "wright," *Oxford English Dictionary*: 3.
4. Jon D. Rossini, *Contemporary Latina/o Theater: Wrighting Ethnicity* (Carbondale: Southern Illinois University Press, 2008), 10. See also Harry Elam's use of "(w)right" to describe

how August Wilson "(w)rights history" in *The Past as Present in the Drama of August Wilson* (Ann Arbor: University of Michigan Press, 2004), 3.

5. A crucial distinction that is frequently lost on the general public is the fact that witchcraft is a practice that is untethered to a particular dogma. Witches have a wide variety of religious or spiritual beliefs, the most documented of which is Wicca, popularized in large part by Gerald B. Gardner's publications. See Margot Adler, *Drawing Down the Moon: Witches, Druids, Goddess-Worshippers and Other Pagans in America* (New York: Penguin, 1986).
6. Legal records for witch trials are flawed because the testimonies they include are rarely transcribed in first person, nor is it possible to know when "confessions" of witchcraft were made under duress. For more on this, see Ronald Hutton, *The Triumph of the Moon: A History of Modern Pagan Witchcraft* (Oxford: Oxford University Press, 1999).
7. Hutton, *The Triumph of the Moon*, 199. See Margaret A. Murray's *The Witch Cult in Modern Europe* and *The God of the Witches* for her theory regarding the origin of witchcraft. For those who have debunked Murray, see Norman Cohn, *Europe's Inner Demons* (Falmer: Sussex University Press, 1975), 102–25, and Jacqueline Simpson, "Margaret Murray: Who Believed Her, and Why?" in *Folklore* 105 (1994): 89–96.
8. Lindy West, "Yes, This Is a Witch Hunt. I'm a Witch and I'm Hunting You." *New York Times*, October 17, 2017, https://www.nytimes.com/2017/10/17/opinion/columnists/weinstein-harassment-witchunt.html.
9. While in the West, Dionysian rituals are frequently cited as part of theatre's origin narrative, rituals combining performance and religion also occurred throughout Asia and Africa, many of which predate the Theatre of Dionysus.
10. Pam Grossman, personal interview with author via Skype, December 13, 2019.
11. By stating that witchcraft is practiced in connection to religious beliefs that predate Christianity, rather than the Murray hypothesis discussed earlier, I base this observation on two things: (1) the definition Margot Adler provides of "Neo-Pagan Witchcraft . . . as one of a number of modern polytheistic religions," (11); and (2) the appearance of witchy characters in ancient epics such as *Gilgamesh* (the "prostitute" who civilizes Enkidu), *The Odyssey* (Circe), and the Bible (the witch of Endor, 1 Samuel 28: 3–25).
12. For more on these ancient witches, see Daniel Ogden, *Magic, Witchcraft, and Ghosts in the Greek and Roman Worlds: A Sourcebook* (Oxford: Oxford University Press, 2009).
13. Grossman, interview with author.
14. Baillie was encouraged to write by her aunt Anne Hunter, who was an amateur poet herself, as well as a member of the Blue Stockings Society. Baillie attended these literary salons, where they enjoyed conversations about literature, philosophy, and politics. For more on Bluestockings, see Elizabeth Eger, *Brilliant Women: 18th-Century Bluestockings* (New Haven, CT: Yale University Press, 2008).
15. The three plays Baillie set in Scotland include *Family Legend* (produced in 1810 at the Theatre Royal, Edinburgh), *Metrical Legends* (1821), and *Witchcraft*. She also set the musical play *The Phantom* in Scotland. *Witchcraft* and *The Phantom* were both published in her 1836 three-volume collection of drama, Joanna Baillie, *Dramas in Three Volumes*. London: 1836.
16. Brian P. Levack, *The Witch-Hunt in Early Modern Europe* (Essex: Longman, 1987), 184. These numbers are necessarily an estimate, since the first census records come from 1801,

but based on those numbers, Scotland's population (in 1801) was 19.3 percent that of England's. See the Office of National Statistics for England and the General Register Office for Scotland for this data.

17. James VI in Scotland became King James I in 1603, unifying England, Ireland, and Scotland under one monarch, although Scotland and England maintained individual sovereignties.
18. Hutton, *The Triumph of the Moon*, 107. Emphasis in original.
19. At first, Baillie did not want to publish her poems and plays, and her first volume of plays she published under a pseudonym. Baillie did have the opportunity to see a handful of her plays produced during her lifetime, including *De Monfort*, produced at Drury Lane in 1800 starring John Kemble and Sarah Siddons, and *Family Legend*, produced in Edinburgh (1810) and Drury Lane (1815). For more about these plays, see Susan Bennett, "Genre Trouble: Joanna Baillie, Elizabeth Polack; Tragic Subjects, Melodramatic Subjects" in *Women and Playwriting in Nineteenth-Century Britain* (Cambridge: Cambridge University Press, 1999).
20. I am not the first to make this observation. See Bennett, "Genre Trouble," 215–32.
21. Lady Annabella does not deign to place the fabric herself—instead, she enlists the assistance of the Dungarren's herdboy, Black Bawldy, to borrow Violet's dress from her maid, telling him that she has learned (from Grizeld Bane) that a scrap of fabric from a murderer's daughter placed under the sick child's pillow will cure them.
22. Joanna Baillie, *The Dramatic and Poetical Works of Joanna Baillie: Complete in One Volume* (London: Longman, Brown, Green, and Longmans, 1851), 618.
23. Baillie, *The Dramatic and Poetical Works of Joanna Baillie*, 613.
24. Baillie, *The Dramatic and Poetical Works of Joanna Baillie*, 641.
25. Quoted in Hutton, *The Triumph of the Moon*, 107.
26. For more on this production and its history, see "Hypertext and Performance: A Resonant Response to Joanna Baillie's Witchcraft," by the Resonance Lab, directed by Patrick Leroux, at: http://resonance.hexagram.ca/witchcraft/#/home.
27. Concordia's resonance on the passions was in keeping with Baillie's lifelong project of using drama to reveal the influence of how "different emotions of the mind are also conveyed along nerves to different muscles of the body," as her brother Matthew stated in his 1794 Gulstonian lectures (qtd. in Alan Richardson, "A Neural Theatre: Joanna Baillie's 'Plays on the Passions,'" in Crochunis [2004], 134).
28. Dorothy McMillan, "Unromantic Caledon: Representing Scotland in the Family Legend, Metrical Legends, and Witchcraft," *Joanna Baillie, Romantic Dramatist: Critical Essays*, ed. Thomas C. Crochunis (London: Routledge, 2004), 83–84.
29. The Eye of Horus was both an amulet (commonly called the *wedjat* or *ujat* eye) to be worn for protection and a graphic design for cosmetics to protect and beautify the (elite and powerful) human eye. In makeup usage, the left eye represented Horus and the right (with a mirrored design) was the Eye of Ra (or Re). See: Jenny Hill, "Eye of Horus," Ancient Egypt Online, https://ancientegyptonline.co.uk/eye/.
30. Jennifer Park, "Discandying Cleopatra: Preserving Cleopatra's Infinite Variety in Shakespeare's 'Antony and Cleopatra,'" *Studies in Philology* 113, no. 3 (2016): 599.
31. Grossman, interview with Author.
32. Baillie, *The Dramatic and Poetical Works of Joanna Baillie*, 630.
33. Baillie, *The Dramatic and Poetical Works of Joanna Baillie*, 642.

34. Baillie, *The Dramatic and Poetical Works of Joanna Baillie*, 642.
35. McMillan, "Unromantic Caledon," 85.
36. It is common practice in witchcraft rituals and in spellcasting to begin the process by casting (or creating) a circle, also referred to as "calling the quarters" or invoking the elements. In short, it is a way of establishing a safe space for the magic work and those who practice it.
37. Baillie, *The Dramatic and Poetical Works of Joanna Baillie*, 643.

Nothing Wicked This Way Comes

Shakespeare's Subversion of Archetypal Witches in *The Winter's Tale*

—JESSICA ANN HOLT

In the fall of 1485, the Inquisitor Heinrich Kramer began the trial of Helena Scheuberin, a woman of Innsbruck and an accused witch. Her trial did not go as planned. The Inquisitor insisted on focusing not on Scheuberin's links to malevolent acts, heresy, or the practicing of magic but, rather, on her sexual history. Local authorities quickly put an end to the trial and dismissed the charges, leaving Kramer humiliated. Following this incident, Kramer, along with Jacob Sprenger, began writing their seminal work on witchcraft, the *Malleus Maleficarum,* first published in 1487. Kramer and Sprenger's work links the practice of witchcraft almost exclusively to women and what they view as disordered female sexuality.[1] The claims of the *Malleus* circulated widely. By the mid-1500s, witchcraft was linked explicitly to worship of and sexual congress with Satan, acts almost always perpetrated by women due to women's inherently weak and sexually voracious natures. Years later, these views were echoed in the beliefs, writings, and actions of King James I. By the time King James of Scotland ascended the English throne in 1603, his obsession with witchcraft was well established. Under James's reign, witchcraft persecutions increased and the punishments became far more stringent than they were under the reign of Elizabeth I.[2] Though it is not the first, nor the most overt, depiction of witchcraft found in Shakespeare's writings, *The Winter's Tale,* written in 1610, is nonetheless influenced by the witch hysteria of his time.[3] Shakespeare creates three female protagonists—Paulina, Perdita, and Hermione—and then links each to characteristics considered common to witchcraft. Shakespeare created these female characters in the midst of King James's fascination with witchcraft and his intractable opinions on the reality and malevolence of witches. I argue that the characters in *The Winter's Tale* might be understood as an author's attempt to capitalize on public fascination with witchcraft. Whether Shakespeare intended it or not, I suggest, these characters also rebuke King James's intense animosity toward women in general and female witches specifically.[4] Though this is certainly not the first study to explore the link between *The Winter's Tale* and witchcraft, by approaching *The Winter's Tale* with a more comprehensive understanding of the links between each major female character and witchcraft, modern readers with both academic and artistic intentions are able to explore a broader range of potential meanings and themes.

Women's inferior status and the belief that women were more susceptible to the lures of witchcraft are found in the writings of King James. According to historian Tracey Borman, the number of witchcraft cases in England increased significantly as a result of King James's influence.[5] James states in his *Daemonologie*, first published in 1597, "The reason is easie, for as that sexe is frailer than man is, so is it easier to be intrapped in these grosse snares of the Devill, as was over well proved to be true, by the Serpents deceiving of Eva at the beginning, which makes him the homelier with that sexe sensine [since then]."[6] Though it can be argued that overall King James approached the subject of witchcraft from a more humanistic perspective than that found in the *Malleus*, his writings make it clear that he had both an unshakable belief in witchcraft and that women, through their assumed inherent weakness and inferiority, were the most likely agents thereof.[7]

Both the *Malleus Maleficarum* and the writings of King James are rife with links between women and witchcraft. In general, Elizabethan views on witchcraft were deeply misogynistic in nature. Satan's employment of witchcraft to achieve his evil aims was considered especially effective because of the following threefold effect: damning the soul of the witch, potentially impregnating the witch to create new followers, and creating an environment of unease, suspicion, and disharmony in society.[8] As witchcraft came to be more closely linked to Satanic practices, it "became a gender-linked offense; women, the witch-hunting manuals repeated, were morally weaker than men and therefore were more likely to succumb to satanic temptation."[9] The *Malleus* in particular supports misogynistic views on women by linking the very nature of womankind with inferiority and weakness. In *The Malleus Maleficarum: Theology and Popular Belief*, Hans Broedel translates Kramer and Sprenger's rationale for women's weakness: "Their minds are warped, twisted like the rib from which Eve was first formed; and just as the first woman could not keep faith with God, so all women are faithless."[10] The blame here attributed to Eve is then extended to all women. In essence: because the mother of all was faithless before God, then all women must share her shame, guilt, and faithlessness.

The death of Queen Elizabeth I in 1603 ended an incredibly powerful and long-standing period of female rule. The transition from the reign of Elizabeth I to that of King James represents a profound shift in the power structure and cultural climate of England. As James ascended the throne, his own misogynistic views mingled with a backlash against the female-led court. In this environment, women could be demonized in ways that would have been much more difficult under Queen Elizabeth. To tar all women as inferior could have been tantamount to treason in a kingdom ruled by a woman. Additionally, James's obsession with witchcraft and the increasing popularity and circulation of the *Malleus* contributed to an increasingly damaging view of women. It is in this context that Shakespeare's *The Winter's Tale* presents Perdita, Hermione, and Paulina in a manner that subtly links the three women to elements commonly associated with witchcraft, including a close link with the natural or green world, female sexuality, maternity, and outspokenness. At the same time, the prevailing negative view of womankind is confronted in the play through Shakespeare's creation of three female characters who are eventually proven vital to the survival and strength of their kingdom. In the following paragraphs, I examine these three characters (Perdita, Hermione, and Paulina) in turn, exploring the tension between expected witchy behavior and reality, to demonstrate the complicated dance between protection and protest that Shakespeare negotiates under James's rule.

Perdita is the primary female character linked to the natural world. This is first demonstrated by the abrupt shift in locale in act 3, scene 3. At this point, the fate of Perdita comes to the forefront of the plot and the setting shifts from the civilized world of Leontes's court at Sicilia to the pastoral realm of Bohemia. During the Elizabethan era, views on nature changed profoundly. Previously, nature had generally been considered all-powerful, mysterious, and beyond reproach. As science progressed, nature became something to be controlled, studied, and subdued.[11] Because women were largely associated with the natural world, they were more likely to be affected by this shift. Within *The Winter's Tale*, however, nature is shown to be nurturing, benevolent to the innocent, and a force for justice. The natural world is a positive environment for Perdita, one in which she is safe and able to develop into a beautiful and righteous young woman. As ecofeminists Banu Akçeşme and Behiye Çelik Karahan argue, "When compared to the wickedness at court, the natural setting provides regeneration, renewal and purification for people . . . nature eliminates the wickedness of the court and provides shelter for Perdita."[12] Crucially, the natural world also exhibits destructive power. Upon abandoning the infant to the elements of the natural world, Antigonus is killed by a bear, and the ship that transported the newborn is beset by a raging tempest. Though nature protects the infant Perdita, it also destroys the men who wronged her. Leontes specifically is punished by the natural world for his hubris and wrongdoing through the death of Mamillius, Antigonus, and the loss of his ship.[13] Shakespeare ties the most vulnerable character—a young, unmarried woman—to the natural world, demonstrating that nature, and therefore womanhood, are strong forces.

Perdita's link to the natural world is enhanced by her status as a young and beautiful woman, which also relates to the issues surrounding female sexuality within the play. The deeply rooted misogyny found in the early church is strongly linked to human sexuality. Christianity itself focuses on the dual nature of humanity in that each individual is made up of both a temporal, human body and an immortal soul. It is only by avoiding sin and mastering the sinful nature of one's human body that the immortal soul can be saved. Therefore, human sexuality is linked to sin. In what were likely efforts to absolve themselves of their own feelings of sin related to sexual desire, church fathers attributed the blame to womankind. Women were tied to sexuality and thereby sin through Eve's original sin in the Garden of Eden, their physical beauty, and the physiological differences between men and women. Women's physical bodies were thought to make them hysterical, irrational, and filled with unnatural levels of lust. By embracing such deeply misogynistic views on women, church leaders in essence created a scapegoat for their own lust and the sexual sins of men. Though witches were accused of a variety of magical impulses, they were commonly tied to love magic. This included interfering in the relationships of others as well as shaping their own romantic lives. As Broedel states, "Love magic of various sorts was invariably recognized as the specific provenance of female magicians. . . . The constant insistence on the part of theologians that such magic was, indeed, diabolical cast women's magic in an increasingly sinister light from the thirteenth century onwards."[14] Catherine Rider explores a contradicting view of this in her essay "Women, Men, and Love Magic in Late Medieval Pastoral Manuals." Rider argues that while the *Malleus* focused on the prevalence of female witches using love magic, other sources, particularly pastoral manuals, suggest that both men and women were potential practitioners. Men were more commonly associated with *erōs*-magic, which was tied to seduction and sexual relationships, while women were linked with *philia*-magic, which focused on strengthening existing romantic and/or marital bonds.[15]

Love magic and female sexuality are further explored through Perdita by virtue of her ties to fertility and assumed power over Florizel. When Perdita is first introduced as a young adult, she is presented as the love of Florizel. Shakespeare demonstrates the guileless love in the relationship between the two, yet the king Polixenes refuses to accept this, believing instead that Florizel is bewitched. As director and Shakespeare scholar Kirstie Gulick Rosenfield explains, "Perdita maintains the witch's sin of poverty and from Polixenes's accusing view entraps his son with sexuality for her own gain. He calls upon popular witchcraft belief, painting her as the social-climbing, sexually-deviant, order-threatening woman. Perdita, however, is already firmly associated with the natural order; likened to the fertility goddess Proserpina, she presides over the rustic feast."[16] The idea of witches entrapping men is a recurring theme, especially in the *Malleus.* It is also important to note that Perdita is accused of witchcraft based on sexuality, just as her mother, Hermione, was. This demonstrates that for both Polixines and Leontes, it is not their own desire but the disordered and uncontrollable female sexuality that is the cause of sin.[17] Thus through Polixines's insistence that Perdita has bewitched Florizel through her sexuality and used her powers to safeguard a relationship that will provide her with security, Perdita demonstrates both the *erōs*-magic and *philia*-magic discussed previously. In addition to Polixenes's fears regarding Perdita bewitching Florizel, Perdita is also linked to witchcraft through her ties to the festival wherein she is first introduced as an adult. In Shakespeare's time, such feasts were heavily criticized by the same religious reformers involved in the persecution of suspected witches. As Klaits describes, "the great seasonal festivals, including Carnival, May Day, Michaelmas, and Midsummer's Eve, which were grand occasions in the life of the people, came under heavy attack by reformers, who condemned them as lewd and pagan profanations . . . to the reformers these festivals seemed circuses of sin."[18] As mistress of the feast, Perdita is the public image of the festival, representing the sexual and pagan aspects of the event and thus linking her to witchcraft.

The Winter's Tale further confronts the societal and religious fear of female sexuality and its connection to witchcraft through the character of Hermione. Social anxieties concerning female infidelity, illegitimate children, and maternity are all interrogated through Hermione and her interactions with the male characters in the play. Leontes is of course aware of Hermione's sexual nature by virtue of their relationship as husband and wife, the presence of their son Mamillius, and Hermione's pregnancy. The pregnancy serves as a stark reminder of Hermione's dual nature as maternal nurturer and sexual being. In addition to Leontes's concerns about Hermione's sexual nature in general, he is specifically concerned about Hermione in regard to what he believes to be her infidelity. While watching Hermione interact with Polixenes, Leontes is abruptly overcome with suspicion and exclaims:

Too hot, too hot!
To mingle friendship far is mingling bloods.
I have a *tremor cordis* on me. My heart dances,
But not for joy, not joy.[19]

Much like witchcraft accusations of Shakespeare's time, Leontes becomes convinced of Hermione and Polixenes's crime with no proof and very little evidence. Shortly after becoming convinced of the affair, Leontes reveals his views on the fidelity of women, saying:

—women say so
That will say anything but they were false.[20]

Leontes's lament echoes the *Malleus*'s assertion that all women are faithless and deceptive.

The attribution of sexual deviance to women made them highly susceptible to accusations of witchcraft as the relationship between Satan and supposed witches shifted from that of simply being associated with the devil into something more physical. This led to the highly invasive and degrading practice of the forced stripping and searching of bodies, including the genitals, of women accused of witchcraft for physical marks that would supposedly prove the woman's relationship and subservience to Satan. Again we see the female body being both shamed and made an object of lust by patriarchal governmental and religious power structures. Women's sexual practices and sexuality became a key part of witch trials and beliefs surrounding witchcraft. The idea of witches as not only worshippers of and dealers with Satan but also his willing sexual slaves became firmly entrenched in the ideologies surrounding witch hunts by 1550.[21]

Though Hermione is spared the cruelty of being stripped naked and searched for signs of a witch's mark, the comparison is nonetheless impactful. As Rosenfield suggests, "Both accusation and trial, the public displays of Hermione's infidelity, invoke the format of the witch hunt, displaying then effacing the body of the powerless."[22] Shakespeare also mocks the proceedings of witchcraft trials with Leontes's lines:

Let us be cleared
Of being tyrannous, since we so openly

> Proceed in justice, which shall have due course
> Even to the guilt or the purgation.[23]

The trial under Leontes is clearly unjust and governed by nothing but his own paranoia. Cultural critic Kirby Farrell argues, "By imprisoning his pregnant wife, Leontes acts to police his fears as the authorities would do on behalf of their communities by mastering witches through shackles, torture, and burning."[24] Shakespeare destroys any hint of validity in Leontes's accusations by showing that Hermione is innocent of the charges, vindicating her through her death and her eventual return to life.

Setting up the persecution of Hermione in a way that mirrors the trials of suspected witches allows Shakespeare to highlight the absurdity of the witch trials by reflecting the unfounded basis for the proceedings, as well as the highly unjust nature of the trials. Though she is the queen, she is brought to stand trial in public, stripped of royal accoutrements, publicly shamed and embarrassed with no one to rise to her public defense. The imagery of a woman standing alone against an all-powerful accuser provides a compelling indictment of the system of prosecution faced by accused witches. Yet at the conclusion of the trial, Hermione is proven faultless through a prophecy from the female oracle. Interestingly, Shakespeare chooses to have Leontes deny even a sacred prophecy as truth. By doing so, he draws attention to action that simultaneously represents the undermining of female contributions to society while recognizing and providing a dramaturgical link to the pagan world. Despite his claims that he will listen to the verdict from the oracle, Leontes—upon learning that the prophecy refutes his own opinion—refuses to believe. It is not until his own son is dead, proving a component of the prophecy, that he is willing to accept the Queen's innocence. This minor component of the play demonstrates an early and dire warning for the future of the kingdom. In essence, when a righteous female is not listened to, in this case the oracle, the continuance and strength of the kingdom is affected.

Hermione further suffers as a result of her role as a mother. Her status as an accused adulterer notwithstanding, even the most faithful of married women faced hostility, as any nonvirginal woman was devalued in Jacobean society.[25] If a woman's primary role in a society, namely that of mother, is no longer sacred and revered, this lack of respect leaves even upstanding women more vulnerable to accusations of witchcraft.[26] This dichotomy between the sexual and nurturing aspects of maternity was only one facet of femininity that made women suspect during the English Renaissance. On the one hand, fears abounded about a woman using her sexuality for anything other than mothering, while, on the other hand, even the natural process of creating, birthing, and rearing a child was seen as suspect. According to Rosenfield: "Contemporary cultural anxiety about the power that women assumed through maternity surfaced in common concerns about ills transmitted through nursing. Colostrum, the mother's first milk, was conventionally referred to as 'witch's milk' and thought to convey both disease and female blood to the helpless male infant. Strengthening the imaginative connection between the nursing woman and the witch was the belief that witches fed their familiars on milk from supernumerary nipples."[27] The archetype of the devilish mother is a result of societal and religious apprehensions about the dichotomy between the sexual and maternal aspects of femininity required to produce offspring.

The mysterious realm of childbearing and its links to deviant sexuality have long been suspect in patriarchal societies. The condition of motherhood invited intense scrutiny for any pregnancy, but the general public's fascination transformed into fixation and often fear at the notion of a witch giving birth. As previously discussed, Satan achieved multiple evil goals through sexual congress with a witch. Not only does such an act damn the witch, but it has the potential to create a pregnancy resulting in future servants of the devil. By having Hermione pregnant during her trial, Shakespeare reinforces the concept of the monstrous mother archetype. Furthermore, when Perdita is of childbearing age, she too is accused of witchcraft, relating to the mythology surrounding witches birthing future witches.

The ways in which witchcraft intersects with maternity and the female-centric realm of childbirth is further illustrated through Paulina and her role as a pseudo-midwife. Though not technically serving as midwife to Hermione as she gives birth to Perdita, Paulina fulfills several key responsibilities of the traditional role. She acts as a conduit between mother (Hermione) and father (Leontes) upon the birth of the child, delivering the infant safely. Paulina proclaims the legitimacy of the birth, despite Leontes's refusal to accept this information. As Hermione's fidelity and the paternity of the infant are vital elements of *The Winter's Tale*, Paulina's involvement in Perdita's birth proves especially relevant. According to Caroline Bicks in *Midwiving Subjects in Shakespeare's England*, the midwife's "perceived closeness to the mother also led to her official role as a paternity testifier, the theory being that women under the duress of labor were more likely to speak freely and truthfully about their behavior and partners."[28] Thus, as Paulina defends the legitimacy of the infant's status as heir, she is fulfilling a key component of midwifery duties. Furthermore, questions of legitimacy and royal lineage during Shakespeare's time were complicated and had far-reaching consequences. Henry VIII began the disruption of traditional patterns of royal succession, and this was further complicated by Elizabeth I's lifelong choice to remain childless. By the time Shakespeare wrote *The Winter's Tale*, King James had succeeded to the throne, effectively ending the Tudor dynasty.[29] The references to illegitimate children, a lack of an heir, and questions regarding monarchal continuity are of particular significance when considered within the context of James's relatively new reign.[30]

In addition to her involvement with the infant Perdita, Paulina is further linked to midwifery because she is responsible at least in part for Hermione's return to life, essentially acting as midwife for the rebirth of the Queen. She carefully creates a situation allowing for her beloved mistress's return to life. Paulina invites Leontes, Perdita, and others to visit her home, where she tells them of a statue she has commissioned as a tribute to Hermione. Paulina informs the group:

> As she lived peerless,
> So her dead likeness I do well believe
> Excels whatever yet you looked upon,
> Or hand of man hath done. Therefore I keep it
> Lonely, apart. But here it is: prepare
> To see the life as lively mocked as ever
> Still sleep mocked death. Behold, and say 'tis well.[31]

Much as a midwife does in the birth of a child, Paulina prepares the way for Hermione, ensures a safe environment for her delivery, and carefully conveys the reborn Hermione to her waiting family.

By linking Paulina with the role of midwife, Shakespeare capitalizes on the public's often imagined concept of the midwife as witch. Though recent scholarship argues that midwives were not the victims of witchcraft persecution and were instead trusted members of society, a public fascination with the link between the two female-centric roles exists.[32] Regarding the linkage between midwives and witchcraft, Broedel describes Kramer and Sprenger's views on the matter, stating, "The most formidable kind of witch, possessing the most impressive occult arsenal, is the midwife-witch, who specializes in killing and eating unbaptized children."[33] The midwife's involvement and command of the female-centric realm of childbirth put them at risk for being accused of witchcraft. Klaits argues, "As one of the few important events in the life of the community that was given over entirely to female control, birthing may well have been a source of unsettling emotions for men accustomed to supervising every aspect of women's lives. Accusations of witchcraft lodged against midwives are a possible indication of male discomfiture with the competent female."[34] Because Paulina fulfills the role of midwife through her involvement in the birth of the infant Perdita, as well as the rebirth of Hermione, she is indelibly linked to the concept of the midwife witch.

In addition to the aforementioned issues of the natural world, female sexuality, and midwifery, witchcraft was also linked to the image of the shrew, or outspoken woman. Shakespeare gives voice to this particular viewpoint again through the character of Paulina. Paulina's bold and assertive way of speaking to powerful men puts her in a precarious position in a society wherein women are already suspect. Klaits explains: "Frequently in witch trials the accused was someone said to be lacking in deference for her betters. This was precisely the sort of person of whom it could be believed, in the words of a Scottish indictment, that she had 'shaken off all fear of God, reverence and regard to the laws of this Kingdome.' Such women, who seemed to threaten conventional opinions of 'woman's place,' were accused not only by men but also by other women whose sense of security may have depended on conforming to the standards of acceptable female behavior set by men."[35] Despite the danger of being punished, when Leontes accuses Hermione of adultery, Paulina boldly defends the queen. Though defense of the queen should fall to the men, Paulina enters the court against their commands and rebukes them, saying:

> Nay rather, good my lords, be second to me.
> Fear you his tyrannous passion more, alas,
> Than the queen's life?[36]

Paulina displays the attributes associated with a shrew witch by chastising the lords and calling her sovereign a tyrant. As Leontes's rage grows, Paulina alone stands strong against him despite the king calling her a "mankind witch" and a "crone."[37] Leontes goes so far as to threaten Paulina with a punishment sometimes meted out to convicted witches: that of being burned to death. Though threatened, Paulina again demonstrates her courage and her willingness to speak truth to power, saying to the king:

> I care not.
> It is an heretic that makes the fire,
> Not she which burns in't.
> I'll not call you tyrant;
> But this most cruel usage of your queen,
> Not able to produce more accusation

Than your own weak-hinged fancy, something savours
Of tyranny, and will ignoble make you,
Yea, scandalous to the world.[38]

Paulina shows strength in the face of incredible societal pressure and at great personal risk. Shakespeare repeatedly demonstrates through Paulina's actions that an outspoken woman can be righteous, powerful, and a force for healing and good. This is in direct opposition to the common views of the time, in particular the linkage between outspoken women and witchcraft. By ascribing these characteristics to Paulina, in many ways the heroine of the play, Shakespeare demonstrates the fallacies inherent in this particular witchcraft characterization.[39]

Paulina is bold in her dealings with Leontes and ultimately shown to be correct and knowledgeable. Leontes realizes his errors and enlists Paulina's counsel, whereupon she becomes his most trusted advisor. Paulina's forthrightness, which began as a trait linking her to witchcraft, is eventually recognized as a powerful force for good. Leontes accepts the counsel and advice of a woman he formerly cast aside. As Shakespearean scholar Cristina León Alfar argues, "Thus, Paulina's role as healer, advisor, and conscience—spanning more than a decade and a half in time as well as four acts of the play . . . makes her a powerful and victorious rebel against the inequities not only between men and women in marriage but also between kings and subjects under monarchy."[40] Shakespeare carefully crafts the character of Paulina so that the archetypal characteristics of the shrew witch that she displays are revealed later as positive aspects of her character. Paulina's daring nature is ultimately the salvation of the entire royal family. It is Paulina's influence that leads to Leontes's change of heart, and it is her guidance over the intervening sixteen years that prepares the way for Hermione's return to life. Through Paulina, Shakespeare again capitalizes on the public fascination with witches while subverting audience expectations by demonstrating that a woman with witchlike qualities can in fact be a healer, a protector, and ultimately a savior of the kingdom.

All three female characters in *The Winter's Tale* are thus linked to witchcraft based on seventeenth-century English views regarding seduction, fidelity, and maternity (both actual motherhood and women's involvement with it via midwifery). By linking these three important aspects of the female sexual experience to witchcraft, religious and societal leaders attempted to maintain authority and absolve themselves of their own perceived sexual sin by shifting the blame to women. Shakespeare, however, demonstrates a dissenting view on female sexuality. Perdita and Florizel's marriage is emblematic of true love, rather than any form of magical interference. Hermione is revealed as the ideal married woman, innocent of infidelity and also a loving mother. Finally, fearless Paulina fulfills the role of midwife and is ultimately responsible for the safe delivery of Perdita, the reborn Hermione, and in many ways the rebirth of the kingdom itself.

Tracing the changes in English witchcraft beliefs from the publication of the *Malleus Maleficarum* through the Renaissance provides a great deal of information about the overwhelming majority of witchcraft accusations being leveled toward women. The expansion of scientific inquiry invited keener attention to the significance of the natural world and women's place in it. Religious reformation from both the Catholic and Protestant churches had a profound effect on societal views on women as well. At the same time, shifting views on the interactions between supposed witches and the devil served to focus on women's sexuality, putting women in an increasingly vulnerable state in terms of the likelihood of being accused of witchcraft. Though he lived and wrote during a time of extreme misogyny and furor over witchcraft, Shakespeare's three female characters in *The Winter's Tale* are each shown to be of noble character, righteous, powerful, and innocent of all accused crimes.

By analyzing the female characters, a potential reading of *The Winter's Tale* emerges wherein Shakespeare capitalizes on the public fascination with witchcraft, a specific obsession of the newly crowned King James I, while at the same time including elements that challenge the era's pervasive negative views on women—particularly pointed, given the recent reign of Elizabeth. Firstly, Shakespeare creates three women that are linked to various aspects of witchcraft, this being a popular topic of the time based on the increased circulation of the *Malleus*, James's own *Daemonologie*, and works of Shakespeare's literary contemporaries. Despite the growing acceptance of the satanic witch archetype, Paulina, Perdita, and Hermione are vindicated and shown to be innocent of any malevolence, thereby subverting the denigrated image of the female witch. Additionally, the issues surrounding royal lineage within this play are a potential reference to King James. His ascension to the English throne was not the result of a seamless transition between father and son. Shakespeare's use of a kingdom without an heir and questions of legitimacy of a royal line cannot be ignored given the events of the era. Finally King James's well-documented fixation on witchcraft, specifically as it applies to women, is explored in a way that exposes lingering anxieties about gender, power, royal legitimacy, and sexuality. Though James's ascension to the throne complicates the lingering societal and cultural effects of Elizabeth's reign, *The Winter's Tale* argues that women are necessary for the survival of a kingdom. When left in the hands of Leontes, his kingdom is nearly destroyed due to his paranoia, selfishness, and stubbornness. Though Leontes recognizes his grave error and begins repenting early in the play, the damage lingers for the next sixteen years. During this time, Leontes accepts the wise counsel of Paulina, without which the reunion at the end of the play would not be possible. Paulina's acceptance into a position of power validates the exigency of outspoken women in society. It is not until the disgraced and displaced royal women are vindicated and returned to their rightful place in the monarchy that the kingdom is healed. As the play was first produced in the years following the death of Elizabeth I, this implication of the necessity for a powerful feminine presence in the running of the country is especially pointed. When considered with the political and societal factors of the time in mind, *The Winter's Tale* contrasts other plays of the period, using witchcraft to demonstrate the goodness of women as well as their capability for public service while simultaneously offering incisive commentary that raises concerns about the young reign of King James.

Notes

1. Hans Peter Broedel, *The Malleus Maleficarum: Theology and Popular Belief* (Manchester, UK: Manchester University Press, 2003), 176.
2. Tracy Borman, "James VI and I: The King Who Hunted Witches." History Extra. Accessed April 1, 2019: https://www.historyextra.com/period/stuart/king-james-vi-i-hunted-witches-hunter-devilry-daemonologue/.
3. William Shakespeare, *The Winter's Tale*, ed. John Pitcher (London: Bloomsbury Arden Shakespeare, 2014) 158–59, 1.2.108–11. According to the introduction to the Arden edition, *The Winter's Tale* was written in late 1610, though other sources debate the actual date. The date of the first performance is also in question.
4. See Borman, "James VI and I."
5. Borman, "James VI and I."
6. Author's clarification in brackets; Neil Rhodes and Jennifer Richards, *King James VI and I: Selected Writings*, ed. Dr. Joseph Marshall (Abingdon, UK: Routledge, 2016) ProQuest Ebook Central, http://ebookcentral.proquest.com/lib/bayloru/detail.action?docID=4817373.
7. Elizabeth Mack. "*The Malleus Maleficarum* and King James: Defining Witchcraft," *Voces Novae* 1, no. 9. Available at: https://digitalcommons.chapman.edu/vocesnovae/vol1/iss1/9
8. Mack, "*The Malleus Maleficarum* and King James," 45.
9. Mack, "*The Malleus Maleficarum* and King James," 59.
10. Broedel, *The Malleus Maleficarum*, 176.

11. Banu Akçeşme and Behiya Çelik Karahan, "An Ecofeminist Reading of Shakespeare's *The Winter's Tale*," *International Journal of Languages' Education and Teaching* 6, no. 1 (2018): 84.
12. Akçeşme and Karahan, "An Ecofeminist Reading of Shakespeare's *The Winter's Tale*," 81.
13. Akçeşme and Karahan, "An Ecofeminist Reading of Shakespeare's *The Winter's Tale*," 85.
14. Broedel, *The Malleus Maleficarum*, 172.
15. Catherine Rider, "Women, Men, and Love Magic in Late Medieval English Pastoral Manuals," *Magic, Ritual and Witchcraft* 7, no. 2 (Winter 2012): 195–97.
16. Kirstie Gulick Rosenfield, "Nursing Nothing: Witchcraft and Female Sexuality in *The Winter's Tale*," *Mosaic: A Journal for the Interdisciplinary Study of Literature* 35, no. 1 (2002): 103. Although Rosenfield does not explicitly define the phrase "witch's sin of poverty" in this essay, one may assume she is referring to the high number of accused witches that lived in poverty.
17. Rosenfield, "Nursing Nothing," 97.
18. Joseph Klaits, *Servants of Satan: The Age of the Witch Hunts* (Bloomington: Indiana University Press, 1985), 81.
19. Shakespeare, *The Winter's Tale*, 158–59, 1.2.108–11.
20. Shakespeare, *The Winter's Tale*, 161, 1.2.130–31.
21. Klaits, *Servants of Satan*, 50–51.
22. Rosenfield, "Nursing Nothing," 101.
23. Shakespeare, *The Winter's Tale*, 221–22, 3.2.4–7.
24. Kirby Farrell. "Witchcraft and Wonder in *The Winter's Tale*," *Renaissance Historicisms: Essays in Honor of Arthur F. Kinney*, ed. James M. Dutcher and Anne Lake Prescott (Newark: University of Delaware Press, 2008): 159–72. Quoted in *Shakespearean Criticism*, ed. Michelle Lee, vol. 138, Gale, 2011. *Literature Resource Center*, accessed December 1, 2018: http://link.galegroup.com/apps/doc/H1420103568/LitRC?u=txshracd2488&sid=LitRC&xid=ae08ea04.
25. For further discussion of women and their roles in society, see Johann Weyer, *Witches, Devils, and Doctors in the Renaissance: Johann Weyer, De Praestigiis Daemonum*, ed. George Mora et al., trans. John Shea (Binghamton, NY: Medieval and Renaissance Texts and Studies, 1991).
26. Klaits, *Servants of Satan*, 66. This disregard for the role of mothers was also seen within the Catholic Church. As Klaits describes, "Although the cult of Mary developed in the Middle Ages, the church insisted that only the status of virginity and the role of motherhood could glorify the female condition. In the serious business of sanctification, even motherhood has disturbed Catholic leaders; there have been very few female saints who were not virgins throughout their lives." Additional information and analysis regarding how Catholicism, witchcraft, and the reign of King James are related can be found in Garry Will's *Witches and Jesuits: Shakespeare's Macbeth* (New York: New York Public Library, 1995).
27. Rosenfield, "Nursing Nothing," 99.
28. Caroline Bicks, *Midwiving Subjects in Shakespeare's England* (Abingdon-on-Thames, UK: Taylor and Francis, 2003), 3.
29. Bicks, *Midwiving Subjects in Shakespeare's England*, 32–33.
30. For more information regarding the use of pregnancy as a literary device in plays during James's reign, see Sara B. T. Thiel's work, "'Cushion Come Forth': Materializing Preg-

nancy on the Stuart Stage," in *Stage Matters: Props, Bodies, and Space in Shakespearean Performance*, ed. Annalisa Castaldo and Rhonda Knight (Madison, NJ: Fairleigh Dickinson University Press, 2018), 143–58.

31. Shakespeare, *The Winter's Tale*, 338, 5.3.14–20.
32. For more information regarding the dismantling of the connection between midwifery and witchcraft, see David Harley's essay "Historians as Demonologists: The Myth of the Midwife-witch," *Social History of Medicine* 3, no. 1 (April 1990).
33. Broedel, *The Malleus Maleficarum*, 30.
34. Klaits, *Servants of Satan*, 96.
35. Klaits, *Servants of Satan*, 98.
36. Shakespeare, *The Winter's Tale*, 207–8, 2.3.26–28.
37. Shakespeare, *The Winter's Tale*, 210–11, 2.366, 2.3.74.
38. Shakespeare, *The Winter's Tale*, 213–14, 2.3.113–19.
39. I use the term "heroine" here as it pertains to the structure of the play. Though each of the three main female characters have great importance, Paulina's actions do the most to help drive the play forward. She is willing to stand outside the constraints of her society, an act of supreme bravery. Additionally, her actions bring about the triumphant return of Hermione.
40. Cristina León Alfar, *Women and Shakespeare's Cuckoldry Plays: Shifting Narratives of Marital Betrayal* (New York: Routledge, 2017): 175, ProQuest Ebook Central, http://ebookcentral.proquest.com/lib/bayloru/detail.action?docID=4803311.

Of Women and Witches

Performing the Female Body in Caryl Churchill's *Vinegar Tom*

—MAMATA SENGUPTA

In patriarchy, women's attempts at recording their personal and collective stories against the metanarrative of recorded history have often been met with severe sociocultural prohibitions. From Lilith and Medusa to Joan of Arc, the examples of female persecution in mythology and history on grounds of their exceptionality and defiance are numerous. The British playwright Caryl Churchill takes issue with the seventeenth-century tradition of witch hunting in her 1976 play *Vinegar Tom*. The present article attempts to reread the play to understand how patriarchy interprets women's attempts at self-actualization as symptomatic of different incurable and inbred "feminine" abnormalities like physical sickness, psychological derangement, and spiritual corruption. I also address how Churchill's female characters in the play revolt against all such patriarchal stereotypes and thereby register the tales of their potentially disruptive experiences in the official history of the "malekind."

Vinegar Tom premiered on October 12, 1976, at the Humberside Theatre, Hull, under the direction of Pam Brighton. The play, as Churchill notes, is the first of her collaborative projects: "Early in 1976 I met some of the Monstrous Regiment, who were thinking they would like to do a play about witches. . . . Soon I met the whole company to talk about working with them. . . . I left the meeting exhilarated. My previous work had been completely solitary—I never discussed my ideas while I was writing or showed anyone anything earlier than a final polished draft."[1] *Vinegar Tom*, therefore, is a product as much of Churchill's creative imagination as of Monstrous Regiment's critical instinct. On the one hand, Churchill's reading of books such as *Witches, Midwives and Nurses: A History of Women Healers*, by the American writers Barbara Ehrenreich and Deirdre English, and *Witchcraft in Tudor and Stuart England: A Regional and Comparative Study*, by the British anthropologist and historian Alan Macfarlane, provided the play with its theoretical/thematic background. On the other hand, the decidedly socio-feminist stance of the Monstrous Regiment guided Churchill's treatment of the theme. Two other notable influences were the 1968 Ford sewing machinist strike by the female employees against Ford's discriminatory wage structure and the 1970 Equal Pay Act that came into effect as a direct offshoot of the 1968 strike. Undoubtedly, the "witches" of *Vinegar Tom* have inherited a lot from these deviant female employees of Ford whose sheer determination, persistence, and hope for a better tomorrow paved the way for the 1970s Equal Pay Bill.

Set in a small seventeenth-century English village, *Vinegar Tom* deals with the struggle between truth and superstition. It attempts to see through the sociocultural discourses of female insanity and corruption to show how patriarchy manipulates these categories in order to fulfill its sexual, social, and religious needs and aspirations. As the alternative theatre critic Catherine Itzin comments, Churchill's *Vinegar Tom* "may be set in the world of seventeenth-century witchcraft, but it speaks, through its striking images and its plethora of ironic contradictions, of and to this century's still deep-rooted anti-feminism and women's oppression."[2] *Vinegar Tom* is divided into twenty-one scenes that tell the tale of five women—Alice, Joan, Susan, Ellen, and Betty—who are accused of practicing witchcraft. The first of these "witchy" women is the twenty-year-old village girl Alice, whose headstrong nature, uninhibited sexuality, and constant questioning of the social givens attempts to dismantle the patriarchal categorization of women as either "bloody whores" or "pious virgins." As a self-assertive woman, Alice rejects both these categories and demands a place in society independent of her gender-identity. The play opens with her postcoital conversation with an anonymous man regarding the "sin"-fullness of their relation.[3] While the man, as a representative patriarch, has no qualms in using Alice as a sexual object but refuses to accept her responsibility or to take her to London, Alice has no such problems in acknowledging both her sexual needs and the absence of paternal affiliation to her child, "I'll do what gives us pleasure."[4] And again,

ALICE: I've a child, mind, I'll not leave the child.
MAN: Has it a father?
ALICE: No, never had.[5]

According to the American feminist thinker Adrienne Rich, "Motherhood is 'sacred' so long as its offspring are 'legitimate'—that is, as long as the child bears the name of a father who legally controls the mother."[6] Alice's uninhibited acceptance of both her sexuality and the absence of her child's paternal affiliation punctures this "sacred" image of the mother. To add to this, her assertions such as, "If it [sex] was [sin] I don't care," and, "Any time I'm happy someone says it's a sin," betray her stern rejection of the patriarchal codes of female morality, chastity, and modesty.[7] This rejection, however, is not a symbol of Alice's inability either to control her body or to ascertain the paternity of her child. It is rather her resistance against an utterly irrelevant symbolic order that judges the worth of a person through his/her sexuality or socio-familial affiliations. This rejection also highlights her ability to become the signifier through which both she and her child can perceive their own selves and their respective worlds without having to remain tethered to the name of the husband or of the father.

The man's urge to make Alice "kiss" his "arse" like the "devil" makes his "witches" do highlights both his perversion and his will to control the female.[8] It also stems from the patriarchal desire to commodify the female body and utilize it without any regard for a woman's own wishes or desires. It is for this reason that the French feminist Luce Irigaray sees the "characteristics of feminine sexuality" as deriving from "a passive acceptance of men's [sexual] activity" without "getting pleasure herself," for "neither as mother nor as virgin nor as prostitute has woman any right to her own pleasure."[9] What follows is a heated argument about a witch-burning scene the man witnessed in Scotland. The enthusiastic description of the spectacle that the man blurts out is continuously counterpointed by Alice's repeated queries regarding the veracity of such beliefs, "Was she a real one? . . . Did you see her flying? . . . What did she say?"[10] That the man is unable to answer a single of her queries in unequivocal affirmatives and instead has to resort to approximations like "I think so" or "I may have done" clearly highlights his confusion and lack of knowledge.[11] The man, however, can hardly accept his failure to silence Alice. Desperately, therefore, he starts equating her to a witch on the grounds of their socially deviant nature.

According to the American radical feminist Mary Daly, "Witch Burning" is among the most prominent of "Western and Christian manifestation[s] of the androcentric state of atrocity" against women.[12] In *Vinegar Tom*, it is primarily through the persistent queries of Alice about the witch-hunting episode witnessed by the man that Churchill attempts to destabilize the myth of patriarchy's infallibility. In fact, what frustrates the man about Alice's repeated queries is her access to free speech and his failure to silence her. If the witch has transgressed the permissible limits of femininity by practicing witchcraft and thereby trying to control or challenge the patriarchy, then by daring to question the paternal authority (the man in this case) and nullifying the need of the father's name for her child, Alice too has situated herself against the patriarchal order. For patriarchy, therefore, both these acts puncture the prevalent image of the woman as weak and submissive. The quarrel between Alice and the man here serves a significant purpose. It highlights Alice's strong sense of individual identity that patriarchy neither expects from nor accepts in a woman. The witch's narrative actually prepares ground for Alice's questions to which the man has no answers. These questions instead make him visualize Alice as another "witch" threatening to overthrow all patriarchal names and norms to categorize and control her: "What are you then? What name would you put to yourself? You're not a wife or a widow. You're not a virgin. Tell me a name for what you are."[13] The fact that Alice or women like her cannot be forced to conform to any socially preferred categories of femininity, such as "virgins," "wives," or "whores," highlights these women's subversive individuality. It is this individuality that unnerves the man. In a patriarchy, women are allowed to exist only in relation to men (as wives, virgins, or whores). Anyone daring to go beyond these parameters or falling short of attaining them is fated to become what Maxine Hong Kingston would have called a "No Name Woman"—a deviant woman who is forbidden and hence forgotten.[14]

Alice's mother, Joan, is the next female character we meet in the play. Despite her supremely important role in the dramatic structure of *Vinegar Tom*, she leads a marginal life both literally and metaphorically. In fact, her stage time is commensurate with and evocative of her status in the youth-oriented and productivity-driven society she inhabits. Her brief conversation with Alice in the third scene of the play highlights her double marginalization as a *woman* and as an *old woman* who has grown out of usefulness:

ALICE: You go out?
JOAN: Funny, isn't it? What would I do going out?
ALICE: I'll stay in if you like.
JOAN: Where would I go? Who wants an old woman?[15]

Churchill strategically places the first song of the play, "Nobody Sings," at this point. According to the playwright, the songs of *Vinegar Tom* are "not part of the action and not sung by the characters."[16] As structural additions to the play's Brechtian episodic narrative, they exist on a separate dramatic plane to highlight the prevalent themes of torture and suffering in our society. Churchill's next instruction that these songs are all "contemporary" and should be sung by "actors in modern dress" offers insight into their meaning and purpose.[17] Songs are Churchill's method of highlighting the continuity of the play's historical past. The "modern" dress of the singer-actors at once dissociates the play from the songs and highlights the persistence of patriarchal oppression across ages. This is why dramaturg Robert L. Neblett calls the songs "metatheatrical devices" for critical-distancing and commentary.[18] In fact, in the structure of *Vinegar Tom*, the songs exist like postdramatic fragments through which the play is released from the shackles of dramatic composition and performance is allowed to carry forward the meaning.

While the early productions of the play mostly followed the original music score by Helen Glavin, a member of the Monstrous Regiment, contemporary directors have often experimented with different forms of pop, jazz, rock, and the blues. Glavin's composition was predominantly melodious with a hint of plaintive-yet-rhythmic country tunes, and her main instruments were piano, guitar, and the conga. Modern productions of the play, however, frequently use a lot of other string, wind, and percussion instruments to bring in new flavors. For example, while the 2013 Whistler in the Dark production of *Vinegar Tom* strategically used a subdued and monotonous score to highlight the cultural silencing of women,[19] the 2019 Indiana University production of the play employed an elaborate musical arrangement inspired by Justin Timberlake, Ariana Grande, Britney Spears, and Lady Gaga to celebrate the unflinching courage of the "witchy" female characters of the play.[20] Another 2019 production by director Ariel Craft attempted to revamp the original songs with a combination of elements from piano ragtime, music hall, and the blues.[21]

The song "Nobody Sings" deals with the theme of menstruation, which happens to be one of the most important yet disquieting experiences of a woman within patriarchy:

> I woke up in the morning,
> Blood was on the sheet,
> I looked at all the women
> When I passed them in the street.
> Nobody sings about it[22]

Churchill explains that this opening verse of the song was actually "left out in the original production [of the play] because the song seemed too long."[23] However, intensely aware of the physical as well as the cultural relevance of menstruation, Churchill later "put it back" into the play.[24] Since patriarchy visualizes women primarily as procreation machines, their worth in society is always determined in reference to their ability to menstruate. "Nobody Sings," therefore, becomes a lot more than a mere expression of a woman's "first period."[25] The song reflects the experiences of women's entire lives—how they grow up, attain puberty, and ultimately grow old and become unnecessary for both the family and society.

According to Gail Weiss, an American embodiment theorist, human beings perceive their bodies neither anatomically nor cognitively but through phenomenological accounts of people who surround them: "The touches of others, the interest others take in the different parts of our body, will be of enormous importance in the postural model of the body."[26] The "postural model" of the body as experienced and emotionally invested by the family or society casts a lasting influence on the person's intra and interpersonal relationships. This is how patriarchy makes the male body aware of its position of power, privilege, and supremacy across all sociocultural situations and institutions. The female body, on the other side, is similarly inscribed with an overpowering sense of shame, helplessness, and inferiority. According to Neblett, in patriarchy, women's "reproductive capacity is an embarrassment to be hidden away in shame."[27] The blood that could have attracted familial attention, medical care, and sociocultural adulation for men highlights for women the "shameful" vulnerabilities of their body that need to be kept in secret. This makes women maintain a studied silence regarding menstruation and allied troubles that, in turn, nullifies their possibilities of finding support from solidarity groups or medical professionals. In fact, a menstruating woman under patriarchy embodies the same disabled female body that the American disability theorist, Nancy Mairs, describes as "crippled" and "doubly other."[28] Menstruation not only frustrates all patriarchal standards of desirability but also transforms the female body into a sociocultural taboo that remains strictly unspeakable. However, the menstruating body is of great value to patriarchy since it possesses the unique capacity to reproduce.

The next stanzas of "Nobody Sings" discuss old age and the sufferings it entails:

> Do you want your skin to wrinkle
> And your cunt get sore and dry?
> ....
> Nobody ever saw me
> She whispered in a rage.
> They were blinded by my beauty, now
> They're blinded by my age.[29]

Neblett opines that "Nobody Sings" gives voice to "the internalized desperation of the women . . . who are ensnared by the patriarchal customs of judging a woman's worth by her physical beauty and reproductive capacity."[30] The claim that society that was once blinded by the woman's "beauty" is now blinded by her "age" bolsters the point. Such an attitude also overlooks the fact that the human need for love and care has nothing to do with age or beauty. This results in the marginalization of "old" or "ugly" people both within the family and in society. The situation worsens for a woman like Joan due to her economic instability. The song ends with the sad recounting of the compulsory silence that women learn to maintain about themselves: "Nobody sings about it / But it happens all the time."[31] Glavin's soft-sounding folk melody here brings out the utter helplessness of women in patriarchal society.

Vinegar Tom next introduces us to sixteen-year-old Betty, whose repeated failed attempts to escape from her house, just like Alice's wish to visit London, are indicative of her strong desire to disentangle herself from the clutches of an overpowering patriarchal family.[32] Similarly, Betty's refusal to marry is symptomatic of her resistance to submit to a relationship that thrives on erasing her individual identity by merging it into that of its legal and sexual owner (i.e., the husband). However, Betty's doctor interprets her growing sense of individuality as an indication of hysteria caused by an excess of blood. He prescribes purging as a means to cure Betty, which, he thinks, will render her marriageable once again:

> DOCTOR: The noxious gases that form inwardly every month rise to the brain and cause behaviour quite contrary to the patient's real feelings. After bleeding you must be purged. Tonight you shall be blistered. You will soon be well enough to be married.[33]

According to American scientist and writer Rachel P. Maines, "Hysteria as a disease paradigm has been variously constructed over time by physicians and their patients, but at all times and places it has retained its focus on the intrinsic pathology of the feminine."[34] While this feminization of hysteria is fueled by the term's etymological association with the Greek *hystera*, meaning "that which proceeds from the uterus," the sufferer's lack of self-control and need for constant monitoring are identified pejoratively as peculiar to the nature and the demands of femininity. Undoubtedly, this provides patriarchy with the excuse to brand all acts of female subversion as expressions of their "abnormality" and therefore "diseased" states of being.

During the seventeenth century, the causes of female hysteria were variously diagnosed as sexual deprivation, resulting in retention of the so-called female semen; sexual indulgence, resulting in over-excretion of it; lack of proper socialization or feminization; hyper-socialization or sexual immorality; heretical beliefs or corruption by the Devil; menstrual problems; or other bodily imbalances.[35] Resultantly, the most common treatment of hysteria focused either on suppressive measures like "normalization" of the "sick" woman through marriage and pregnancy[36] or on corrective procedures like getting rid of the "suppressed menstrual blood" through cutting and bleeding.[37] In *Vinegar Tom*, the audience witnesses such a corrective procedure when the doctor's blistering of Betty renders her temporarily unable to resist her family's wish to get her married.

The audience next meets Susan, who happens to be a friend of Alice. The inarticulate fears that haunt Betty and the unfulfilled desires that torture Alice find their full expression in Susan's disrupted body. She is a woman in her early twenties. The two children that Alice bore and the three miscarriages that she endured make her impervious to the demands of yet another forced pregnancy that is caused by her husband's desire to have another "fine child."[38] Susan's Christian indoctrination, however, makes her too scared to attempt to change her life until Alice awakens her to her rights over her own body:

> SUSAN: They do say the pain is what's sent to a woman for her sins. I complained last time after churching, and he said I must think on Eve who brought the sin into the world that got me pregnant. I must think on how woman tempts man, and how she pays God with her pain having the baby. So if we try to get round the pain, we're going against God.[39]

Susan's words point out how Christianity tries to control the female body by identifying all their sufferings as punishments for Eve's original sin. The female, therefore, learns to accept her physical troubles, including menstrual and labor pains, as divine punishment. This is what makes the American feminist Kate Millet observe, "Patriarchy has God on its side."[40]

There is, however, more to Susan's perfectly domesticated exterior. Her mechanical recounting of her last church visit and the reference to her multiple "complaints" highlights her deep-seated disbelief of everything patriarchy professes or preaches.[41] It is at this point that Alice's reply, "Blood every month, and no way out of that but to be sick and swell up," shocks Susan out of her resignation.[42] For the first time in her life, she starts assessing her real condition and looks for alternatives to end her sufferings, even though such an act might mean "going against God" or against His incarnation in the family—that is, her husband.

Susan's search for alternatives brings the next female character, Ellen, onstage. Ellen is a healer in her mid-thirties who has a great knowledge of and mastery over medicinal herbs that can heal wounds and cure different health conditions. It is this knowledge that differentiates Ellen from the other characters in the play and establishes her as a demigod for her patients. When she offers to share her knowledge with Alice, it is her empathic understanding of women's lot in patriarchy that inspires this act of solidarity. The potion that she administers to Susan terminates her pregnancy, and with this, Susan's control of her own body is reestablished. It is, however, this very act of terminating Susan's pregnancy that brings both Ellen and Susan under patriarchal surveillance; for in daring to interrupt the patriarchal bloodline, they have committed a crime against their sociocultural "masters" that cannot go unnoticed and unpunished. As feminist critic Lisa Merrill puts it, "women's autonomous desires are seen as punishable offences because they are committed without official sanctions."[43]

Churchill brings in her second song, "Oh Doctor," at this precise dramatic turn. The song is divided into two parts. The first half is positioned at the end of the fifth scene, where Susan instinctively decides to terminate her pregnancy, while the second section is placed just after the sixth scene, wherein the doctor diagnoses Betty to be hysteric:

> Oh, doctor, tell
> me, make me well.
> What's wrong with me
> the way I am[44]

And again:

> Oh, doctor, tell
> me, make me well.
> What's wrong with me
> ....
> I can't wait
> To see myself.
> Give me back my body.[45]

The song, as we see, revolves around Susan's and Betty's desperate queries regarding their "illness" and their intense desire to get "cured." While Susan is able to find out the right medicine to end her pregnancy through an empowering female bonding, Betty's search is answered by a male doctor who drags her further into confusion and suffering. The musical arrangement of this song in the original production, comments Neblett, typifies "the internalized desperation of the women in the play."[46]

The seventh scene of *Vinegar Tom* introduces two minor but extremely important characters—Jack and Margery—who happen to be Alice's neighbors. Apparently naive and harmless, they are, to the contrary, the ones to accuse Alice and Joan of practicing witchcraft. The third song of the play, "Something to Burn," highlights the seventeenth-century mass hysteria regarding witch hunting. The song with its strategic indexing of "women" with "witches," "lunatics," "blacks," and "Jews" highlights how these categories have been traditionally ostracized and marginalized by the supremacist discourse of patriarchy:

Sometimes it's witches, or what will you choose?
Sometimes it's lunatics, shut them away.
It's blacks and it's women and often it's Jews.
We'd be quite happy if they'd go away.
Find something to burn.[47]

According to theatre critic Phyllis R. Randall, by "placing witch-burning in the context of holocaust and genocide, Churchill forces her audience to confront the socio-economic basis of fear and prejudice."[48] To put Randall's comment into perspective, this song subtextually highlights the basic similarity between different episodes of human oppression. This similarity, in its turn, emphasizes how the discourses of sexism, ageism, ethnocentrism, capitalism, and religion divide humanity against itself.

As the women of Churchill's play try to escape the prying eyes of patriarchy, the fourth song, "If Everybody Worked as Hard as Me," enumerates both the rules for women's successful integration into society and the possible reasons for their exclusion from it:

Nobody loves you
unless you keep your mouth shut.
Nobody loves you
if you don't support your man.[49]

That a woman's acceptability in the family depends on her ability to perform the role of wife, mother, or grandmother indicates the normative existence that society prescribes for women. Similarly, age and speech are considered to be negative attributes for a woman; for, according to patriarchy, it is only through her sexual appeal and unquestioning submission to the male-superior that a woman can be accepted into society. The song also underlines patriarchy's discourse about the importance of socio-familial bonds in the lives of women, "So nobody comes knocking at your door in the night / So the horrors that are done will not be done to you."[50] Sarcastic as they are, the statements point out how patriarchy denies basic human rights such as the right to physical safety and the right to personal freedom to women who do not commit themselves to the service of men. It is this awareness of the dangers of a "man-less" female existence that makes Joan exclaim before Alice, "If we'd each got a man we'd be better off. . . . We'd have more to eat, that's one thing"[51] and causes Ellen to advise Betty to marry, "You get married, Betty, that's safest."[52]

The fifth song of the play, "If You Float," occurs at the end of the sixteenth scene immediately after Betty leaves Ellen with an apparent promise to get married:

> If you float you're a witch
> If you scream you're a witch
> If you sink, then you're dead anyway.
> If you cure you're a witch
> Or impure you're a witch
> Whatever you do, you must pay.[53]

If the song "If Everybody Worked as Hard as Me" spells out the patriarchal conditions for a woman's acceptance in society, then "If You Float" punctures all such assurances with the reality of wholesale female persecution in the name of witch burning. That every female attempt at self-assertion or self-preservation is foredoomed to be identified as witchcraft highlights the male paranoia that visualizes the female as an essentially deceptive, dangerous, and loathsome being that can at best be controlled by penetration and possession and at worst be eradicated by force or strategy.

As agents of that strategy, the utter illogic of the witch hunters of the play (Harry Packer and Goody) to identify Alice, Joan, and Susan as witches by searching their bodies, pricking them in public, and identifying their blood or the absence of it as symptomatic of their corruption is nothing but a mockery of justice.[54] Instead of serving any religious or judicial purposes, these procedures only gratify Packer and Goody's sexual perversion: "Devil hides his marks all kinds of places. The more secret the better he likes it. . . . And a woman last week with a big lump in her breast like another whole teat where she sucked her imps. . . . And when I squeezed it first white stuff came out like milk and then blood, for she fed those horrid creatures on milk and blood and they sucked her secret parts in the night too. Now let's see your secret parts and see what the devil does there."[55] Ultimately, when these men have satisfied themselves with voyeuristic and tactile pleasures, Packer's announcement, "Though a mark is a sure sign of a witch's guilt having no mark is no sign of innocence for the devil can take marks off," leaves no option for the women to escape patriarchal punishment.[56]

The convicted women, at this point, try to evade their fate through performing three different forms of subversion. Joan initially fakes pregnancy and then turns completely silent upon realizing her failure to deceive the patriarchy. Susan first resorts to a blame game and then tries to perform a penitent self, "Oh God, I know now I'm loathsome and a sinner and Mr. Packer has shown me how bad I am and I repent . . . don't make me go to hell and be burnt forever."[57] Alice, the third of the convicts, is the only one to perform her deviance and express her subversive intent: "I'm not a witch. But I wish I was. If I could live I'd be a witch now after what they've done. . . . I shouldn't have been frightened of Ellen, I should have learnt. Oh, if I could meet with the devil now I'd give him anything if he'd give me power. There's no way for us except by the devil. If I only did have magic, I'd make them feel it."[58] According to theatre critic Amelia Howe Kritzer, Alice's is an important political statement whereby she at once "breaks the silence that has aided her oppressors throughout history" and renounces "powerlessness even at the price of embracing an imagined evil."[59] That Alice is now desperate to "learn" things even from the devil indicates her readiness to avenge herself and her ilk at all costs. This is a truly transformative moment in Alice's story in which she finally comes out of her constrictive personal existence and starts representing an entire womankind.

The sixth song, "Lament for the Witches," appears at the end of the twentieth scene when Joan and Ellen have already been hanged and the other "witches" of the play are awaiting punishment. The song, therefore, becomes a call for the entire womankind to come out of their complacent femininity and give voice to their silenced tales of injustice and oppression:

Look in the mirror tonight
Would they have hanged you then?
Ask how they're stopping you now.
Where have the witches gone?
Who are the witches now?
Ask how they're stopping you now.
Here we are.[60]

That the witches have not died but are actually "Here" is not due to their supernatural powers. They are kept alive by the persistence of patriarchal oppression on women and likewise by women's indomitable desire for freedom.

The concluding song of *Vinegar Tom*, "Evil Women," heralds the advent of these new age witches who are hailed as "Satan's lady, Satan's pride / Satan's baby, Satan's bride":

> Evil Women
> Is that what you want?
> Is that what you want to see?
> On the movie screen
> Of your own wet dream
> Evil women.[61]

Unlike the song "Lament for the Witches," which is addressed to the intertextual and intratextual female audience of the play, "Evil Women" addresses patriarchy directly. It identifies the male obsession with "evil" women as a classic case of ambivalence. On the one hand, the male is attracted by the unpredictable and mysterious "witch," and, on the other hand, he is appalled by this same unpredictability and mysteriousness. The male is, therefore, incited to "know" and "control" the female through sexual means, and this is what accounts for the sexual nature of punishment meted out to deviant women across ages and cultures. The song "Evil Women," here, becomes an expression of the Freudian castration anxiety of the man vis-à-vis a self-assertive woman.

Vinegar Tom ends with a brief lecture by Heinrich Kramer and Jacob Sprenger, authors of the infamous 1487 treatise *Malleus Maleficarum* (*The Hammer of Witches*), dealing with procedures of finding and persecuting witches. Played by two female actors, Kramer and Sprenger lecture about women's inherent susceptibility to sin and demonic temptations as resulting from their biological weaknesses:

> SPRENGER: Women are feebler in both body and mind so it's not surprising
> KRAMER: In intellect they seem to be of a different nature from men—
> SPRENGER: like children[62]

According to feminist philosopher Sally L. Kitch, men have always "considered themselves the human model and solipsistically regarded women as unfortunate imitations of, appendages to, or even curses upon the male norm."[63] The belief derives from the patriarchal need to establish and justify itself as the one and the only potent representative of humanity. Patriarchy, in fact, always attempts to dislocate and/or substitute the feminine for a hegemonic set of fantasies and beliefs, confining the woman within a compulsory inferiority while conferring to the man a psychosomatic superiority. When Kramer and Sprenger talk about women's intellectual and physical inferiority, they seem only to repeat what Euripides stated centuries ago: "Women are a huge natural calamity, / against which men must take / strenuous measures."[64] Their further observations about women's "carnal desires," "defect of intelligence," "inordinate passion," "weak memories," "vengeance," "insatiable malice,'" and "unfaithfulness" highlight similar patriarchal stereotypes.[65]

In our society, women have always been relegated to a second-class citizenship thanks to the historical stereotyping of the woman as the archetypal Other to the dominant male Self. The image of the self-effacing woman who can neither dare nor desire at once sustained the dominant patriarchal imagination and legitimized the hegemonic gender hierarchy that patriarchy warrants and on which society thrives. While patriarchy has always thwarted and punished all female attempts at free expression and free will, it is this repression that has provided women with both the incentive and the occasion for telling their tales and reaching out to one another. In *Vinegar Tom*, though the women cannot escape the social radar and have to sacrifice their lives, the eternal spirit of their chainless minds immortalizes them. According to Ehrenreich and English, "Unfortunately, the witch herself—poor and illiterate—did not leave us her story. . . . It was recorded, like all history, by the educated elite, so that today we know the witch only through the eyes of her persecutors."[66] Quite mindful of this, Churchill's "witches" in *Vinegar Tom* do not depend on others to tell their tales. They register their stories through their own acts of defiance and deviance; for, as the Native American writer Leslie Marmon Silko has put it, "tales must be told / they are all we have, you see, / all we have to fight off / illness and death."[67] It is this valiant act of telling that ultimately liberates Churchill's "witchy" women from their silenced existence into the freedom and empowerment of expression and sharing.

Notes

1. Caryl Churchill, *Plays: One* (London: Methuen, 1985), 129.
2. Catherein Itzin, "Survival—by Sinking without Drowning," *Tribune* (1976): 8–9, 8.
3. Churchill, *Plays: One*, 135.
4. Churchill, *Plays: One*, 136.
5. Churchill, *Plays: One*, 135.

6. Adrienne Rich, *Of Woman Born: Motherhood as Experience and Institution* (London: W. W. Norton, 1995), 42.
7. Churchill, *Plays: One*, 136.
8. Churchill, *Plays: One*, 136.
9. Luce Irigaray, *This Sex Which Is Not One*, trans. Catherine Porter and Carolyn Burke (Ithaca, NY: Cornell University Press, 1985), 186–87.
10. Churchill, *Plays: One*, 136–37.
11. Churchill, *Plays: One*, 137.
12. Mary Daly, *Gyn/Ecology: The Metaethics of Radical Feminism* (Boston: Beacon, 1990), 179.
13. Churchill, *Plays: One*, 137.
14. Maxine Hong Kingston, "No Name Woman," *The Woman Warrior: Memoirs of a Girlhood among Ghosts* (London: Vintage, 1976), 1–20.
15. Churchill, *Plays: One*, 141.
16. Churchill, *Plays: One*, 133.
17. Churchill, *Plays: One*, 133.
18. Robert L. Neblett, "'Nobody Sings about It': In Defense of the Songs in Caryl Churchill's *Vinegar Tom*," *New England Theatre Journal* 14 (2003): 101–22, 106.
19. Jeffrey Gantz, "'Vinegar Tom' Emphasizes the Dark in Witch Hunt Tale," *Boston Globe*, January 14, 2013: https://www.bostonglobe.com/arts/2013/01/14/stage-review-vinegar-tom-presented-whistler-dark/dYglN2FssIxDDpvllYYXdO/story.html.
20. Clark Gudas, "*Vinegar Tom* at IU Theatre Brings Pop, Electronica to 17th-Century England," *Indiana Daily Student*, March 20, 2019: https://www.idsnews.com/article/2019/03/vinegar-tom-at-iu-theatre-brings-pop-electronica-to-17th-century-england.
21. Victor Cordell, "Caryl Churchill's *Vinegar Tom*: At Ashby Stage in Berkley," *Berkshire Fine Arts*, December 14, 2019: https://www.berkshirefinearts.com/12-24-2019_caryl-churchill-s-vinegar-tom.htm.
22. Churchill, *Plays: One*, 141.
23. Churchill, *Plays: One*, 133.
24. Churchill, *Plays: One*, 133.
25. Churchill, *Plays: One*, 133.
26. Gail Weiss, *Body Images: Embodiment as Intercorporeality* (London: Routledge, 1999), 16.
27. Neblett, "Nobody Sings about It," 105.
28. Nancy Mairs, "Carnal Acts," in *Writing on the Body: Female Embodiment and Feminist Theory*, ed. Katie Conboy, Nadia Medina, and Sarah Stanbury, 296–308 (New York: Columbia University Press, 1997), 299.
29. Churchill, *Plays: One*, 141–42.
30. Neblett, "Nobody Sings about It," 114.
31. Churchill, *Plays: One*, 142.
32. Churchill, *Plays: One*, 149.
33. Churchill, *Plays: One*, 149.
34. Rachel P. Maines, *The Technology of Orgasm: "Hysteria," the Vibrator, and Women's Sexual Satisfaction* (Baltimore, MD: Johns Hopkins University Press, 2001), 21.
35. Cecilia Tasca, Mariangela Rapetti, Mauro Giovanni Carta, and Bianca Fadda, "Women and Hysteria in the History of Mental Health," *Clinical Practice and Epidemiology in Mental Health* 8 (2012): 110–19, 110–11. Theories regarding "female semen" can widely be found in Aristotle, Hippocrates, and Galen, who believed it to be a real substance that

was nonetheless of inferior quality to male semen. In the Galenic model of the human reproductive system, both the male and the female bodies were shown to have seminal vesicles. The belief continued to exist until the late nineteenth century, after which it was gradually replaced by new scientific discoveries. For further information please see Vivien Marx, *The Semen Book* (London: Free Association Press, 2001).

36. Charles Bernheimer and Claire Kahane, *In Dora's Case: Freud—Hysteria—Feminism* (New York: Columbia University Press, 1942), 3.
37. Elaine Showalter, *The Female Malady: Women, Madness and English Culture, 1830–1980* (New York: Penguin, 1985), 56.
38. Churchill, *Plays: One*, 145.
39. Churchill, *Plays: One*, 146.
40. Kate Millet, *Sexual Politics* (New York: Columbia University Press, 2016), 51.
41. Churchill, *Plays: One*, 146.
42. Churchill, *Plays: One*, 146.
43. Lisa Merrill, "Monsters and Heroines: Caryl Churchill's Women," in *Caryl Churchill: A Casebook*, ed. Phyllis R. Randall, 71–90 (London: Garland, 1988), 82.
44. Churchill, *Plays: One*, 149.
45. Churchill, *Plays: One*, 152.
46. Neblett, "Nobody Sings about It," 114.
47. Churchill *Plays: One*, 154.
48. Phyllis R. Randall, ed., *Caryl Churchill: A Casebook* (London: Garland, 1988), 80.
49. Churchill, *Plays: One*, 160.
50. Churchill, *Plays: One*, 161.
51. Churchill, *Plays: One*, 141.
52. Churchill, *Plays: One*, 169.
53. Churchill, *Plays: One*, 170.
54. Churchill, *Plays: One*, 166–67.
55. Churchill, *Plays: One*, 172.
56. Churchill, *Plays: One*, 172.
57. Churchill, *Plays: One*, 174–75.
58. Churchill, *Plays: One*, 175.
59. Amelia Howe Kritzer, *The Plays of Caryl Churchill: Theatre of Empowerment* (Basingstoke: Macmillan, 1991), 94.
60. Churchill, *Plays: One*, 176.
61. Churchill, *Plays: One*, 178.
62. Churchill, *Plays: One*, 177.
63. Sally L. Kitch, *The Specter of Sex: Gendered Foundations of Racial Formation in the United States* (New York: SUNY Press, 2009), 18.
64. Euripides, *Hippolytos*, trans. Robert Bagg (Oxford: Oxford University Press, 1973), 47.
65. Churchill, *Plays: One*, 177.
66. Barbara Ehrenreich and Deirdre English, *Witches, Midwives and Nurses: A History of Women Healers* (Santa Cruz: Quiver distro, 2009 [1973]), 6.
67. Leslie Marmon Silko, *Ceremony* (New York: Signet, 1978), 2.

(Un)Limited

The Influence of Mentorship and Father-Daughter Relationships on Elphaba's Heroine Journey in *Wicked*

—REBECCA K. HAMMONDS

In her *Unbecoming Women: British Women Writers and the Novel of Development*, Susan Fraiman argues: "Becoming a woman may be thought of as, in Judith Butler's rephrasing of Simone de Beauvoir, 'an incessant project, a daily act of reconstruction and interpretation' (131). It is a lifelong act continuing well past any discrete season of youth, and it involves a struggle among diverse narratives: official and also oppositional stories of arriving at adult 'femininity.'"[1] In the present study, I use the libretto and score from the musical *Wicked* (2004) in an attempt to understand how the central character, Elphaba, is constructed by the show's writers as a young witch who undertakes the heroine journey of development. Drawing on my theory of "bookish" heroines in musicals (e.g., Jerusha Abbot, *Daddy Long Legs*; Belle, *Beauty and the Beast*; Jane Porter, *Disney's Tarzan*; Matilda, *Matilda*; Katherine Plummer, *Newsies*, etc.), I analyze the characterological importance of Elphaba's mentors and her use of the magical book of spells known as the *Grimmerie*.[2] I argue that the evolution of her mentor/mentee relationships significantly influence Elphaba's "I Want," or super objective, within the musical and alters the course of her character's identity arc. Specifically, through the use of her bookish powers and identity, she moves from a young heroine searching for acceptance to a social justice advocate fighting systems of oppression.

Heroine journeys in classic literature and fairy tales, from which the musical *Wicked* descends, frequently rely on the absence of the mother as a means of propelling the heroine out into the masculine world.[3] This is true of Elphaba, who loses her mother as a young child. The heroine's "spark of individuality" and drive for significant action and meaningful work in the world lead her to identify with the masculine and to look for role models and allies who will help her on her journey of development and maturation.[4] In her book *The Heroine's Journey: Woman's Quest for Wholeness*, Maureen Murdock writes that the heroine's male role models can include fathers, boyfriends, teachers, and religious leaders as well as a "male-identified woman, perhaps an older childless woman who has played by team [i.e., patriarchal] rules and successfully made her way to the top."[5] While attending Shiz University, Elphaba finds two such mentors who influence her development as a heroine: Madame Morrible and Doctor Dillamond.

Elphaba's need for mentors at school is due almost entirely to her father-daughter relationship at home. Elphaba's green skin reveals her illegitimacy. Elphaba's father hates and regrets Elphaba's birth and blames her for the death of his wife and the lameness of his younger daughter Nessarose. Like a wicked stepmother, he demands she serve and care for Nessarose, chides her sarcastic wit and intelligence, and demeans her abilities. Murdock writes that girls "who suffered from the denial of positive attention from their fathers in childhood look for him in each relationship they have."[6] In light of her father's failure to provide a positive mentoring relationship that supports Elphaba's identity development, she turns to others who recognize her value and encourage her sense of competence.

In *Jane Eyre's Sisters: How Women Live and Write the Heroine's Story*, Jody Bower argues that while witches and "powerful women" are the enemy of the hero, they are helpful and informative guides for the heroine.[7] According to Bower, "Women often have to *prove their worth* to other women in positions of power before those women will consent to mentor them. . . . The powerful woman will only consent to teach if the prospective student makes it clear that she will not be wasting her time."[8] Within minutes of her arrival at Shiz University early on in act 1, Elphaba unwittingly accomplishes this proof process and earns the respect of the older witch. Elphaba explodes in anger when the headmistress, Madame Morrible, assumes responsibility for Nessarose and begins to wheel her away.

ELPHABA. *LET HER GO!!!*

(And suddenly the wheelchair pulls itself out of MORRIBLE's grasp. The students gasp, the chair spins, rises into the air, and then lands gently in front of ELPHABA. MORRIBLE stares at ELPHABA. The other students and faculty stare, dumbfounded, then buzz amongst themselves.)

MORRIBLE. How did you do that? . . .

NESSAROSE. Elphaba, you promised things would be different here!

MORRIBLE. (*Leaning closer*) You mean this has happened before?

ELPHABA. Well, something just comes over me sometimes, it's something I can't describe. I'll try to control myself. I am so sorry, Nessa.

MORRIBLE. What?! Never apologize for talent! Talent is a gift! And that is *my* special talent, *encouraging* talent! (*Studies her closely*) Have you ever considered a career in sorcery?

ELPHABA. Not really . . .

MORRIBLE. I shall tutor you privately—and take no other students![9]

Morrible, a woman who shares Elphaba's ambition for influence, immediately sees how she can benefit from the unschooled talent of the young witch and agrees to teach and mentor her. She will not be a waste of the older woman's time.

Elphaba's magical and intellectual talents are underscored by the show's creators through Elphaba's ongoing contrast with alpha-girl Glinda. Morrible rejects Glinda as an unworthy pupil with little potential ("I do not teach my seminar every semester, of course if someone special were to come along"[10]), choosing instead the unruly power exhibited by Elphaba. The success of Elphaba's tutelage under Morrible is demonstrated when Morrible recommends her to the Wizard and he invites her to come work with him. Morrible navigates the patriarchal system and gets ahead at any cost. Collaborating with the Wizard in his campaign to oppress and silence marginalized communities so that she can preserve her access to power, she tricks Elphaba into using her craft to create flying-monkey spies for the Wizard. In short, although Madame Morrible is a witch mentor, she does not fulfill Bower's description of the witch as modeling "a form of wisdom that defies rational, logical understanding," exhibiting intuitive wisdom, and discerning what "is important through *knowing* on a deep level."[11] Rather, she relies heavily on accepted modes of thinking that value the blunt force of authority and prestige over deep knowing and intuitive wisdom that operate in discernment.

While Morrible ultimately fails as a positive female role model, Elphaba finds a mentor who can identify with her experience of otherness and marginalization and guide her passionate compassion for the vulnerable and oppressed. Elphaba's history teacher, Doctor Dillamond, provides a purpose for her life, intellect, and magic and becomes both her most important mentor and a father figure. The green girl and the goat professor, an activist for "animal" rights in Oz, develop a significant mentoring partnership and community that grows and ultimately shapes the entire story. In her essay "Collaborate, Conspire, Commune:

Academy-Based Activism as Mentorship in Marginalized Communities," sociologist Ailsa Craig argues for a "philosophy" and an egalitarian model of mentorship designed to disrupt the traditional hierarchical model that so frequently leads to the burnout of "stable" mentors who instruct and ground the younger members.[12] This model has three primary components that can be seen in the mentoring relationship at work between Dillamond and Elphaba: to collaborate, to conspire, and to commune.

Collaboration occurs when members of mentoring communities meet together to discuss the issues of concern, *conspire* by assigning tasks to members based on ability, and *commune* by sharing food and spending time with one another. Craig argues that "ability" does not reside solely in the hands of the authoritative elders. Though those members may be able to contribute the four primary kinds of mentor/mentee capital—social capital ("access to social networks"), symbolic capital ("prestige, reputation, authority"), economic capital ("monies"), and cultural capital ("knowing how to navigate different cultural situations")—younger members of the group may be as capable, if not more so, of acquiring or distributing these kinds of resources.[13]

Elphaba finds her mentor at a particularly vulnerable time in his life, and she supports him in all three of the primary components, as seen in scenes 4, 8, 9, and 10 of act 1. In scene 4, Elphaba remains after class to encourage Dillamond, who has received hate speech from students ("Animals should be seen and not heard").[14] She *communes* with him by listening and sharing food with him. She *collaborates* with him by discussing the problem of Animal oppression and arguing that "someone's got to tell the Wizard! He'll make it right! That's why we have a Wizard."[15] Later, in scenes 8, 9, and 10, Elphaba *conspires* by fighting for Dillamond to remain at school and then volunteers to go speak to the Wizard on behalf of the Animals. The supportive, egalitarian mentoring relationship begun in Dillamond's classroom contributes significantly to the complexity of Elphaba's heroine character arc and directly impacts her transition from an insecure student to an active, decisive, and "deeply knowing" witch.

Like many other "bookish" characters, about whom I theorize in my broader research, Elphaba's activities are closely tied up in the use of a book—the ancient book of spells known as the *Grimmerie*—as a tool for personal and group empowerment. Elphaba's ability to read the *Grimmerie* is key to her character, sets her apart from the other magical folk in Oz, and stems from her paternity. In the opening scenes of the musical, we see Elphaba's mother have an affair with a mysterious man who drinks a green elixir and persuades her to do the same. Elphaba's green skin, it is implied, is caused by this green elixir, though such a claim is never explicitly stated. In the final scene of the show, Glinda, who had previously seen the Wizard with a bottle similar to the one prized by Elphaba, confronts him with the truth: that Elphaba is his daughter. Madame Morrible, who is also present, cries out, "So that's it. That's why she had such power! She was a child of—*both worlds*."[16] As a child of an Ozian mother and Earthly father, Elphaba has the power to perform magic and decipher the ancient language of the *Grimmerie*. But how does the relationship between Elphaba and her real father, the Wizard, shape her experience? Is it only through her genetics that he impacts her character? No. Throughout her heroine journey, Elphaba's experience is influenced by her personal relationship with the Wizard. This can be seen clearly by analyzing four songs that connect them: "The Wizard and I," "I Am a Sentimental Man," "Defying Gravity," and "Wonderful."

In their books about the structure of Broadway musicals, Aaron Frankel and Jack Viertel state the importance of the "I Want," and to a lesser extent the "I Am," song. "The hero has to want something that's hard to get" writes Viertel in his *Secret Life of the American Musical*.[17] "The 'I want,' more than the 'I am,' turns the character out and relates them to the world," argues Frankel in his *Writing the Broadway Musical*.[18] In *Wicked*, "The Wizard and I" is Elphaba's "I Want" song. Coming on the heels of Madame Morrible's declaration that Elphaba has a bright future as a witch and might even work for the Wizard himself, Elphaba sings about her desire to meet the Wizard and have a lasting relationship with him.

ELPHABA. When I meet the wizard
Once I prove my worth,
And then I meet the wizard
What I've waited for since—since birth!
And with all his wizard wisdom by my looks, he won't be blinded.
Do you think the wizard is dumb? Or like munchkins, so small-minded?
No! He'll say to me: "I see who you truly are
A girl on whom I can rely!"
And that's how we'll begin
The wizard and I.[19]

Two things are important in this verse. First, Elphaba has been longing to meet the Wizard since she was small. Like any child with a famous role model, Elphaba has dreamed of meeting the Wizard and of being accepted by him—acceptance she never received from the father who raised her. Second, Elphaba does not expect the Wizard's "I see who you truly are, a girl on whom I can rely," to come without having first proven her worth, as she did with Morrible. She will lay her talents at his feet in exchange for his approval and adoption. He will mentor her. He will have the power to, as she sings later, "de-greenify" her—a power she does not herself possess. The bookish heroine is looking for the ultimate guide.

It is only in light of these possibilities that Elphaba first imagines herself to be "unlimited."[25] She envisions herself celebrated and held in high esteem by everyone. She wants the acceptance of a distinguished guide and the adoration of privileged social stakeholders; and her desires do not, at this point in the show, seem impossible. However, there is an unspoken act of foreshadowing in this moment that predicts the Wizard's failure as Elphaba's mentor and father figure. Elphaba is bookish and needs a mentor of the same kind as herself. The *spectacular* Wizard, with his "wonderful" promises, cannot show her how to live in a way that is true to herself. A reality that comes to fruition during "I Am a Sentimental Man" and "Defying Gravity."

When Elphaba *does* meet the Wizard, she is excited and shy.

ELPHABA. (*Shyly*) I'm so happy to meet you.
WIZARD. Well, that's good—cuz that's what I love best—making people happy.
(*Sings*) I am a sentimental man
Who always longed to be a father
That's why I do the best I can
To treat each citizen of Oz as son—
(*beams at Elphaba*) Or daughter.
And Elphaba, I'd like to raise you high
'Cuz I think ev'ryone deserves the chance to fly
And helping you with your ascent allows me to feel so parental
For I am a sentimental man.[20]

That is the entire song. He is willing to take her on and raise her high. He wants to be a father figure. It is everything she had hoped to receive. Stepping forward boldly, therefore, she begins to explain the reason she has come—to protect the Animals from those forces that are harming them. The Wizard quickly cuts her off, promising to help her with whatever she needs, *if she can prove herself*. This is what she anticipated in her "I Want" song. She is not taken by surprise; she calmly waits to be told what to do. He asks her to read a spell from the *Grimmerie* that will make his monkey servant, Chistery, fly. She does so, but the transformation causes Chistery to cry out in pain. In that moment, Elphaba realizes two horrible things: she has done something terrible and irreversible; and, worse, the Wizard and Madame Morrible planned it all along.

ELPHABA. So it's you? You're behind it all?

WIZARD. Elphaba—When I first got here, there was discord and discontent. And where I come from, everyone knows: the best way to bring folks together, is to give them a really good enemy.

ELPHABA. (*The realization is growing*) You can't read this book at all, can you? That's why you need an enemy. And spies. And cages. You have no real power!

WIZARD. Exactly. And that's why I need you! (*Enthusiastically*) Don'cha see—the world's your oyster now! You have so many opportunities ahead of you! (*To Glinda*) You both do.

GLINDA Oh, thank you, you're [*sic*] Ozness!

WIZARD. (*Sings*) The two of you, it's time I raised you high yes, the time has come for you to have the chance to—

ELPHABA. No! (*And with the book of spells still clutched in her hands she runs out of the room . . .*)[21]

Her father figure, the man she has been waiting to guide her bookish growth and magical talent, turns out to be not only unable to guide her but also the perpetuator of the very oppressions she has come there to protest. Jody Bower argues that "a young woman at this stage reveres those she thinks know more than she does and accepts their words without question. More often than not, these idols turn out to have feet of clay. When this happens, the young woman may feel betrayed and stop trusting anyone else."[22] The young woman, Bower suggests, will then begin to "hear and trust her own intuition instead [of theirs]."[23] Elphaba runs away from the Wizard, taking the book as a denial of his rights to it and asserting her own claim to use its power.

In the 2008 edition of his groundbreaking book *The Hero with a Thousand Faces* (1949), Joseph Campbell states that, as a part of his journey, the (male) hero experiences a rivalry with his powerful father figure.[24] To break away and claim a place of self-governance, the hero must overcome the authority of the father. Elphaba, more than most bookish heroines, experiences this severe break with her beloved father figure. At the same time, as Carol Pearson and Katherine Pope argue in *The Female Hero in American and British Literature* (1981), the "dragon" that many female heroes have to overcome is fear: "fear of what other people might think; fear of being different; fear of being isolated."[25] These two powerful experiences culminate for Elphaba in "Defying Gravity."

Having run away, Elphaba and Doctor Dillamond barricade themselves against the Wizard's soldiers and Madame Morrible's declaration that Elphaba is "evil" and a "Wicked Witch." She has been betrayed by two of her greatest mentors, Madame Morrible and the Wizard. Her sense of identity as a young woman with great promise who will work alongside those in power for the good of all has been demolished. Her idols have feet of clay, her friend is pulling away from her, and Elphaba must make a choice: to abandon her previous "I Want" of being in the "Wizard and I" team or to abandon the identity she has developed in her mentoring community with Doctor Dillamond. The "dragon" of fear is at the door, and Elphaba rises to do battle: "It's the Wizard who should be afraid. Of me."[26] Elphaba refuses to back down. She will overcome her fear and stand as the rival to her father figure.

In the succeeding verses and chorus, Elphaba decides that rather than trying to please everyone and obey the rules that Ozian society has dictated, she will defy them and embrace her outsider status. This is in keeping with Pearson and Pope's argument that the "hero who is an outsider because she is female, black, or poor is almost always a *revolutionary*. Simply by being heroic . . . she implicitly challenges the status quo."[27] Once again Elphaba sees herself as "unlimited" and successfully uses the *Grimmerie* to cast a levitation spell that enables her to fly on a broom. From this moment forward, Elphaba will use her bookish abilities *against* the Wizard rather than for him. He flew to Oz in a hot-air balloon and claimed that "everyone deserves a chance to fly."[28] Elphaba will do so, but on her own terms. He wanted her to prove herself by using the *Grimmerie*, and now she will prove herself by using it against him. We learn later, in the song "Thank Goodness," that she leaves the Emerald City and begins to fly across the land of Oz speaking out against the Wizard's abuses and trying to rescue the Animals.

Elphaba is not completely immune to the Wizard, however. Hero(in)es frequently experience a temptation to abandon the journey and give up the battle, and Elphaba experiences this temptation in a particularly bookish way during the song "Wonderful."[29] When Elphaba returns to the Wizard's chambers to free the winged monkeys, he declares that he never meant to harm her and croons that she must be as lonely as he is. "Elphaba . . . you've been so strong through all this. Aren't you tired of being the strong one?"[30] The Wizard then assumes a series of fatherly overtures during this "charm" song whereby he tries to ally her with himself. Not yet ready to comply, she queries, "How do I go back to that time, when I believed in you—in some magic *father* who would drop from the sky and make everything all better. . . . No one believed in you more than I did."[31] Elphaba wishes she could go back to her original "I Want," but her commitment to her mentoring community causes her to resist. The Wizard appeals to her old desire for recognition and praise when he describes how *he*, "one of your dime-a-dozen mediocrities," became the Wonderful Wizard. "They called me 'Wonderful,' so I said 'wonderful'—if you insist I will be wonderful—and they said 'wonderful.' Believe me it's hard to resist."[32]

Over the course of this song, as seen in the musical score, Stephen Schwartz deploys a number of musical techniques designed to draw Elphaba and the audience in and strip them of their defenses. Elphaba accuses him of lying to the citizens, and he counters by saying they were lies the people wanted to hear. "Where I'm from, we believe all sorts of things that aren't true. We call it—'history.'"[33] The bookish heroine's father figure first tempts her by appealing to her intelligence: "A man's called a traitor—or liberator. A rich man's a thief—or philanthropist. Is one a crusader—or ruthless invader? It's all in which label is able to persist."[34] He then quickly follows this up with an appeal to her moral stance: "There are precious few at ease with moral ambiguities, so we act as though they don't exist."[35] The Wizard then finishes with an appeal to her ego: "At long, long last receive your due—long overdue. Elphaba—*the* most celebrated are the rehabilitated. There'll be such a whoop-de-doo. A celebration throughout Oz that's all to do with *you*."[36] In this final line, the Wizard actually reprises Elphaba's "I Want" song. He appeals to her intellect, her morals, and her pride. Why should she, he is asking, hold herself to a different standard than everyone else? She could rejoin the normative group and enjoy the privilege of power.

The music itself works toward the goal of wooing Elphaba and the audience over. It begins in a higher key (G major) and slower more tentative tempo (with musical directions such as "freely," "colla voce," and "rit.") that indicate a tentative wooing.[37] Then, as the Wizard grows in confidence, the music moves down to F major and then finally C major and speeds up with "a temp" and "grand" tempos.[38] The Wizard charms Elphaba with his fatherly performance and reasoning. In performance, Joel Grey, the original Wizard, comes across not as a menacing dictator but as a goofy and proud father who simply wants to rescue his daughter from the path she has strayed onto.[39] He might even be compared to other goofy fathers of bookish women such as Professor Porter in Disney's *Tarzan* or Maurice in Disney's *Beauty and the Beast*.[40] To top it off, there is a father-daughter dance at the end of the song, and Elphaba succumbs to his invitation ("It does sound wonderful") with the condition that the Wizard set the monkeys free. "Done!" he cries as he does so.[41]

Elphaba's relationship with the Wizard would have been restored in this moment if she had not suddenly noticed a "figure, trembling under a blanket" in the corner.[42] It is Doctor Dillamond, her history teacher and mentor who first inspired her to fight for Animals' rights. Compared to the Wizard's simplistic and revisionist history lesson, Doctor Dillamond had presented a complex history that included the experiences of oppressed and unrepresented groups.

Compared to the Wizard's relativistic and selfish morality, Doctor Dillamond represented a self-sacrificing morality that was loyal to those in need of representation. He was the first being Elphaba met who could be a role model for her as a marginalized person—both because of her body and because of her intelligence and abilities. In this moment, Elphaba must choose which father figure and mentor she wants to follow and which she will renounce. Turning to the Wizard "with growing fury" she says, "You and I have nothing in common. I'm nothing like you and I will never be. And I'll fight you till the day I die!"[43] Here we see Elphaba renew the "I Want" she began with "Defying Gravity"—to defeat the Wizard—but it is not a task she is able to accomplish herself.

In *Jane Eyre's Sisters*, cultural mythologist Jody Bower describes the role of the "frenemy" within the heroine's journey. This friend-enemy "forces the heroine to look at her own behavior—a process that, while painful, can also be clarifying. Sometimes the criticism of such a friend provokes the heroine into standing up for herself. The frenemy can also act as a sort of contrary muse."[44] The relationship between Elphaba and her frenemy Glinda is one of the methods used by the show's creators to mark Elphaba's difference and otherness.

While Madame Morrible embodies Maureen Murdock's "male-identifying woman's" power, Glinda performs and deploys her power with stereotypical white and blonde femininity. According to race and whiteness scholars, the white blonde woman "can signal youth, beauty, privilege and conformity," is considered the normative "visual ideal," and "often served in visual media texts as the source of desire for the red-blooded American male."[45] At the same time, Glinda's feminine "goodness" limits the kind of power she can access. When Elphaba and Glinda stand before the Wizard and the *Grimmerie* is brought out, Glinda reverently asks if she can touch it and receives a curt "no" from Madame Morrible as the book is passed to Elphaba. As in university, Elphaba, rather than Glinda, is designated the suitable person to engage in magical bookishness.

Several scholars have debated the influence of Elphaba's potential racialization and how her oppression represents an experience of color. In *The Subaltern Status of Elphaba in* Wicked: *The Untold Story of the Witches of Oz*, Yoyo Chuang argues that Elphaba is a subaltern woman of color who "is not allowed to represent herself" but is instead represented through the normative white woman's narration of events.[46] By setting Glinda's normative whiteness against Elphaba's green skin, Chuang equates her skin with experiences of race, specifically the subaltern experience of voicelessness in the face of overwhelming white (colonizing) power. On the other hand, both Stacy Wolf in *Changed for Good* and Alissa Burger in *From* "The Wizard of Oz" *to* "Wicked": *Trajectory of American Myth* argue against Elphaba's specifically racial difference and understand her to represent difference more broadly.[47] Race, they argue, is culturally specific and Elphaba's greenness is not. In other words, she is not part of an oppressed group of green people. Elphaba's difference is the individual difference with which the writers of the show encourage audiences to personally identify, which contributes to the musical's successful deployment of specific experience for broad or universal appeal.

I agree with Wolf and Burger but add the following suggestion: Unlike many heroines who experience various obstacles on their journey of development, Elphaba encounters insurmountable *systemic* obstacles—an experience associated with marginalized communities. During the first half of the musical, Elphaba's anger is significantly lessened as she is honored and supported by her guides and friends.[48] Her individual successes and talent are encouraged as long as they remain separate from the general uplift of other marginalized and oppressed individuals and groups. In light of her determination to help the Animals, however, the Wizard and Morrible's political machine turns entirely against Elphaba and she never recovers her feeling of being "unlimited."

Elphaba's marginalized status is foregrounded in the score of the musical as well. In his analysis of *Wicked*'s score, musical dramatist and composer Robert Vieira describes how Stephen Schwartz represented the theme of fate in the show through the use of the "Wicked Witch Theme" leitmotif (a reoccurring musical theme connected to a character).[49] Vieira suggests that fate is used in the show as a kind of antagonist against which the characters fight. From the beginning of the show to the end, the "Wicked Witch Theme" reminds the audience that Elphaba is fated to be seen as a danger to society. I argue that given the political undercurrent of the show, the idea of fate is a mask for the systemic oppression against those accused of endangering society and government in Oz (e.g., Animals and the Wicked Witch). After her flight from the Wizard and Madame Morrible in "Defying Gravity," Elphaba becomes a pariah. Morrible turns public opinion against her while false information and fearmongering abound.

The score shows the Ozian chorus frantically changing keys and tempo multiple times during the one-minute-and-ten-second "Act II Opening." They accuse her of becoming more wicked and terrifying, seeking out victims to hurt, and "defaming our poor wizard with her calumnies and lies!" Madame Morrible and the Ozians later provide more specific "evidence" of her wicked behavior: namely, that she is sneaky, is wrathfully jealous, has an extra eye, can shed her skin, and has a soul so unclean that pure water can melt her. Analysis of the score shows Schwartz using both key and tempo changes to create a sense of growing urgency and fanaticism against the witch whose primary crime, underneath all the hype, is her campaign to speak out against the Wizard's oppression of Animals. This experience of systemic oppression, though experienced by Elphaba as an individual, is one of the elements of Elphaba's character that may lead members of oppressed and marginalized communities to identify with her.

Toward the end of the show, Glinda realizes she is complicit in Elphaba's oppression and goes to warn her that a mob of Ozians is coming to destroy her. The exchange is laced with frenemy humor ("Let the little girl go. And that poor little dog—Dodo. Elphaba—I'm sorry, but somebody has to say it: You are out of control! I mean, come on. They're just shoes!") and Glinda swears to tell all of Oz what has truly happened and clear Elphaba's name.[50] When Elphaba refuses, Glinda insists that she doesn't understand. Elphaba reestablishes the collaborating and conspiring functions of the mentoring community she had begun with Doctor Dillamond.

ELPHABA. (*Singing*) I'm limited. Just look at me—I'm limited.
And just look at you—you can do all I couldn't do, Glinda . . .
She signals to Chistery, and he brings the Book of Spells. Elphaba holds the Book out to Glinda.
ELPHABA. Here. (*Glinda stares at the Book, stunned*) Go on. Take it.
GLINDA. Elphie . . . you know I can't read this.
ELPHABA. Well, then—you'll have to learn.(*Sings*) Because now it's up to you. For both of us. Now it's up to you.[51]

Just as Elphaba became the recipient of the "cause" from Doctor Dillamond, Elphaba empowers Glinda and bequeaths her bookishness—as well as the book —to her. The blonde, who has been told throughout the entire show that she is unworthy of interacting with the book and of having serious magical power, must take on the heroine's mantle and finish the journey. Until this moment, Glinda's access to bookishness (taking classes in sorcery, touching or using the *Grimmerie*) has been negated and thus led to a hesitancy on her part ("Elphie . . . you know I can't read this."). It is only after bookishness is encouraged, and married to her experiences of privilege, that she accomplishes her greatest successes. As Elphaba warns, however, it will not be without effort. While Elphaba seemed to have an innate ability, Glinda will have to *learn* to read the *Grimmerie* and *work* to use the spells.

After Elphaba is "melted," Glinda returns to the Wizard and confronts him. *Grimmerie* in hand, she assumes control of the land—banishing the Wizard, imprisoning Madame Morrible, and accepting the mantle of responsibility as "Glinda the Good." Elphaba has changed Glinda and empowered her. Rather than the shallow and vain girl who always needed to be popular and get her own way, Glinda is able to have compassion and serve others.

One may well ask why I have spent so much space discussing the relationship of the heroine with men when *Wicked* remains such a haven for womanist and feminist pleasure? I confess that at times this research has felt decidedly androcentric despite its heroine subject. The answer is that by clarifying the way mentoring and father-daughter relationships function within *Wicked*, I gain a more specific understanding of Elphaba's journey as a heroine. Because of the popularity of *Wicked*, and musicals in general, we run a risk of trivializing and generalizing the elements at work within its structure, and I suggest that close character and dramaturgical readings of this and other productions provide much-needed analysis for scholars, practitioners, and general viewers alike.

Notes

1. Susan Fraiman, *Unbecoming Women: British Women Writers and the Novel of Development* (New York: Columbia University Press, 1993), x. The parenthetical 131 is original to the Fraiman, noting the Beauvoir page number that Fraiman is quoting.
2. Rebecca K. Hammonds, *Bookish Women: Examining the Textual and Embodied Construction of Scholarly and Literary Women in American Musicals*, electronic thesis or dissertation (Bowling Green, OH: Bowling Green State University, 2019), https://etd.ohiolink.edu/.
3. Jody Bower, *Jane Eyre's Sisters: How Women Live and Write the Heroine's Story* (Wheaton, IL: Quest, 2015), 77; Maureen Murdock, *The Heroine's Journey: Woman's Quest for Wholeness* (Berkeley, CA: Shambhala, 1990), 19–21.
4. Murdock, *The Heroine's Journey*, 39–40.
5. Murdock, *The Heroine's Journey*, 39–40.
6. Murdock, *The Heroine's Journey*, 40–44.
7. Bower, *Jane Eyre's Sisters*, 165. For Murdock, this is the male-identifying older woman who succeeds because of her participation in the patriarchal rules of society.
8. Bower, *Jane Eyre's Sisters*, 171. Italics added.
9. Winnie Holzman and Stephen Schwartz, *Wicked* (New York Rehearsal Script-2003), 14–15. https://www.scribd.com/document/371302924/Wicked-Broadway-Libretto-pdf.
10. Holzman and Schwartz, *Wicked* (New York Rehearsal Script-2003), 12.
11. Bower, *Jane Eyre's Sisters*, 169.
12. Ailsa Craig, "Collaborate, Conspire, Commune: Academy-Based Activism as Mentorship in Marginalized Communities," *Proceedings of the 2016 Atlantic Universities' Teaching Showcase 20* (Association of Atlantic Universities, 2016), 79.
13. Craig, "Collaborate, Conspire, Commune," 78.
14. Holzman and Schwartz, *Wicked*, 22.
15. Holzman and Schwartz, *Wicked*, 25.

16. Holzman and Schwartz, *Wicked*, 119. Italics original.
17. Jack Viertel, *Secret Life of the American Musical: How Broadway Shows Are Built* (New York: Farrar, Straus, and Giroux, 2016), 53.
18. Aaron Frankel, *Writing the Broadway Musical* (Boston: Da Capo, 2000), 95–96.
19. Holzman and Schwartz, *Wicked*, 16.
20. Holzman and Schwartz, *Wicked*, 60.
21. Holzman and Schwartz, *Wicked*, 65.
22. Bower, *Jane Eyre's Sisters*, 179.
23. Bower, *Jane Eyre's Sisters*, 179.
24. Joseph Campbell, *The Hero with a Thousand Faces*, 3rd ed. (Novato, CA: New World Library, 2008), 125.
25. Carol Pearson and Katherine Pope, *The Female Hero in American and British Literature* (New York: R. R. Bowker, 1981), 17.
26. Holzman and Schwartz, *Wicked*, 68.
27. Pearson and Pope, *The Female Hero in American and British Literature*, 9.
28. Holzman and Schwartz, *Wicked*, 89.
29. Bower, *Jane Eyre's Sisters*, 42.
30. Holzman and Schwartz, *Wicked*, 89.
31. Stephen Schwartz, "Wonderful," *Wicked: Piano/Vocal Score [Rev. 9/23/03]*. https://pdfslide.net/download/link/wicked-musical-piano-conductor-score-complete-565f47e689a67. Italics added.
32. Holzman and Schwartz, *Wicked*, 89.
33. Holzman and Schwartz, *Wicked*, 90.
34. Holzman and Schwartz, *Wicked*, 90.
35. Holzman and Schwartz, *Wicked*, 90.
36. Holzman and Schwartz, *Wicked*, 90.
37. Notation for the soloist to sing freely while the instruments follow their lead.
38. Stephen Schwartz. "Wonderful," *Wicked: Piano/Vocal Score.*
39. Musical Slimes, *The Tale of the Wicked Witch of the West (ft. Wicked OBC)*, Youtube video, 2:24:26, April 21, 2020, https://www.youtube.com/watch?v=ahEAkDHBV2Q.
40. Linda Woolverton (book), Alan Menken (composer), Howard Ashman (lyrics), Tim Rice (lyrics), *Disney's Beauty and the Beast: The Broadway Musical* (New York: Palace Theater, 1994); Phil Collins (music and lyrics), David Henry Hwang (book), *Disney's Tarzan: The Broadway Musical* (New York: Richard Rogers Theater, 2006).
41. Holzman and Schwartz, *Wicked*, 91.
42. Holzman and Schwartz, *Wicked*, 91.
43. Holzman and Schwartz, *Wicked*, 92.
44. Bower, *Jane Eyre's Sisters*, 115.
45. Phil Chidester. "May the Circle Stay Unbroken: Friends, the Presence of Absence, and the Rhetorical Reinforcement of Whiteness," *Critical Studies in Media Communication* 25, no. 2 (2008): 165.
46. Yoyo Chuang, *The Subaltern Status of Elphaba in Wicked: The Untold Story of the Witches of Oz* (New Taipei City, Taiwan: Fu Jen Catholic University, 2016), 1.
47. Stacy Wolf, *Changed for Good: A Feminist History of the Broadway Musical* (New York: Oxford University Press, 2011); Alissa Burger, *From "The Wizard of Oz" to "Wicked": Trajectory of American Myth* (OhioLink, 2009).

48. Michael Lewis. "Chapter 11: The Development of Anger," in *International Handbook of Anger*, ed. Michael Potegal, Gerhard Stemmler, and Charles Spielberger (New York: Springer, 2010), 177. According to Michael Lewis, "anger is the consequence of the blockage of a goal-directed action." Elphaba experienced a great deal of anger before her time at Shiz University, and it caused her magical ability to pulse out of her in uncontrolled emotional moments. With the help and acceptance of her mentors and frenemies, she learns to control her anger and magic, though not always with successful consequences.
49. Robert Vieira, "Wicked the Musical's Groundbreaking Score—Act 2," *Musical Writers*, https://www.musicalwriters.com/studying-broadway-musicals/wicked-the-musicals-groundbreaking-score-act-2/.
50. Vieira, "Wicked the Musical's Groundbreaking Score," 112.
51. Holzman and Schwartz, *Wicked*, 115.

Immersive Witches

New York City under the Spell of *Sleep No More* and *Then She Fell*

—DAVID BISAHA

Immersed in Witchcraft

I'm sitting in a darkened room, waiting for someone to show up. I'm surrounded by elaborately designed rooms: an office, a hospital, a boudoir, a cemetery, a hotel lobby. Curiosity, fear, and excitement fill me. Characters enter the room, performing dance sequences solo and in pairs, and I'm drawn to the fantastic among them: covens of witches, White Rabbits, Mad Hatters, Red Queens. As I explore the five-story McKittrick Hotel complex or the corridors of the Kingsland Ward asylum, I lose myself, not knowing what lies behind a curtain, through a door, atop a staircase. Powerful female characters ignite my wonder; these witches contest "normalcy" with a set of upside-down rules and rituals. As I reflect on the ten-year history of commercially successful and widespread immersive theatre in the United States, I observe that two of the longest-running such experiences in New York City depend on themes of witchcraft. By aligning authoritative witchlike characters with an audience encouraged into childlike exploration and submission, creators of the performances *Sleep No More* (2011) and *Then She Fell* (2012) made use of stage witch tropes to introduce a new phase of immersive theatre.[1]

Both productions take place in large, designed spaces and are inspired by canonical literary works: *Macbeth* and Lewis Carroll's Alice stories, respectively. However, they are not living storybooks; both incorporate other works, such as

Sleep No More's quotation of Alfred Hitchcock films, and both take place within fictional institutions of an earlier time: the 1930s-themed McKittrick Hotel and the Victorian hospital Kingsland Ward. Accompanied by a constant soundtrack, dancer-performers engage each other using a dance vocabulary full of contemporary technique and contact improvisation. *Then She Fell* consists of several audience tracks in which characters lead audience members by ones or twos through three floors of rooms. *Sleep No More* is a free-for-all, as characters perform predetermined, one-hour tracks across the six-floor, 100,000-square-foot warehouse and audiences pursue whichever of the twenty-some characters they choose. Daring audience members are rewarded with intimate, "one-on-one" performances in *Sleep No More*, and *Then She Fell* provides many personalized experiences. Both have attracted significant internet-based fan followings, and both are frequently contrasted in criticism of New York's immersive scene, due to their roughly contemporary openings, long open-ended runs, and choreographic similarity. To these comparisons I add that they share witchy themes.

The current wave of immersive performance in New York City began around 2010 with the work of several dance- and nightclub-based innovators. The UK-based company Punchdrunk and management company Emursive invested in a major, open-run production of *Sleep No More* in Chelsea in 2011. Joining Punchdrunk in New York were Third Rail Projects (*Then She Fell*) and Cynthia Von Buhler's Speakeasy Dollhouse (*The Bloody Beginning*, 2011). According to *American Theatre* magazine, similar immersive works had emerged throughout the country by 2013.[2] The immersive theatre trend was not unique to New York City, but it took on unique shapes due to the environment and talent pool of the city. In particular, early New York immersives from 2011 to 2015 tended to eschew site-responsive or outdoor performances and instead modeled their work on the type of open "sandbox" or warehouse model, as Punchdrunk did, or else in the nightclub model begun a decade earlier with *The Donkey Show* (1999).[3]

However, with their nearly completely emancipated spectators, emphasis on one-on-one experiences, and nonlinear structure, the new immersives of the 2010s sold spectacle over story. It was often an expensive ticket, and as a result, Punchdrunk and Third Rail Projects attracted an economically well-off audience but not necessarily an intellectual or high-art one. New York already boasted a rich history of nightlife entertainment and cabaret, site-specific experiments emerging from performance art discourses, and a tradition of relational, community-based, and participatory art in the gallery. Immersive theatre took on a new niche by embracing a more commercial mindset early on. These performances offered exclusive invitation and attention from a host, spectacular entertainment, and the frisson of downtown nightlife—all wrapped in the general atmosphere of the macabre or the mysterious. Witches and the occult were not the only organizing theme behind this wave of performances, but they did play a significant part in several early, influential pieces.

With this brief history, and this article, I aim to bring together two cultural strands of the early 2010s. The figure of the witch stands alongside other supernatural fads in American popular culture. While zombies and vampires dominated film, books, and television from the mid-2000s until the mid-2010s, witches began overtaking them in the early 2010s.[4] The rebirth of the witch has been read as an expression of rage against misogyny and sexual assault in mid-to-late-2010s culture, as a desire for female leadership and community, and as an opportunity to enact fantasies of control and women's empowerment. Taking a historical view, Kelsea Stahler writes that "when women's resistance is at a fever pitch (as it was in the 1960s, the 1990s, and now) and women are seeking empowering stories that allow them to control their own narratives, stories about witchcraft seem to become more popularized."[5] And indeed, since 2013, witches have become more popular horror archetypes, from several seasons' focus on *American Horror Story* (Seasons 3, 6, and 8, 2013–2018) to reboots of *Sabrina the Teenage Witch* and *Charmed* franchises and the Robert Eggers film *The Witch* (2015). In some ways, witches after #MeToo and the 2016 election of Donald Trump (the subject of his own self-proclaimed "witch hunt") engage more with human politics than the fantasy-based witches of earlier witch-trope revivals. In the 2010s, immersive theatrical witches aligned with their pop culture cousins through their desire to resist male power and institutions, the existence of efficacious "magic" outside the sphere of the digital, and the allure of occult rituals and practices.

A distinction: The occult and witchcraft are related, overlapping, but not synonymous concepts. Often scholars have conflated the two, as has popular culture of recent decades. Occult simply refers to hidden knowledge, outside of religious mainstream practice, while witchcraft may often refer to the historical European "witch craze" and fairy-tale witch archetypes, or also (somewhat imprecisely) to several modern religions, including Neopaganism, Wicca, even LaVeyan Satanism.[6] In this paper, I use "witch" to refer to the cultural archetype derived from European/British witch traditions, and I use "occult" to refer to a larger network of hidden knowledge, which includes both nonmainstream religions and knowledge such as spiritualism, magic, alchemy, folk medicine, divination, and the paranormal. These two domains are commonly blended. The early-2010s wave of immersive theatre participated in a pop culture trend that combined European witchcraft with mysterious or esoteric practices: astrology, spiritualism, herbalism, shamanism, Afro-American religions such as Voodoo, and fantasy figures (vampires/fairies).

In *Sleep No More* and *Then She Fell*, witches and witchlike characters adapted concepts of the occult and the fairy tale into expressions of neoliberal, mediatized, early-twenty-first-century culture. Part of the success of these long-running New York City productions was that they used the witch to introduce a new type of immersive theatre spectatorship. Audiences entered a dimly lit space with new rules, gave themselves over to the "spell" of immersive environments and intimate experiences, and watched as arcane dance-rituals unfolded. Through these performances, the figure of the witch came to encompass the marketability of personalized, gamified experiences, the search for comfort and order in new universes. In this paper, I call upon the figure of the witch as a midwife of an immersive theatre era. For a generation of theatregoers dazzled by the dual sirens of social media and popular culture depictions of the occult, witches became useful, profitable figures.

Childhood and Initiation

Through the witch figure, these performances link childlike wonder with the pleasures of initiation, ritual behavior, and voyeurism. As knowledgeable, powerful creatures, witches position themselves as links to the "other" world. At times, this passage is directly invoked; for instance, *Then She Fell* begins with an invocation of the concept of liminality, a seductive introduction that paraphrases Arnold Van Gennep and Victor Turner, inviting them to experience "the landscapes of dream, myth, wonder, intoxication." Having just consumed a wine cocktail, and seated in a wooden chair reminiscent of elementary school furniture, I'm reminded by the head doctor of Kingsland Ward that liminality "is precisely that state of falling, in any of its myriad meanings: falling ill, falling apart, falling in love, falling out of love, falling into madness, falling from innocence."[7] Across town, at the McKittrick, *Sleep No More* packs the audience into an elevator and simply instructs its "hotel guests" to keep their masks on, to remain silent, and to turn off cell phones. Then, advice: "Fortune favors the bold."

The historical witch has drawn much of her power from her mirror-image identity, the inverted mother, virgin, or nun. These women maintain control over reproduction, sexuality, and even the future (through dominance over children); this power is seen strongly in European fairy tales. Fittingly, control over childhood is deeply embedded into both immersive pieces. *Sleep No More* makes much of Macbeth's fatal birth prophecy and highlights the childlessness of protagonists in both the Scottish play and Hitchcock's *Rebecca*. One culmination of this child obsession is the spectacular rave-orgy, a popular element of *Sleep No More* fandom. The famous prophecies are delivered by the three witches: One witch hands Macbeth a tree over a table in a darkened bar, at which point EDM-rave music rises, strobe lights and green lasers flicker. The Boy Witch character reveals himself naked, bloody, wearing a goat-head mask; another witch births a figure of a small child.[8] Other missing children appear elsewhere in the performance, from the inclusion of Agnes Naismith, a character from the historical Paisley witch trials in Scotland, who wanders the town square looking for her lost sister, to the mournful dances of Lady Macbeth, whose child, presumably, has died, or never existed, and the MacDuffs, who perform a mournful duet in a nursery, underscored by Vera Lynn's 1940 song "Goodnight Children, Everywhere." Further, several of the audience one-on-ones associated with younger characters (Agnes, Lady Macbeth, Lady Macduff) place the complacent audience member in the role of a child through bedtime stories, caressing gestures, or other soothing phrases. Strong, older female characters are one of the main power centers of the performance. Their actions direct large portions of the performance, particularly those of witch-queen Hecate, who orchestrates the witches' behavior but rarely leaves her own bower, but also those of nurse/maid/servant characters, such as Catherine Campbell, also named for a Paisley trials figure. Like other witches who exact revenge through control over birth (the Witch in *Into the Woods* comes to mind), in *Sleep No More* childlessness is thematized while the audience comes to take the place of a child, exploring unfamiliar terrain.

Then She Fell similarly creates a world in which older women have control over the young. In contrast to *Sleep No More*, this world contains children (Alices, two of them) and engages the liminality of growing up. And while the Queens are not explicitly coded as witches in a European early modern model, I consider them witchlike here. The paired Red and White Queens possess magical powers and invert male authority. Lewis Carroll/Charles Dodgson himself was personally obsessed with the occult; he owned a library of esoteric volumes, and scholars have read the "nonsense" world of the Alice stories as a secularized version of witchcraft.[9] In Kingsland Ward, witches embody adulthood and authority from a child's perspective. In one scene, I look through glass medicine chests mounted on the wall as the Red Queen dances a solo in which she cannot hold up her head and her body flails. A clipboard on the wall identifies the "patient" as Alice's mother, Lorina Hannah Liddell. She invites me in and explains how growing up tends to wear one down. This fraught relationship of mother and daughter animates the rest of the production, from the sudden breakage of the relationship between Carroll/Dodgson, which seems to be Alice's mother's doing, to a series of duets in which the Red Queen instructs Alice on proper behavior (bowing, holding dresses, combing hair) and ties a red ribbon around her neck. The other maternal character in the production is the White Queen, who nurtures: I begin the evening by being invited to lie in a bed while she tells me a story about a girl who ages backward. In another vignette, the White Queen feeds fruit and potions to Alice and me in a room full of flowers and herbs, and then later dances a loving, romantic duet with the White Rabbit—a polar opposite to the Red Queen.

Contemporary witch narratives in the European folklore model frequently rely on childhood and initiation tropes. In some stories, young witches discover their powers; in others, the discovery of witchy rites (sabbaths, orgies, initiations) is made by young people. Either way, the audience is meant to be thrilled and fascinated by the disorientation and discovery of a new set of rules. In many witchcraft narratives, devil worship and an inversion of Christian concepts and hierarchy fascinate the audience, as well. This element of witchcraft derives from early modern conceptions of witches as agents of Satan; this was articulated in the *Malleus Maleficarum* of 1486, a work that underpinned the witch trials and crazes of England, France, and Germany through the seventeenth century.[10] In the early modern period, witchcraft was regularly associated with a standard characterization, which included a ride by night, a pact with the Devil, a secret meeting/orgy that desecrated Christian sacraments, and the sacrifice of infants and children.[11] Depictions onstage and in writing of witches' anti-Christian rituals have repeatedly attracted audiences, historically and today. An inverted relationship to mainstream religion, morality, even logic and physics has provided both comic relief and dark, deep mythologies in contemporary representations of witchcraft.[12]

Such discovery of an unfamiliar world replicates a sense of childlike wonder and fear, and this emotion similarly animates the worlds of *Sleep No More* and *Then She Fell*. While only partially created by witches, a general spooky feeling authorizes audience members to enjoy risk. Choreographer Maxine Doyle has explained that *Sleep No More* "kind of goes back to the ethos of trying to rediscover the child within. . . . We all remember the things that we shouldn't touch but do and then the excitement when we have. I think that this work is about that—inviting the sort of forbidden touch."[13] Through combining "the role of the powerful female, creeping paranoia, and lust for control," immersive productions use witches to place us once more in a submissive, quiet, childlike receptivity.[14] Piecing it together, in your own way, is very much a part of the fun.

Analog Magics, Digital Desires

In the years after opening their major New York productions, creators of *Then She Fell* and *Sleep No More* explained the success of their productions in terms of digital isolation. "People are striving for the analog in this digital world," according to Punchdrunk founder Felix Barrett. Zach Morris, cofounder of Third Rail Projects, found similar inspiration for *Then She Fell*: "We crave those sensory experiences, we crave tactile experiences, we crave intimacy." When these works were in development, the smartphone, mobile computing, and social media were all rapidly gaining wide user bases. Capitalizing on this, creators frequently positioned immersive theatre as a response to an increasingly digital culture. Accordingly, both productions eschew digital trickery, video projection, and screens of all types; instead, text is handwritten or typewritten on pages, and speakers and audio apparatuses are hidden. The effect is cinematic, but not digital; the goal is to create an illusion of authenticity, a designed yet fully sensory and overwhelming experience.[15]

The figure of the witch, then, is a handy archetype for the analog production of sensory desire. Having renounced digital special effects, these productions have landed on objects that have similar efficacious, even magical powers—witchy items—and ones that don't require a battery. Dominant decorative elements are analog objects associated with transformation, healing, liminality, or magic. Both use playing cards as specific plot elements, for instance. As tools of change, luck, divination, and sin, they connect Alice and the McKittrick to the occult, if not directly to the European witch. Other such "magics" that are used are collections of herbs and dried plants, mirrors, water, blood, charts of plant or animal anatomies, taxidermy, anachronistic glassware, apothecaries, and pills. These objects all have some relationship to divination, prophesy, healing, or potion-making. They are witches' tools. Such alternative forms of power have been historically hidden, feminized, or demonized, and these productions revel in them. Audiences find themselves in a land of not-now, not-here, and perhaps not-natural.

Perhaps the strongest anti-digital aspect of these performances has to do with their erotic and tactile elements. Speaking of *Then She Fell*, theatre critic Benjamin Brantley observed that "you're tainted by a certain relationship—

something on the one hand that creates enchantment, and on the other hand is perhaps a dubious act of seduction."[16] Touch connects spectator to environment, yet the charged atmosphere of these productions makes one aware of one's body, hands, voice, and, potentially, desire. The aesthetic pleasures of athletic, lithe dancers are part of both productions' draw, and multiple critics refer to the erotic energy exchanged, especially in private, one-on-one performances. According to Shakespeare scholar Todd Barnes: "I've never been to a 'gentleman's club,' but suddenly become aware of the rules that govern that space: be touched but do not touch. Yet, this immersive theatre experience [*Sleep No More*] seems to rely on my participation." Immersive scholar Adam Alston adds that "risk, for some, is sexy."[17] In the words of critic Agnes Silvestre, "of the one-on-ones . . . the defining features seemed to be seduction and fear, and through both, a rendering of the spectator powerless." A Punchdrunk artistic associate interviewed by Silvestre remarked that "a good one-on-one should perhaps make you fall in love."[18] Such aesthetics link the power of certain witches to seduce and control with the pleasurable feeling of losing oneself, of falling, of liminality highlighted by *Then She Fell*'s doctor. For these productions' audiences, which do skew younger and "edgier" than Broadway, young and attractive performers seduce the audience into participation, intimacy, even complicity. Of course, the association of beauty with seductive witchcraft rests on the socially constructed beauty ideals that produce the idea of feminine allure and associate it with compulsion. These predominantly young and young-looking performers reflect twenty-first-century biases toward the types of bodies seen to be most pleasurable to view and marketable to sell to mainstream, affluent Off-Broadway or nightclub audiences.

Sometimes, participation and complicity tip over into unwanted touch. Most audience members in *Sleep No More* maintain at least some distance from the dancers unless invited to touch, yet there have also been numerous allegations that audience members have sexually assaulted actors during performances of *Sleep No More*.[19] Third Rail Projects have claimed that their lack of masks and structure of one-on-one encounters makes assault less of a problem in *Then She Fell*. In both performances, though, negotiations of space, intimacy, and consent are very much part of the artwork. One reading of this is that their dark, private space, sensuous content, and intimate experiences may encourage some spectators to step over the line. Spectators who assume that touch is permitted break the rules of performance and consent, certainly. Yet, these performances derive power from toeing that line. The creation of such intimacy is one of the particular gifts of the immersive-trained performer, and despite the protests of critics who view such encounters as mechanical and false, the aesthetic pleasure of the actor being present with an individual audience member can be captivating. The feeling of being chosen for a one-on-one provides a thrill aligned with the seductive side of witchcraft. Witches, after all, can be deceivers, wielding the power of glamorous illusions, seducing subjects into otherworldly experiences. In the words of a song covered by several spooky performers, "I put a spell on you / And now you're mine."

Compulsion, Seduction, and Neoliberal Spectatorship

The witch's glamour isn't simply an illusion in these performances; witches are some of their most beautiful and mysterious figures, especially in the case of *Sleep No More*. They seem to rule the productions, and they guide participation with an oblique smile, eye contact, words whispered in the ear. Their costume design plays with gender presentation, especially for the witches, who present as androgynous, queer, or nonbinary. Most performers are young and attractive—a departure from the ugly, outcast witches of some fairy tales. The witch has transformed from someone to avoid, a figure of fascination and revulsion, to a main attraction. In both their choreographic languages and in their mode of audience engagement, the immersive stage witches enchant. For audiences, the experience is pleasurable; most spectators do not see how they are being cued, scripted, and manipulated. A large part of the enchantment, too, is the sale of the individualized, private, experience-driven entertainment product that compels repeat visits.

The choreographic style differs between the two productions, yet expressions of compulsion pervade both. *Sleep No More*'s choreography must engage with large spaces and differing architectures and also maintain the perimeter of a "performance area" within which the audience will not cross. This preservation and negotiation of space results in a series of push-pull partner sequences, thrusts, throws, and extensions of the limbs along the major axes of a given interaction; fights, romantic duets, and addresses occur along a few dominant lines, especially when they take place in the more open areas of the experience.[20] A preoccupation with lead-follow and dominance comes through in Doyle's work, as the witches lead and the earthly characters follow, and the space leads and the dancers follow, improvise, and partner. *Then She Fell*, jointly choreographed by Zach Morris, Tom Pearson, and Jennine Willett, similarly features close, daring duets with furniture, other actors, and scenic architecture. Characters are thrown across rooms, climb walls and furniture, and hold and pull each other in expressions of desire. Both productions rely heavily on weight sharing, close partnering, and an emphasis on physical contact, whether through the often explosive or violent movements of *Sleep No More* or the controlled, intentionally doubled and dualistic movements of *Then She Fell*.

Audiences are similarly compelled as well, though in less obvious ways. Theorists of immersive theatre have critiqued claims that open-world immersives such as *Sleep No More* provide true freedom to act, as in massively multiplayer online role-player games such as *World of Warcraft*. Rather than affording the participant agency to experience the production in any way he or she likes, the options are actually limited by fairly narrow rules. Explicit rules spoken early on the array of options in both productions, assuring (relatively) docile and compliant audience members. But implicitly, audience members are also gently guided by the performers to engage in a certain way and are structurally blocked from "acting out" by black-masked stewards or crew dressed as nurses and orderlies. The presence of these boundaries enables seemingly free play inside the performance while maintaining the necessary communication network and distribution of authority.

Much published criticism of these productions has connected immersive theatre to global neoliberalism. Neoliberalism itself is seductive, as under its banner values of freedom, entrepreneurship, and individualism, systemic capital relations constrain the individual and promote, above all, the profit of the business over the welfare of the subject. David Harvey's definition provides a useful gloss: "A theory of political economic practices that proposes human well-being can be best advanced by liberating individual entrepreneurial freedoms and skills within an institutional framework characterized by strong private property rights, free markets, and free trade."[21] Inducements toward individual and privatized action, and the accumulation of capital by those at the top, result in an unequal distribution of wealth and power. Jen Harvie notes that any art practice that promotes such entrepreneurialism will "exacerbate inequalities." And as Adam Alston has noted, the neoliberal ideology of immersive theatre hinges on the concept of risk: "It is not so much risk-as-danger which is co-opted, as it is a desire held by some to enjoy the perception of risk as a hedonistic thrill." Worthen, too, connects the online performances of immersive superfans to the "experience economy" of postshow social media sharing, which is both a record and a re-performance of audience autonomy that further returns social capital to the audience member—and, ultimately, moves more financial capital toward the production itself.[22] Beautiful, seductive witches provide hedonic, intimate experiences to the select few, those who dare and risk, while permeating the theatrical environment with mysterious atmosphere and unstated rules. They are the traffic-cops of experience economies. The immersive witch is the mirror image of the outsider, historical stage witch: she is instead the very source of private experiences to be consumed and recycled.[23]

And so, I theorize that the witches emerging from these immersive performances are networked, neoliberal witches. They are neoliberal because they reward individual risk and prize the consumption by the individual, rather than the group. They establish hierarchies of access, value, and success across the audiences they establish. Time with the witches is available for a relatively high price; especially in *Sleep No More*, the rarest encounters depend on repeat attendance and foreknowledge, "winning" is both expensive and elusive. (Third Rail Projects, to their credit, has experimented with less expensive immersive experiences since *Then She Fell* opened, but their flagship production remains a $100–$200 ticket.) Immersive witches also appeal to audiences more comfortable with technologically managed encounters and social media than with community life. They pit us against each other, all in a mode of consumption. These witches are network beings, too. The occult and the mysterious permeate the environments of these productions, and witches tease the viewer with hidden meaning, but they obscure, rather than reveal, coherent narratives. No single meaning or story is shared among audience participants; rather, discrete encounters assemble into different constellations of meaning for each viewer. The productions are built to encourage divergent spectatorship. As such, the network, the rhizome, the cloud, and the cluster are better metaphors for the types of experience one engages in than a plot or linear narrative. The witch is a suitable metaphor because witches as an archetype oppose structure, normativity, and linearity. The mystery, chaos, and power of immersive witches is in the fragmentation they spread, made palatable by the control they exercise over others.

Twenty-First-Century Values

The seductive cry of witchcraft is, to some degree, the call of power through alternate means. Antiestablishment, radical desire has been placed onto the figure of the witch across time, but in these productions, the figure of the witch and the environment of the occult commodify the supernatural. The long runs of *Sleep No More* and *Then She Fell* have multiple causes, of course; their success is as likely due to their companies' savvy business practices as to the dark themes of their content. To be sure, the companies purchased permanent performance spaces, train their own performers, and maintain robust volunteer and internship programs, all of which helps make long, open-ended runs possible. Both companies, too, have diversified their income streams. Emursive/Punchdrunk renovated the McKittrick Hotel to include other revenue-generating ventures, and the complex includes secondary performance spaces, cabaret events, and a rooftop restaurant. Third Rail Projects maintains an active workshop, education, and residency program, helping the company employ core performers as teachers. Yet, none of their canny business approach would have mattered had the performances themselves not captured something important in 2010s culture: a desire for connection, intimacy, and authenticity. For this, the figure of the witch was a familiar framework on which creators, and audiences, could organize their experiences as a new performance form grew.

The witch character may have become particularly strong in New York immersive theatre due to the city's emphasis on commercial theatre production models. Immersive work from the UK, Europe, and Australia predated the New York premieres of *Sleep No More* and *Then She Fell*, as Josephine Machon has helpfully charted.[24] The translation to New York City, perhaps, and its commercial, Broadway-fueled fantasy of the open run and long-standing nightlife parties turned immersive theatre from gallery art project to entertainment institution. The success of occult themes in early New York productions inspired imitators. Companies began to extend their runs—not only *Sleep No More* and *Then She Fell* but also similarly weird- or nostalgia-themed nightlife experiences such as Speakeasy Dollhouse/Cynthia Von Buehler's performances, *Queen of the Night*, and Woodshed Collective. Many of these performances, though not all, included themes of witches or magic. *Sleep No More* and others proved that strange and esoteric themes could help sell performances in New York and led to performances centered around witches, devils, and the occult such as Von Buhler's *The Illuminati Ball*, Company XIV's burlesque circus performances, and others. While the field has undoubtedly broadened beyond the weird since 2011, in its initial phases there was a good deal of witchiness in the movement.

Witch characters in *Sleep No More* and *Then She Fell* embody the emergent values of the twenty-first century. Their athletic bodies danced, enchanted, and seduced, filling a need for contact between humans in a moment of expanding mobile technology and social media. The witch presided over a hyperreal, networked, gamified performance environment. Like the subjects of the early modern witch craze, the world of the immersive witch paralleled or inverted the "real" world. They sold escapism, the loss of self, and fantasy. But, unlike witches in previous historical moments, these witch characters were ultimately in the service of a commercial production, rather than representing some possible departure from it. Despite their veneer of woman-centered, antiauthoritarian power, these witches primarily existed to elicit desire out of the audience, to provide fleeting sensory experiences, and to encourage risk-taking, entrepreneurial participation.[25] As such, the witch reflects back elements of contemporary American culture: an ambivalent relationship to the virtual, the desire for authenticity based in the senses, and the commodification of women's bodies and those of nonbinary and genderqueer persons. As other expressions of neoliberal capitalism do, immersive theatre provides the illusion of choice, freedom, intimacy, liberation, when in fact one's choices are trammeled and profits accrue to the ones who set the terms. The witch is a useful conduit for such affective sleight of hand. Witches are objects of fascination, prescriptions for the perceived lack of authenticity plaguing the twenty-first-century urbanite. Held within the framework of the immersive experience, however, these stage witches repackage the thrill of the occult but have little power to challenge the larger structures that put the witch to use in the first place.

Notes

1. Punchdrunk has created several performances with the title *Sleep No More*. The 2011 version, a collaboration with production company Emursive, is the longest-running iteration. It was preceded by a 2003 production in London and a 2009 production in Boston in collaboration with the American Repertory Theatre.
2. Other pioneering US companies included Chicago's Dog and Pony, Pittsburgh's Bricolage Production Company, We Players in San Francisco, and La Jolla's Without Walls festival. Diep Tran, "In Immersive Theatre, The Audience Members Are the Actors," *American Theatre*, July 6, 2013, https://www.americantheatre.org/2013/07/06/in-immersive-theatre-the-audience-are-the-actors/.
3. For further discussion, see Arnold Aronson, *The History and Theory of Environmental Scenography*, 2nd ed. (London: Methuen, 2018).
4. *28 Days Later* (2002), *World War Z* (book 2007, film 2013), *Pride and Prejudice and Zombies* (book 2009, film 2016), and *The Walking Dead* (2010–2020) illuminate a trend peaking around 2010–2013. A similar time frame animates the most recent vampire trend, which includes the Twilight series (books 2005–2008, films 2008–2012), *True Blood* (2008–2014), and *The Vampire Diaries* (2009–2017). A major exception to this chronology is the Harry Potter universe, which uses the term "witch" to denote a female wizard but without many associations with European early modern folklore.
5. Kelsea Stahler, "The Resurgence of Witches," *Teen Vogue*, November 14, 2018, https://www.teenvogue.com/story/witches-pop-culture-sabrina-ahs-charmed-real-world.
6. The occult includes "diverse nonmainstream religions such as spiritualism, theosophy, UFO cults, NeoPaganism, Scientology, and any other group that might be labelled as secret or hidden." NeoPagans, in particular, are often incorrectly conflated with Satanic religions. Christel J. Manning, "Embracing Jesus and The Goddess: Towards a Representation of Conversion to Sycretistic Religion," in *Magical Religion and Modern Witchcraft*, ed. James R. Lewis (Albany, NY: SUNY Press, 1996), 302.
7. This introductory speech of the Kingsland Ward doctor is preserved in the film *Between*

Yourself and Me, Dance Films Association in collaboration with Third Rail Projects, producer, New York, 2017.

8. "For none of woman born / Shall harm Macbeth" and "Macbeth shall never vanquish'd be until / Great Birnam wood to high Dunsinane hill / Shall come against him." *Macbeth*, act 4, scene 1.
9. Kevin Shortsleeve, "Nonsense, Magic, Religion, and Superstition," *Bookbird: A Journal of International Children's Literature* 5, no. 3 (2015): 28–36; Phyllis Stowell, "We're All Mad Here," *Children's Literature Association Quarterly* 8, no. 2 (1983): 5–8.
10. Christopher S. Mackay, *The Hammer of Witches: A Complete Translation* (Cambridge: Cambridge University Press, 2009); Malcolm Gaskill, *Witchcraft: A Very Short Introduction* (Oxford: Oxford University Press, 2010), 30–35. See also Diane Purkiss, *The Witch in History* (New York: Routledge, 1996).
11. Jeffrey B. Russell, *A History of Witchcraft: Sorcerers, Heretics and Pagans* (New York: Thames and Hudson, 1982), 55.
12. Television lends itself to deeper mythologies, and comic and/or dark "parallel" worlds populate the universes of *American Horror Story: Coven* (2013), *Sabrina the Teenage Witch* (both the 1996–2003 sitcom and 2018 Netflix reboot), *Buffy the Vampire Slayer* (1997–2003), *Supernatural* (2005–2020), and *Game of Thrones* (2011–2019).
13. Doyle quoted in Mark Kennedy, "UK Theater Company Finds Success in Jaded New York," *Backstage*, July 15, 2011, https://www.backstage.com/magazine/article/uk-theater-company-finds-success-jaded-new-york-61390/
14. Kennedy, "UK Theatre Company Finds Success in Jaded New York."
15. Felix Barrett, "Punchdrunk: Making a Show as Addictive as Candy Crush," Fora.tv, June 1, 2014, https://www.youtube.com/watch?v=4r-V5fMCUqg; Margarita Jimeno, director. "Working in the Theatre: Immersive Theatre," American Theatre Wing, May 7, 2014, https://americantheatrewing.org/working-in-the-theatre/immersive-theatre-wit/
16. *Between Yourself and Me*, Dance Films Association.
17. Quoted in W. B. Worthen, "'The Written Troubles of the Brain': *Sleep No More* and the Space of Character," *Theatre Journal* 64, no. 1 (2012): 94; Adam Alston, "Audience Participation and Neoliberal Value: Risk, Agency and Responsibility in Immersive Theatre," *Performance Research* 18, no. 2 (2013): 136.
18. Agnes Silvestre, "Punchdrunk and the Politics of Spectatorship," Culturebot, http://www.culturebot.org/2012/11/14997/punchdrunk-and-the-politics-of-spectatorship/.
19. As a nonunion production, *Sleep No More* relies heavily on early-career and intern labor, making some performers and other workers particularly vulnerable to abuse, without the recourses available to professional union performers. Amber Jamieson, "Performers and Staffers at 'Sleep No More' Say Audience Members Have Sexually Assaulted Them," BuzzFeed News, February 6, 2018, https://www.buzzfeednews.com/article/amberjamieson/sleep-no-more; Alexis Soloski, "The Problem with Immersive Theatre: Why Actors Need Extra Protection from Sexual Assault," *Guardian*, February 12, 2018, https://www.theguardian.com/stage/2018/feb/12/immersive-theatre-punchdrunk-sleep-no-more.
20. In devising the choreography, Doyle "was interested in looking at how violent the body could be." Dancer Jordan Morely (Boy Witch/Bellhop/Mr. Barragan) states that "there's a lot of thrash, but it's controlled. . . . It's really about having honest reactions to almost torturous events, like someone shaking your bones or tossing you against the wall or trying to strangle you." Gia Kourlas, "'Sleep No More,' but Move Nonstop," *New York Times*,

September 6, 2011, http://www.nytimes.com/2011/09/07/arts/dance/sleep-no-more-is-theater-embedded-with-dancers.html.

21. David Harvey, *A Brief History of Neoliberalism* (Oxford: Oxford University Press, 2007), 2.
22. Jen Harvie, quoted in Alston, "Audience Participation," 133; Alston, "Audience Participation," 136; W. B. Worthen, "Free Reign?: Designing the Spectator in Immersive Theatre," *Routledge Companion to Scenography*, ed. Arnold Aronson (London: Routledge, 2018), 304.
23. See also Jen Harvie, *Fair Play: Art, Performance and Neoliberalism* (New York: Palgrave Macmillan, 2013); Paul Masters, *Constructing the Sensorium: Neoliberalism and Aesthetics Practice in Immersive Theatre* (PhD dissertation, Tufts University, 2016); and Keren Zaiontz, "Narcissistic Spectatorship in Immersive and One-on-one Performance," *Theatre Journal* 66, no. 3 (2014): 405–25.
24. Mike Pearson's Brith Gof, dreamthinkspeak, and artist Adrian Howells are several key UK-based examples. Josephine Machon, *Immersive Theatres: Intimacy and Immediacy in Contemporary Performance* (Basingstoke: Palgrave, 2013); Masters, *Constructing the Sensorium*.
25. This term was coined in Alston, "Audience Participation."

Part III

ESSAY FROM THE CONFERENCE

The Robert A. Schanke Award-Winning Essay, MATC 2020

New Conventions for a New Generation

High School Musicals and Broadway in the 2010s

—LINDSEY MANTOAN

Scholars of musical theatre often point to midcentury musicals as constituting the so-called golden age of the art form, and the legacy of the time period looms large when studying subsequent musical genres and trends.[1] In *Changed for Good: A Feminist History of the Broadway Musical*, Stacy Wolf offers a survey of musicals that she organizes by decade and analyzes through feminist and critical race lenses, beginning with the golden age. While gesturing to a broad range of musical styles and conventions, Wolf demonstrates that 1960s musicals often featured the Single Girl who sang and danced solo onstage but was often punished for her independence. The radical politics of the 1970s gave rise to the ensemble musical that negotiated the inward reflection of individual characters and the cohesion of communities. The megamusical dominated the 1980s, with imports from the United Kingdom such as *Les Misérables* and *Phantom of the Opera* dramatically altering musical theatre values, shifting focus from characters to scenery and spectacle. To conclude the book, Wolf spans the 1990s and the first decade of the 2000s, analyzing musicals centering women of color and mapping out "the interdependence of race, gender, and sexuality" in those musicals.[2]

Wolf's book, published in 2011, takes readers up to 2008's *In the Heights* in its study of trends and conventions in Broadway musicals. This paper extends Wolf's work into the 2010s. Here, I suggest that there is a new category that in part defines musicals of the 2010s—the high school musical—and that comparing its values to those of previous eras can demonstrate the changing character of the musical form as well as changing values in US culture. If the musical is almost always about national and individual identity (see Raymond Knapp),[3] these 2010s high school texts, including *Bring it On: The Musical*, *Mean Girls*, *Heathers*, *The Prom*, *Dear Evan Hansen*, *Be More Chill*, *Carrie*, *Clueless*, and *Bare*, signal a shift in what constitutes a community, which individuals are valued, and what integration might truly mean. These musicals put forward body positive messages and embrace queerness and trans identities, and in so doing, they develop a new genre of US musical theatre. They dismantle the firmly entrenched social cliques of 1990s high school films through incorporating social media into the narrative and production design, foregrounding female friendship, framing identity as performative and mutable, and developing nuanced and collaborative adult characters who had previously occupied tyrannical, static positions in these types of narratives. The longer version of this project develops these ideas across multiple high school musicals. Here, I focus on the way *Bring It On: The Musical* revises and recuperates the figure of the "queen bee," the popular, pretty girl who sits atop the high school social pyramid and bullies the other students. Next, I examine how the musical *Mean Girls* celebrates social egalitarianism through performance.

High school musicals on Broadway draw from a genealogy that includes 1980s John Hughes high school films and their legacy in the 1990s, along with a couple of high school musicals during earlier eras (specifically *Bye, Bye Birdie* [1960] and *Grease* [1971]), and three musicals of the 2000s: *Hairspray* (2003), *Spring Awakening* (2006), and Disney's made-for-television *High School Musical* (2006). Beginning with John Hughes's *Sixteen Candles* (1984), *The Breakfast Club* (1985), *Ferris Bueller's Day Off* (1986), and *Pretty in Pink* (1986), conventions of high school narratives carefully delineate the social status of archetypes such as the nerd and the jock, yet all the characters are presented as conventionally attractive, even if they wear glasses and refer to themselves as a geek or a loser. Staunchly antiauthoritarian, Hughes's films situate grown-ups as out of touch, occasionally harmless, but always a force to be overcome. Heterosexual romance is the raison d'être of these high school films; the lovers hail from different social circles, and these differences constitute part of the attraction they share. Writing about the effect Hughes's films have had on subsequent high school movies, cultural studies critic Roz Kaveney argues, "The mere fact that films consciously imitated him, or consciously subverted tropes that he established, is crucial to the existence of teen films as a genre. . . . After Hughes, teen movies would always be knowing."[4] Indeed, there's a self-referentiality to works of this genre that almost constitutes a break with realism.

Self-consciously aware of the ways in which they negotiate the tropes established by Hughes, the high school films of the '90s such as *Clueless* (1995), *10 Things I Hate About You* (1999), *She's All That* (1999), and *American Pie* (1999) continue to center heterosexual romance that requires core characters to navigate a clique culture separating them from their love interest. Teen films of the 1990s, according to film critic Robin Wood, are "extremely conservative, for all their determination to shock; the ideal remains true love and monogamy, the women are divided into 'nice girls' (usually virgins) and 'bitches,' depending upon whether they attach themselves to the central male character or dump him; notions of sexual freedom or 'free love' are never offered as desirable alternatives to the traditional forms of sexual organization."[5] Even a film seemingly promoting girl power and riot grrrl culture like *10 Things I Hate About You* sees its fiercely independent female protagonist forgive the boy who only asked her out because someone paid him to and settle into a traditional romance with him.

The three dominant high school musicals of the first decade of the 2000s, *Hairspray*, *Spring Awakening*, and *High School Musical*, vary significantly in their approaches to understanding adolescence. *Hairspray* posits that a young, white teenager can be at the forefront of racial integration. *Spring Awakening* offers a poetic yet bleak take on the oppression of young people by the adults with power over them, while *High School Musical* celebrates school unity during a pep rally. These three musicals of the 2000s mark a significant increase in musical theatre's interest in the high school experience and establish the groundwork for the next decade. Since the early 2010s, musicals about the high school experience have proliferated both on Broadway and Off Broadway. In a 2019 blog post on *Medium*, Alexandra Middleditch writes, "Ask just about anyone who keeps up with Broadway, and most people will agree that it's having a bit of a teen musical moment."[6]

Middleditch broadly addresses any musical featuring a teenage protagonist. I wish to distinguish the 2010s high school musical as a distinct genre—one that features scenes set in the hallways or classrooms; grapples with major high school events such as the prom, the house party, or the school play; and foregrounds negotiating school cliques as central to students' understanding of the world and their place in it. While *The Breakfast Club* allows audiences the chance to see representatives from various cliques come to understand and even like each other, it concludes with each student departing alone. Popular-girl Claire gives a speech about what will happen on Monday, predicting that the students who had bonded during Saturday detention would avoid or make fun of each other once school resumes. Through Claire's speech, the film signals that any breakdown in the social order was temporary.[7] The musicals of the 2010s, however, resist Hughes's pessimism and rigidity. They frame relationships with adults as more collaborative than oppressive, revel in the fluidity of identity, and celebrate a more egalitarian social structure—a structure that the characters achieve via performance.

While *Bring It On: The Musical*'s opening number, "What I Was Born to Do," engages with themes of popularity and belonging, it also sets up a departure from the centrality of the queen bee figure. The song is sung from the perspective of protagonist Campbell, and she informs the audience that she's become a cheerleader and "now my life is every adolescent's favorite dream. Slow motion down the hall, as kids all stop and stare. I feel like I'm a part of it all for the first time."[8] In earlier versions of high school narratives, Campbell would structurally be positioned as a typical queen bee or mean girl, which literary scholar Sara K. Day defines as "the popular girl who maintains her status in the high-school hierarchy through bullying, manipulation, and emotional blackmail." According to Day, this figure "can be traced back to at least the mid-twentieth century, and characters such as *Grease*'s Rizzo and Cha Cha DiGregorio. . . . Over time, these characters evolved away from near-juvenile delinquent status to a more polished and upscale model. . . . She is, almost without exception, white, straight, and economically privileged."[9] Yet *Bring It On*'s narrative arc avoids perpetuating the mean girl trope and ignores the clique structure of high schools in favor of a more inclusive community that values friendship rather than division, and building each other up rather than diminishing others to increase social standing.

Bring It On, book by Jeff Whitty and lyrics by Amanda Green and Lin-Manuel Miranda, premiered on Broadway in 2012 and was nominated for two Tony Awards, Best Musical and Best Choreography. With Miranda's trademark wordsmithing and Andy Blankenbuehler's hip-hop and cheer choreography, the musical veered from the original narrative of the 2000 film by the same name. In the musical, the story follows Campbell's journey from the top of the predominately white Truman High School social structure (and cheer pyramid) as she's redistricted to the majority-minority Jackson High School, which doesn't even have a cheer squad. Desperate to return to her sport and to best her former squad, now led by sophomore Eva, Campbell lies and tells Jackson students that the prize for winning the national cheer competition is a college scholarship, inspiring Danielle, the leader of the Jackson dance crew, to recruit students into a cheer squad.

Unlike golden age musicals, in which the community is often divided into two groups (farmers and cowhands in *Oklahoma!*, Jets and Sharks in *West Side Story*, gamblers and missionaries in *Guys and Dolls*), the opening songs of 2010s high school musicals often reveal a highly fractured and ossified environment, with many small communities situated in a rigid hierarchy ruled by a queen bee, a gatekeeper girl with all the social capital and who determines others' social status. And yet, unlike the films on which many of these musicals are based, 2010s musicals evacuate the trope of the queen bee of its oppressive power over both the characters within the story and the structure of the genre's narratives. *Bring It On: The Musical*'s Jackson High doesn't even have a queen bee.

The song that introduces Campbell and the audience to Jackson High School, "Do Your Own Thing," establishes immediately that the predictable social structures of white high school narratives don't exist at Jackson. Students reprimand Campbell, "don't follow me, why you on top of me, leave me alone, do your own thing," and when she confesses, "I'm so confused about who's in whose clique, who are the surfer dudes, where are the cool kids," she's told, "we don't travel in groups."[10] Potentially unmooring audiences who are accustomed to compartmentalizing characters, *Bring it On* asserts that the strength of the community comes not from conforming to expected norms but from embracing individualism.

"Do Your Own Thing" also introduces the lead members of Jackson High's dance crew, Danielle, Nautica, and La Cienega, the first trans high school student on Broadway.[11] The choreography of the song avoids full-ensemble unison dancing. Instead, the characters express their individuality through unique movement. They encourage Campbell to do the same. The students at Jackson more readily accept Bridget, the unpopular girl from Truman who played the school mascot at games and was also redistricted to Jackson, than they do Campbell, praising Bridget's "junk in the trunk," welcoming her to the dance crew, and later singing "It Ain't No Thing" with her, an anthem of body positivity. The narrative sets adrift both Campbell and the stale high school structures established by the movies of John Hughes.

The musical also resists the white savior trope (unlike, say, *Hairspray*). Most narratives with a similar premise would see Campbell assume a leadership position over students of color and transform Jackson's hip-hop crew into an award-winning cheer squad. Instead, Danielle remains the leader of the crew and the one who decides how much access and power to give the new white girl. This dynamic might seem to position Danielle as the mean girl, but she's never cruel or manipulative. Her power comes from her honesty and her skill as a dancer, and both she and the musical value hard work and perseverance as vital to both friendship and performance (dance and cheering). Danielle flips burgers at a fast-food joint and speaks openly about how hard she's working in multiple arenas in order to go to college, but the musical doesn't pity or condescend to her. In this way, Danielle's character resists "the larger discourse of adolescent womanhood as conflict-oriented and survival-driven" and "impressions of the queen bee as . . . necessarily ill-intentioned."[12] Rather, Danielle exhibits a great deal of care toward her fellow students, and Jackson High functions in a healthy way—without the presence of a queen bee.

Indeed, rather than the cat fights or relational aggression foregrounded in the female friendships of 1990s–2000s high school narratives, Campbell and Danielle's relationship provides the emotional heart of the show. In the song "Friday Night, Jackson," Campbell attempts to prove herself to Danielle by donning the school's leprechaun mascot suit and dancing after the football game. Impressed that Campbell's not too proud to be goofy and dorky, Danielle sings, "Look at this little rich white girl turning it out, wow, I can't be mad at that, look at her go. Look at this little rich white girl movin' the crowd, wow, she's not half bad at that. Look at her go!"[13] Although Danielle and Campbell become friends, conflict arises after Danielle discovers Campbell's deception about the college scholarships and she essentially ends their friendship.

With Danielle's introduction to the story coming midway through "Do Your Own Thing," during which she pushes Campbell aside singing, "I said move!," and their eleven o'clock number staging their emotional reunion, the trajectory of their narrative arcs draws more from *Wicked* than from the high school film genre. The initial friction that defined their relationship transforms into deep feeling, a painful rupture, and a moving reconciliation culminating in the duet "We're Not Done" in which Danielle sings, "It's easy to ignore you when I see you down the hall. It's easy to be angry. It's easy not to call. To throw away this thing we had, and blame it all on you. It's harder to admit, I miss it too." Their voices braid complementary melodies and intertwine in harmony until they end in unison on "we're not done."[14] This eleven o'clock number, which reads as queerly as *Wicked*'s "For Good," situates friendship in terms of collaboration, empathy, and emotional honestly. Wolf defines an eleven o'clock number as "an emotional tour de force," arguing, "this number tends to be when the heterosexual couple sings of their finally achieved love for one another," and she persuasively demonstrates the ways in which "For Good" positions Elphaba and Glinda as the romantic couple at the center of *Wicked*.[15] While *Wicked*'s conclusion permanently separates its two leading ladies, *Bring It On* makes an optimistic claim for Danielle and Campbell's future. Reunited, they compete in nationals, and after losing to the Truman squad, they, along with other Jackson students, sing "I Got

You," a song about valuing friendship above winning. In this way, *Bring It On* situates the high school experience as rooted in inclusive performance—friendships are made and lost via dance, and while cheering has a reputation for rigid gender binaries and excluding nonnormative bodies, their crew celebrates bodies of various sizes and nonbinary genders.

The character that most closely approximates the mean girl in *Bring It On* is Eva, the Truman sophomore who blackmails her school board mother to redistrict Campbell, then steals Campbell's cheer squad, boyfriend, and hairstyle. But while Eva is cruel and manipulative, she never occupies a position as gatekeeper of social capital (apart from the redistricting), and although members of Campbell's former squad defend Eva when Campbell accuses her of lying her way to squad captain, no one worships her and Eva cannot be said to be the queen bee. Through its structural differences from the standard narrative arc of this genre, and its racial and gender politics, *Bring It On* puts forward a new model for understanding the high school experience.

Mean Girls likewise dismantles the reductive social units so entrenched in the high school genre, although it does so through foregrounding the performance of everyday life (whereas *Bring It On: The Musical* foregrounds cheerleading and dance performance) as a way to resist the essentialism embedded in popular understandings of the high school experience. Tina Fey's 2004 film of the same name, on which the musical is based, directly tackles the teen film conventions. Film studies scholar Joseph Walderzak writes, "in perhaps no other film of the genre has the relationship between popularity and power been so resolutely revealed."[16] The musical's emphasis on performance as vital to maintaining, revealing, and dismantling hierarchies takes the film's self-consciousness one step further. With music by Jeff Richmond, lyrics by Nell Benjamin, and book by Tina Fey, *Mean Girls* tells the story of Cady Heron's transfer from Africa, where her American parents conducted field research, to North Shore High School in Chicago. Befriended by art kids Damien and Janis, Cady goes on a mission to topple queen bee Regina and the Plastics and in so doing becomes a "mean girl" herself.

Cady's journey to becoming a Plastic involves layers of performance, including masquerading as a true friend of Regina and the two other Plastics, Gretchen and Karen. But the lines between performance and authenticity collapse as Cady begins to feel affection for the Plastics and superiority to all other North Shore students. In other words, the musical suggests that what high schoolers "put on" becomes their reality, even as audiences are given a front-row view to the beauty regimes and social routines that the Plastics perform every day to accumulate status. As Cady's star rises, she strips away the trappings of popularity from Regina, including her looks, her friends, and her boyfriend, revealing the ways in which these layers are not innate but a carefully crafted performance.

Mean Girls puts forward multiple understandings of the way performance can operate in a high school setting. While Cady's performance as a Plastic demonstrates the dangers of pretending, Damien's character basks in the playfulness of theatrical performance and Gretchen's character reveals the painful cost of trying to perform the role of "woman." Damien is conscious of his own singing and dancing, interjecting "Kick! Layout! Fosse!" into the first verse of the opening song, "A Cautionary Tale."[17] His musical style is solidly classic Broadway, his dance is jazz, and he quotes musicals like *Funny Girl* to emphasize his points. Damien isn't a buff leading man, nor does he buy into that kind of hype. Instead, he finds joy in his own performance and locates authenticity in theatricality.

Gretchen, on the other hand, understands the relation between performance, gender, and the debilitating effects of trying to maintain power as a woman in high school. Her song "What's Wrong with Me," directed in part at Regina, includes the questions: "What's wrong with me? How I speak? How I dress? . . . What's wrong with me? What can I do? What's wrong with me? Could it be you? It's probably me."[18] Significantly, one of the few lines that isn't a question is Gretchen's assertion that her own deficiencies are probably what's wrong with her. Yet through the way the women of *Mean Girls* sing their feelings, the audience is positioned to understand that the problem lies not with Gretchen or even Regina but with impossible standards of beauty for women.

Mean Girls demonstrates how far the high school genre has come in terms of recognizing the performativity of identity—that gender and even social status requires iterative performance, repetition of individual behavior solidifying the social hierarchy—as opposed to the genre's former essentialist understanding of identity rooted in innateness. In her anthem "I'd Rather Be Me," Janice sings, "We're supposed to all be ladies and be nurturing and care. Is that really fair? Boys get to fight, we have to share. Here's the way that turns out: We always understand how to slap someone down with our underhand. So here's my right finger to how girls should behave, cause sometimes what's meant to break you, makes you brave. So I will not act all innocent. I won't fake apologize. Let's just fight and then make up, not tell these lies."[19] Janice redirects the audience's attention away from who people *are* (the mean girl, the new girl, etc.) toward how people *behave*. In other words, unlike *The Breakfast Club*'s letter to the principal, which focuses on identity categories ("a brain, and an athlete, and a basket case, a princess, and a criminal"), Janice focuses on what students *do*.

In so doing, *Mean Girls* suggests that categories are fluid, mistakes can be forgiven, and mean girls can be redeemed.

From introducing new tropes such as the Party Song, in which students reveal their innermost hopes and fears while on mind-altering substances at a party at another student's house ("Who's House Is This" in *Mean Girls*, "Big Fun" in *Heathers*, "Halloween" in *Be More Chill*); braiding cell phone use, social media, and cyber bullying into the fabric of the narrative (*Dear Evan Hansen*, *Bare*, *Mean Girls*); and more constructive relationships between teenagers and adults (the principal and Emma in *The Prom*, Sister Joan and Peter in *Bare*), high school musicals of the 2010s respond to changing cultural understandings about adolescence. These musicals are wildly popular; *Be More Chill* ranked five on the list of most-streamed musical cast albums of 2019 and four on the list of most-streamed cast albums of the decade, besting megamusicals such as *Les Mis* and *The Lion King*. *Dear Evan Hansen* took the number two slot on both lists, and *Mean Girls* took number eight on the 2019 list.[20] While the longer version of this project delves into other characteristics of this genre, such as the ones I list above, what I want to emphasize here is that musicals of the 2010s decenter the heterosexual romance at the heart of the teen films and golden age musicals that came before and productively embrace multiplicity and fluidity of identity as integral to building lasting community. They're also loads of fun.

Notes

1. For a thorough explication of the category "golden age," the various ways scholars have deployed the term, and the benefits and drawbacks of its continued use, see Jessica Sternfeld and Elizabeth L. Wollman, "After the 'Golden Age,'" in *The Oxford Handbook of the American Musical*, ed. Raymond Knapp, Mitchell Morris, and Stacy Wolf (Oxford: Oxford University Press, 2011), 111–24.
2. Stacy Wolf, *Changed for Good: A Feminist History of the Broadway Musical* (New York: Oxford, 2011), 22.
3. See Raymond Knapp, *The American Musical and the Formation of National Identity* (Princeton, NJ: Princeton University Press, 2005); and Raymond Knapp, *The American Musical and the Performance of Personal Identity* (Princeton, NJ: Princeton University Press, 2006).
4. Roz Kaveney, *Teen Dreams; Reading Teen Film and Television from Heathers to Veronica Mars* (New York: Palgrave Macmillan, 2006), 12.
5. Robin Wood, "Party Time, or Can't Hardly Wait for that American Pie: Hollywood High School Movies of the 90s," *Cineaction*, 2002, 5.
6. Alexandra Middleditch, "Broadway Critics Have a Problem with Teen Musicals. How Do

We Solve It?" *Medium*, October 17, 2019, https://medium.com/@alexandra.middleditch/broadway-critics-have-a-problem-with-teen-musicals-how-do-we-solve-it-95bd08788adc.

7. *The Breakfast Club*, directed by John Hughes. USA: Universal Pictures, 1985.
8. Jeff Whitty, "What I Was Born to Do," Spotify track, with Taylor Louderman, *Bring It On: The Musical* (Original Broadway Cast), 2012.
9. Sara K. Day, "Mean Girls End Up Dead: The Dismal Fate of Teen Queen Bees in Popular Culture," in *Bad Girls and Transgressive Women in Popular Television, Fiction, and Film*, ed. Julie A. Chappell and Mallory Young (Cham, Switzerland: Palgrave McMillan, 2017), 138.
10. Jeff Whitty, "Do Your Own Thing," Spotify track, with Taylor Louderman and Adrienne Warren, *Bring It On: The Musical* (Original Broadway Cast), 2012.
11. See, for example, Adam Hetrick, "'It Ain't No Thing': *Bring It On: The Musical* Cheers On Broadways' First Transgender Teen Character," Playbill.com, August 15, 2012, https://www.playbill.com/article/it-aint-no-thing-bring-it-on-the-musical-cheers-on-broadways-first-transgender-teen-character-com-196686.
12. Day, "Mean Girls End Up Dead," 137.
13. Jeff Whitty, "Friday Night, Jackson," Spotify track, with Taylor Louderman and Adrienne Warren, *Bring It On: The Musical* (Original Broadway Cast), 2012.
14. Whitty, Jeff, "We're Not Done," Spotify track, with Taylor Louderman and Adrienne Warren, *Bring It On: The Musical* (Original Broadway Cast), 2012.
15. Wolf, *Changed for Good*, 167.
16. Joseph Walderzak, "Man-Candy, Hot Body, and an Army of Skanks: Mean Girls as Revisionist Text and the Teen Film Genre," *Quarterly Review of Film and Video* 36, no. 6 (2019): 500.
17. Tina Fey, "A Cautionary Tale," Spotify track, with Barrett Wilbert Weed and Grey Henson, *Mean Girls* (Original Broadway Cast Recording), 2018.
18. Tina Fey, "What's Wrong with Me?," Spotify track, with Ashley Park, *Mean Girls* (Original Broadway Cast Recording), 2018.
19. Tina Fey, "I'd Rather Be Me," Spotify track, with Barrett Wilbert Weed, *Mean Girls* (Original Broadway Cast Recording), 2018.
20. Ruthie Fierberg, "The 10 Most Streamed Cast Albums of 2019 and of the Decade," Playbill.com, January 31, 2020, https://www.playbill.com/article/the-10-most-streamed-cast-albums-of-2019-and-of-the-decade.

Part IV

BOOK REVIEWS

Edwin Forrest: A Biography and Performance History. By Arthur W. Bloom. Jefferson, NC: McFarland and Co., 2019. Pp. ix + 334. $55, paperback.

Arthur Bloom has done the field of theatre history estimable service with his biographies of Joseph Jefferson (2000) and Edwin Booth (2013). He adds to those achievements with this excellent biography of the great actor Edwin Forrest. The book's first half is a carefully researched biographical narrative. Here, general readers and historians get a clear view of Forrest's life, career, and controversies. Those interested in digging deeper have an admirable resource in its second half, which catalogues Forrest's performances day-by-day, with notes, and the author's sources year-by-year. The narrative includes the number of performances of his prominent roles, including *King Lear*, 353 times, *Metamora*, 392, *The Gladiator*, 403, and *Richelieu*, 385. Today, whether we're fans or not, gushing media gives us a sense of celebrities' careers. Bloom's count similarly suggests the overall shape of the career of the United States' first star actor, plotting the roles he favored and his audiences cheered.

Parsing Forrest's life is no easy task. He's now as much symbol as actor, a site—like Marilyn Monroe, another famous performer with a famous body—on which writers project theories, signs, and body critiques. Agile enough to have been a circus acrobat (15–16), with a barrel chest and legs like tree trunks, Forrest becomes emblematic for historians inclined to see the era's theatre, its crowds, and the country as deplorably crude. His powerful physique fades to stiff poses in photographs, while "rant" is applied so routinely to describe his vocal power that the term seems obligatory. Readings of his personal life dovetail with those of his professional life. For example, his scandalous divorce included credible accusations of infidelity on both sides yet often shrinks in the telling to a blunt dichotomy: American brute vs. sophisticated Englishwoman wronged. The deadly Astor Place Riot of 1849 had social and political causes, which have been analyzed with depth and subtlety, yet the precipitating feud between the British star William Macready and Forrest shrivels to another rudimentary opposition of brawn versus refinement. It's hard to see Forrest for the tree-trunk legs.

Bloom works mightily to untangle these simplifications. While acknowledging criticism of the actor's dynamic style, the author also quotes contemporaries who celebrated his greatness. Considering Forrest's protests that English critics allied against him, Bloom notes both the influence of the actor's ego *and* that he had cause for complaint. Against the image of a self-involved star, he sets Forrest's care for friends and family and his generosity. Most impressively, Bloom veers from the traditional praise of rival Macready as refined to give a fuller picture of Forrest's refinement: his extensive book collection, his intellectual friends, his careful research into roles. He was not the primitive of caricature, blustering his way through his characters. He initiated play contests, Bloom notes, not only to add roles he could play but also to encourage the young country's playwrights. He relished *Richelieu* because it enabled him to exercise his "verbal wit" (61). Edmund Kean praised his talent as a young colleague, while Forrest found in the great English actor a model for his own "impulsive displays of passion, the fiery spurts of eloquence that made the pit tremble, and the realistic bursts of physical movement" (19–20). Forrest disliked depictions of Richard III as a "moody villain," writing in 1837 that he preferred to play him as "dashing," with a "reckless regal jollity" (55), a strikingly modern insight. This evidence shows a more nuanced figure than the historiography tends to recognize.

Bloom's inclusion of Forrest's personal life adds insight into his professional life. Histories regularly comment that his 1852 divorce from Catherine Sinclair Forrest titillated the country; less often noted is that she implicitly took sides, moving out the day Macready arrived in New York for his ill-fated Astor Place engagement (105). Forrest lost two years to the divorce, and another sixteen until final settlement, sapping time, energy, and emotion that he might have otherwise devoted to work (111). Bloom deeply considers Forrest's romantic life, further documenting the actor's diary accounts of his sexual practice. At first, this archive seems to fit the preening of the blunt stereotype: visits to brothels, sending a servant for a condom, and so on (46, 48). Yet, this evidence is more complex, indicating the searching soul that informed his roles. He saved a playful letter to "dear Ed" from "Kitty the Spinner" that suggests a paramour yet also a family friend, who urges him to write to his mother (16). He loved Paris restaurants, "where men and women mixed freely" (41). He conducted a romantic, not sexual, amour with a Russian countess (47–49). Bloom's discussion of Forrest's personal life avoids oversimplification by attending to dynamics of desire that could get lost among the emerging preference for decorum and "subtle" acting.

Bloom doesn't fully escape symbolism's gravitational pull. He quotes a New York paper's declaration in 1837 that "Forrest is all nature and Macready all art" (57), as if the meaning was clear: Forrest as boisterous force of nature, Macready as artistry personified. However, a historicized reading clarifies that "art" hadn't yet acquired its elevated connotation and meant then artifice or craft, what the quotation renders as "finishing touches," while "nature" was what our age might consider emotional realism, an actor following his impulses, expressing feelings, loudly or softly, as the character's situation required. Bloom also echoes an enduring historiographical mistake. Historians repeat that in 1846 Walt Whitman complained of Forrest's "loud mouthed ranting style" (1). However, Whitman wasn't referring to the great actor himself but to less-talented *imitators*. Finally, while Bloom does discuss the formidable cultural forces that sparked the Astor Place Riot, he also paints Forrest as culpable, arguing that Forrest could have stopped this riot because he had stopped earlier riots (96–97). These issues inadvertently reinforce the debatable link often made between Forrest's physicality and the era's violence.

It helps to recall that Forrest flourished in the same soil that nourished Whitman's blend of the exultant "I" and democratic multitudes, in the same air that prompted Ralph Waldo Emerson to advocate for American expression. During Forrest's long career, the United States swung to a preference for a quieter, decorous style of performance, exemplified by Edwin Booth. Though restraint still finds favor—it fits movies perfectly—our contemporary cultural fashion shouldn't obscure the richness and nuance of Forrest's acting. Bloom makes its force clear, as he fashions a well-rounded picture of the dynamic actor who spoke to and for a dynamic culture, then—to use the era's new phrase—aborning.

—DAVID CARLYON
Independent Scholar

Political Dramaturgies and Theatre Spectatorship: Provocations for Change. By Liz Tomlin. London: Methuen Drama, 2019. Pp. ix + 205. $90.00, hardcover.

An important theoretical question animates Liz Tomlin's new book: How, given the swell of interest in enabling an autonomous, liberated spectator in theatre and theatre studies, can we keep sight of dramaturgies that still seek to guide their audiences toward specific liberatory futures? In asking this question, Tomlin pinpoints a crucial tension in recent post-Marxist scholarship on political theatre: the tension between a logic of autonomy, which invests the spectator with new levels of self-determination, and an egalitarian logic, which seeks to convince its audiences of specific political stances, what she calls "ideological steer." Grappling with both current conversations in the field of theatre studies and a range of contemporary performances in the United Kingdom, Tomlin's study offers up a useful counterbalance by resuscitating some key concepts from activist theatre and holding them in careful balance with more recent trends. The result is a book that offers an erudite reframing of how scholars and practitioners both might conceptualize not just the politics of theatrical spectatorship but also the spectator herself.

As much as the study is grounded in the experience of theatrical representation, Tomlin is primarily concerned with the critical conversation, and she is careful to stake out her interlocutors—empirical audience research, the critical work of Jacques Rancière and those that follow, and the theories of Ernesto Laclau and Chantal Mouffe. Hans-Thies Lehmann's work on postdramatic spectatorship lurks in the background here, but Tomlin clearly explains her break from that work, with its tendency to collapse form and politics. This propensity, she asserts, is also true of the logic of autonomy, which is imagined to be political in form, emancipatory in effect, and yet simultaneously supportive of an uncoupling of politics and theatre.

Tomlin's engagement with Rancière's autonomous spectator and her objection to empirical research hinge on a specific observation: that the spectator who might be both observed and emancipated currently exists specifically and inextricably within the commodified and precarious context of neoliberal political economy. In both cases, she sees the logic of autonomy as coincident with the rise of the neoliberal subject, for whom autonomy is also a hallmark of "the precarity of her position . . . and leads to a reduction in her capacity for empathy, agency and ability to make better futures" (7).

Tomlin's move to theorize the "spectator-subject" signals precisely her notion of the spectator as always already interpellated into culture; section one, which contains three chapters—on real and imagined spectators, on the autonomous spectator, and on the precarious spectator—illustrates this context by insisting that the actual autonomous spectator is so bound up in the contexts of neoliberalism that her autonomy can end up being libertarian rather than liberatory. Tomlin's stance, then, is that the autonomy of the spectator must constantly be held in balanced tension with the actual politics of the performance itself, holding that some "ideological steer" is always necessary to stave off the alienating subjectivity of neoliberalism. This is a nuanced revision of Rancière's influential position, and a convincing one.

The second section of the book moves this theorized spectator-subject into the context of specific contemporary performances and employs an analysis that examines the logic of autonomy in specific relationship to the egalitarian politics that a given performance may or may not adopt. After a brief framing of this methodology, Tomlin embarks on concise analyses of several contemporary UK performances along four key vectors: irony and interpellation, autonomy and affect, empathy and agonism, and antagonism and agency. In the first case, Tomlin examines the dramaturgy of ironic interpellation, in which a performance casts audience members as already-complicit subjects of the neoliberal moment, only to expose neoliberalism's discontents within this framework. Using Made in China's *Gym Party* (2013) and Martin Crimp's *In the Republic of Happiness* (2012), she shows how these productions teeter on the tightrope between egalitarian rhetoric and individual autonomy while exposing some of the dangers for individual spectators who might or might not fit comfortably within the ironic subject positions these performances prescribe.

The chapter on autonomy and affect extends and applies Tomlin's engagement with Rancière, bringing Nicholas Ridout's *Passionate Amateurs* into the discussion as a direct stand-in specifically within the context of theatre studies, suggesting that Ridout's examination of the affective form of the *labor* of theatre-making might stand in for the politics of the theatre that is made. This rebuttal might be the book's weakest argument, in part because the case studies of the work of Kieran Hurley (2016) and Andy Smith (2012, 2018) that follow refute by arguing affirmatively for the opposite—for politically effective work that is nonetheless formally disinterested. In this way, she continues to make a case for retaining a sense of political engagement in the content of contemporary performance, while her critique of the limits of emancipated spectatorship, convincing as it is, remains largely theoretical.

The last two chapters, though, escape this trap, as they pick up the work of Mouffe to help frame work in which an egalitarian logic comes to the fore. In these chapters, analyses of the theatre-of-real-people production *Queens of Syria* (2016), Chris Thorpe and Rachel Chavkin's *Confirmation* (2014), and Common Wealth Theatre's *The Deal Versus the People* (2015), retrain a critical eye back on the politics of the performances themselves while holding that gaze simultaneously on the productions' configuration of the spectator-subject as able to ethically engage in the political terms of the performance itself.

The takeaway is, as Tomlin terms it, "a modest corrective," but it is an important one, too: to refrain from completely discarding dramaturgies that seek political change through their content and artistic intention in favor of an otherwise dogged pursuit of spectatorial autonomy (180). It's a false choice, Tomlin argues, and one that (in this political-economic context) may well undermine its own aims. In this focused and thoughtful study, we may land on a mode of understanding political dramaturgies that is not too distant from modes that have held in theatre studies for decades but that is balanced meaningfully with the post-Marxist modes of thinking that populates much of the thinking of recent studies of political theatre.

—**RYAN CLAYCOMB**
Colorado State University

Unfair Labor? American Indians and the 1893 World's Columbian Exposition in Chicago. By David R. M. Beck. Lincoln: University of Nebraska Press, 2019. Pp. ix + 299. $65.00, hardcover.

In August 1891, Emma Reeves wrote to federal officials seeking employment at the Chicago World's Fair, offering her services as an Abenaki basket weaver who would dress in "Indian costume or in citizens dress" as directed (12). She was hired by the fair's anthropology director, Frederic Ward Putnam, to perform in his ethnological village . . . as an Iroquois. During the years 1891–1893, Fort Rupert Kwakwaka'wakw George Hunt traveled the Pacific Northwest, collecting items for the fair's Northwest Coast Canadian Indian exhibit, including ceremonial masks, dishes, tools, and a multifamily house (60). Hunt, who later became a noted ethnographer and linguist, was paid decently for his efforts, and the tribal communities from which he collected were compensated in cash.

Reeves and Hunt were two of the hundreds of American Indians who found employment through the World's Columbian Exposition. Hundreds of additional tribal members engaged with the fair from a distance, selling material culture items to acquisitive exhibitors. David R. M. Beck's *Unfair Labor?: American Indians and the 1893 World's Columbian Exposition in Chicago* is the most comprehensive treatment of Native work at the fair yet written, tracing the varied paths by which American Indians joined and labored in its workforce. In doing so, it closely attends to the economic and social factors that encouraged Indians to partake in the Exposition (and, by extension, its colonialist agenda). As Beck argues, "the fair reflects a pivotal moment in history as American Indians increasingly entered a cash economy that was extending even beyond the nation's borders" (xvi). Given the Office of Indian Affairs' persistent obstructing and weakening of tribal economies, the fair's cash economy allowed some Indians to "gain greater control of the profits of their own labor and production in an increasingly capitalist world" (xviii).

Beck's scholarly interventions in *Unfair Labor?* complicate and deepen conventional readings of American Indian involvement in the fair. ("American Indians"/"Indians" are Beck's preferred terms throughout the book, though he also employs "Indigenous" and "Native" in describing his book's subjects.) First, he proves through expertly applied archival research that while the fair's ethnological villages depended on American Indians to reenact tribal life for millions of visitors, performing was by no means the only job accessible to Native workers. Some operated as agents, securing families of American Indians to inhabit the villages; others "scoured Indian country" (51) for Native handiwork, ceremonial objects, and tools of subsistence for Putnam's anthropological exhibits or served on the Columbian Guard, the fairgrounds' temporary police force. In contradicting the extant literature's suggestion that the Exposition almost exclusively employed Indians to stage their indigeneity, Beck asserts there was a more complex, unsettled, and (at times) mutually beneficial relationship at work between Native Americans and the fair's officials and audiences. Beck does not refute the imperialist ideologies driving the World's Columbian Exposition; rather, he contends that, just as the fair's officials used American Indians, American Indians "used the fair to infuse their lives into the larger American cultural landscape and its globalizing economy through economic means" (xviii).

Second, Beck deliberately toggles between the stories of individuals and groups, emphasizing the heterogenous attitudes, actions, and responses of indigenous peoples to the Chicago World's Fair. This historiographical strategy pairs profitably with one of the book's biggest gifts: an appendix titled "American Indians and Other Indigenous People Affiliated with the United States at the Fair." Organized by tribal affiliation, the appendix includes notes on how each individual was occupied at the fair, whether it be to work or to visit. Beyond its clear benefit to scholars of the Exposition or broader historical disciplines (indigenous studies, labor studies, nineteenth-century popular culture), the appendix is an elegant refutation of broad-strokes treatments of the fair's American Indians. Indeed, Beck's efforts in *Unfair Labor?* complement the scholarly work of Melissa Rinehart, Rosemarie K. Bank, Bridget R. Cooks, Christopher Robert Reed, and Ellen P. Conant, all of whom direct readers to reject narrow explanations of what Black Americans, Native Americans, and foreigners of color thought, felt, and did at the 1893 Exposition.

Unfair Labor? is divided into three parts. In two chapters, part one addresses how the fair constructed its narrative of Native Americans and how, in turn, Native Americans pushed for partial agency over their depictions. Shunning the civilized/primitive binary historians often apply to the Exposition's Native exhibits, Beck proposes that American Indian representation at the fair actually "fell into five categories: Indians as they wanted themselves to be understood, Indians as objects of science, Indians as assimilating into American society, Indians as romantic images and actors reflecting a bygone era, and Indians as savage or wild representations of America's past" (5). Part two focuses on the ways American Indians engaged in preparations for the fair and the financial and social outcomes of this work. Across three chapters, Beck examines the efforts of display organizers, individual collectors, and government bodies to actualize the fair's Native exhibits, as well as the contributions of tribal communities who made or sold objects in advance of the Exposition. These pre-fair activities earned Indians money and access to the US economy, though, as Beck writes, "the benefits were unevenly distributed. Some Native communities—those with a combination of market demand and market savvy—benefited to a greater extent than others. But all were at a disadvantage due to colonial power structures and relations" (101). Part three's three chapters address American Indian labor once the fair began, including staging Native life, participating in special ceremonies, and learning at the onsite educational school, among other positions. Unique among the book's chapters is chapter 8, "Those Left Out," which summarizes the failed attempts of Native individuals or groups to work with or for the Exposition.

There is very little to fault in this readable and well-researched text. Any redundancies appear as a function of the book's organization, as Beck's chronological approach compels him to revisit figures and sites he introduced in earlier chapters. These repetitions are few and unobtrusive. Theatre historians of world's fairs might find themselves perplexed by the relative lack of references to our field's literature on the subject, given the importance of living exhibits to Beck's project. Such texts would have assisted Beck in better articulating how the fair's Native American villagers were laborers who *performed* work for paying audiences. Still, these are insignificant quibbles when compared with the book's many accomplishments.

What makes *Unfair Labor?* especially gratifying to read is that it is both a compelling work of scholarship in its own right *and* an auspicious starting place for future researchers. This dual design feels purposeful on the author's part. Beck, a seasoned historian with a reputation for lucid prose, is modeling (particularly in the appendix but throughout the book as well) a scholarly generosity that tacitly acknowledges how historical knowledge is built, distributed, absorbed, and remade. A meaningful addition to Beck's body of work and the University of Nebraska Press's noteworthy catalogue of Native American and indigenous studies titles, *Unfair Labor?* demystifies, nuances, and legitimizes American Indians' participation in the 1893 Chicago World's Fair.

—MEREDITH CONTI
University at Buffalo, SUNY

Theatres of Contagion: Transmitting Early Modern to Contemporary Performance. Edited by Fintan Walsh. New York: Methuen Drama, 2020. pp. xii + 232. $101.00 hardcover.

As I read through this collection, concerns related to COVID-19 surrounded daily, and I regularly encountered evolving understandings of contagion's powerful and lasting effects. Arguments about transmission and contraction, two overarching themes in the new collection *Theatres of Contagion*, edited by Fintan Walsh, address the urgency of examining contagion on a global scale, including the contagious affective and emotional power of performance. As the collection shows, theatre scholarship should rightly take up contagion as a concept that expands performance's power to invigorate the stage, its audiences, and beyond.

Theatres of Contagion: Transmitting Early Modern to Contemporary Performance speaks to our current moment, when we are surrounded by the effects of contagion. These essays address queer sexualities, race, nation, affect, neurology, and digital technologies, explicating the intricate connections between contagion and theatre, a genre that formally puts the body on display (10). Theatre's engagement with contagion ranges from incorporating this theme into the content of a play to the ways theatre's formal structures transmit affect to theatregoers. Spanning examples from the early modern period to contemporary drama, as well as immersive projects like the *Macbeth*-inspired horror hotel production *Sleep No More* (2011) and virtual reality technologies, the many sites in this collection speak to the significance of performance for understanding the vulnerability and susceptibility we all share to contagion in its various forms.

Walsh's introduction to the collection highlights a central tension in the study of contagion: while contagion elicits fear and anxiety, it also can activate an element of desire. With a recognition of how contagion extends to many different disciplinary sites of knowledge production, Walsh maintains, "These definitions do not account for how contagion morphs under the influence of power and desire, which are crucial to understanding cultural processes or practices" (7). Throughout the collection, essays stage how contagion "shapes our sense of self and other(ness), particularly in terms of identity, community, and belonging" (7). Indeed, this collection offers many insights into the ways that contagion has shaped, and continues to shape, theatre and performance as cultural production, along intersecting vectors of attraction and anxiety.

The volume is broken down into three separate sections and each centers on a primary aspect of contagion in forms of theatre. In the first section, "Infectious Bodies and Behaviours," essays reference early modern theatre's constructions of bodies and affects, beginning with Walsh's essay on Dickie Beau's *Remember Me* (2017), a queer adaptation of *Hamlet* that focuses on AIDS memory and kinship. Moving toward sensory and affective contagion in theatrical spaces, Marcus Cheng Chye Tan and Shani Bans examine how the affective frequencies prevalent in Shakespeare's work affected the bodies of theatre spectators in the early modern period by looking to plays such as *Romeo and Juliet*, *Henry VI*, and *As You Like It*. The contagiousness of embodied affects holds a powerful force onstage via sensory experiences in the theatre, as both authors assert.

The second section, "Sites of Contamination and Containment," explores different forms of media and performance addressing contagion and plague. The chapters range from Sophocles's *Oedipus Rex* all the way to the contemporary moment with *Bio Inc. - Biomedical Plague* (2018), a simulator where players are invited to create the most lethal illness possible, as Kirsten E. Shepherd-Barr describes in her contribution. Essays in this section take up contagion's entanglement with biomedical and social realms. Julius Green focuses on psychogenic and neurological effects of theatre as contagion by examining examples of fainting during performances at Parisian Theatre du Grand (1897–1926). Molly McPhee's treatment of criminality in Clean Break's 2013 *Dream Pill* and *Little on the Inside* and Lynne McCarthy's work on analyzing how environmental racism plays out in 2011 representations of an eviction of three hundred Irish travelers in Dale Farm, Essex, help foreground the importance of the felt effects of race and class when considering contagion and performance.

The final section of the collection, "Conducting Emotions, Moods, and Minds," highlights the sensory experiences of contagion in more experimental performance forms. Ana Pais breaks down the divide between performance and audience participation in the horror hotel production *Sleep No More*, whose dynamics of felt experience, Pais argues, involve the physiological effects of music. Mark Pizzato examines the relationship between inner and outer contagion in theatrical performance by drawing on cognitive and neurological science and the concept of imitative spreading. Liam Jarvis wraps up the collection with a piece that reconsiders affective experiences of disability through online simulation in virtual reality environments.

The wide swath of topics covered in this collection evidences a compelling range of exciting scholarship at the intersection of performance and contagion. Engaged by the many theories this intersection activates, I wanted to see more close readings from the range of texts the collection's authors explore. This collection could not come at a more appropriate moment for a world anxious and curious about what changes contagion will bring on a global scale. These essays fit nicely into the growing body of work on contagion in theatrical forms such as Darryl Clark and Mary Floyd-Wilson's 2019 collection *Contagion and the Shakespearean Stage*. Scholars across many disciplines and fields who focus on interdisciplinary approaches to understanding contagion will benefit from this book, as it centers theatre and performance's contagious effects within many different areas across the humanities, social sciences, and biomedical sciences.

—JEREMY CORNELIUS
Louisiana State University

Women Adapting: Bringing Three Serials of the Roaring Twenties to Stage and Screen. By Bethany Wood. Iowa City: University of Iowa Press, 2019. Pp. viii + 285. $89.69, cloth.

The measure of a piece of scholarship's contribution may be how many other modes of inquiry it inspires. In coining the term "adapturgy," Jane Barnette (2017) not only shed light on the poetics of adaptation but also forced a hard look at the means of production and the structures of labor surrounding a text. In her new book, Bethany Wood connects her work to Barnette's, conducting a case study of three early-twentieth-century adaptations, applying the material considerations of adapturgy to their historicized production processes. Focusing on a moment when film moguls consolidated power and aided and abetted constructions of white nationalist middle-class femininity, her chosen period is as edifying as it is provocative. However, like Barnette before her, the spine of the book also issues a sharp challenge to adaptation studies, emphasizing that "reading with an eye toward production" marks the trail forward for this field and its interdisciplinary reach (211).

In chapter 1, Wood examines the early twentieth century when cinema began to trawl print media for properties to be made into films, thereby commodifying narratives. Women were often victims of uncredited appropriations during this time of nascent copyright law. For example, during her research for what become *Showboat*, Edna Ferber "discovered that the showboat proprietors she was interviewing had dramatized some of her own magazine fiction for their shows" (13). However, copyright law became a more robust category as it concerned dramatization and screenwriting after the infamous *Ben Hur* case, *Kalem Co. v. Harper Bros* (1911). Consequently, a vigorous market for literary products emerged, giving rise to "the agent" as the conduit through which literary properties could be acquired. Initially, this market required writers to have strong literary ties to New York City, a region already dominated by men. However, as Wood recounts, the Kalem ruling left film moguls wary of novice screenwriters. As film studios turned to magazines for adaptable material with clear copyright, women's magazine serials (the subject of Wood's study) became "an important entry point" for women into the film industry (15). While women's right to autonomous creative careers was everywhere challenged, copyright law did enable women some potential creative control over their narrative properties, leading to adaptation as a singular opportunity for women who wished to "influence representations of femininity in mainstream commercial entertainment" (31). To Wood's point: The adaptations themselves are figures, the labor conditions were the ground. Thus, Wood establishes early on that the examination of labor and the means of production is a fruitful mode of inquiry for adaptation studies, particularly for those scholars for whom parity and representation are paramount.

In chapters 2–4, Wood conducts a thorough materialist reading of the adapturgy of Edith Wharton's 1920 novel *The Age of Innocence*. Wood illustrates the way magazine publishers forced an emphasis on romance and a manufactured female nationalism through the figure of the strong US American wife. Further, in 1924 Warner Bros. defied *droit moral* (the right an author has to protect her own work for alteration) to alter Wharton's original story against her wishes, demonstrating that "poor quality adaptations of works by women played into assumptions about gender and writing and thus posed more of a risk for women authors, particularly those without Wharton's venerated professional and social status" (78). The example of *The Age of Innocence* demonstrates the contortion of existing law in which Wharton was both contracted as the original author and its adaptor but had no control or oversight of the product. Warner Bros. was able to advertise her attachment to the project as a selling feature while disempowering Warton.

In chapters 5–7, Wood works through *Showboat*, spanning musical theatre as a genre, the figure of the Ziegfeld Girl, and the jump into adapting for "sound film." Wood depicts the first film adaptation of *Showboat* (Universal Studios,

1929) as a process of manufacturing a male produced version of womanhood from the more unconventional original, a process that almost entirely obscured Edna Ferber's original meditation on gender and race. Although the studio marketing used images of Laura LaPlante (Magnolia) reading the Ferber novel, their adaptation process was interrupted when the 1927 Broadway musical production of *Showboat* presented itself as a commercial opportunity to connect the film to the Ziegfeld musical. Wood claims the musical employed the lightness of the genre and the commercial viability of the hyper-sexualized Ziegfeld Girl as an insurance policy against the controversial nature of the text. Ferber tried to intervene but ultimately felt herself to be constrained by the musical theatre genre itself (147).

In chapters 8 and 9, Wood examines Anita Loos's 1925 novel *Gentlemen Prefer Blondes,* prodding fidelity and consumerist femininity and the reproduction of farce. The media of book, magazines, and live performance onstage influenced the representations of femininity found in the female protagonist, Lorelei, eventually extracting the satire of Loos's original. The 1926 dramatization was overwhelmingly successful, however, and inspired the cinematic adaptations that were to come. Wood concludes on the process, "Adaptations thus underscore larger issues of representation and identity in for-profit entertainment by highlighting the interindustrial systems poised to advance constructs, no matter how problematic, based on profit alone" (205). In this example, Wood successfully advances the notion that interindustriality is an essentially conservative practice, because maintaining the status quo is a reliably profitable endeavor.

Wood concludes that case studies such as hers are illuminating "when read with an eye on production" and light "a path along which adaptation studies might productively adapt" (211). While making her theoretical argument, her penetrating gaze at capitalist constructions of US American femininity reveals that they were manufactured by the publishing-cinema pipeline from the outset (and still influence production today). Yet, I cannot help but wish Wood exploited more of the potential for intersectionality in her discussion of gender. She covers derogatory stereotyping (73), miscegenation (122–23), blackface performance (130, 146, 182), and interindustrial racism (144–46). However, though perhaps most clanging in *Blondes* and *Showboat,* all three texts are rife with intersectional potential and also may expose upper-class white women's complicity in manufacturing US American ideologies of race through the stage and cinema, even at the expense of their own disenfranchisement. This trajectory can be explored not at the expense of gender issues but as a necessary articulation of the way gender ideologies co-function with race ideologies in the United

States. Further case studies from Wood that take a robust intersectional point of view would be welcome.

—**JENNIFER EWING-PIERCE**
Independent Scholar

Irish Drama and Theatre Since 1950. By Patrick Lonergan. London, UK: Methuen Drama, 2019. Pp. 280. $26.95, paperback.

Patrick Lonergan's history of Irish drama and theatre in the second half of the twentieth century begins where one might expect it to: the Abbey Theatre. But Lonergan does not start by calling back to the Irish Literary Revival, or the Abbey's epochal first few decades, when playwrights like J. M. Synge and W. B. Yeats premiered their new plays. Rather, he draws our attention to the hashtagged present, specifically the movement arising from #WakingTheFeminists (#WTF) that emerged following the programming announcement for the Abbey's 2016 season, a centenary remembrance of the 1916 Easter Rising. When this lineup of plays featured just one work by a female dramatist, Irish feminists mobilized to raise awareness about the underrepresentation of women in Irish theatre. As the novelist and playwright Katy Hayes told Lonergan, "We thought we could change the world . . . but the world went back to its old tricks" (4). Well into the new millennium, the Abbey Theatre found itself surrounded by conversations not about how it would progress forward but rather about how it served as a platform for issues in Irish theatre and society that have not yet gone away.

At the core of *Irish Drama and Theatre Since 1950* is a careful mapping of the repetitive patterns of Irish theatre, of how it "moves cyclically rather than teleologically" (110). The #WTF movement is one of many examples in this meticulous study wherein Irish dramatists and theatremakers turn to the past. Lonergan carefully illustrates, however, that "cyclicality" does not mean stale repetition or remaining stuck in place. Rather, these cycles build upon and advance the cycles that came before them. For example, Irish theatrical responses to restrictive Catholic sexual prohibitions in the ostensibly "lost" decade of the 1950s were renewed at the turn of the twentieth century when playwrights and theatre companies tackled the scandal of abuse by priests in the Catholic Church. For Lonergan, the continued return to signature subjects of Irish theatre is a rewarding repetition.

This can be seen most vividly in his book's fourth chapter, "Repeat and Revise," which functions as the cornerstone of Lonergan's larger argument about cyclicality. Here, he examines leading playwrights of the latter half of the twentieth century, such as Marina Carr and Martin McDonagh, and surveys stage reimaginings of canonical Irish writers like Synge and James Joyce. Building on the discussion of #WTF in the introduction, Lonergan centers women playwrights and directors in this chapter, even when discussing adaptations of male writers. Post-1950 Irish theatre and drama, Lonergan asserts, would not be the same without the work of director Garry Hynes, who "transform[ed]" Synge on the stage through her direction of McDongah's *Leenane* Trilogy (1997), which formed the bedrock of the 2004–2006 *DruidSynge* project at the Druid Theatre. "Repeat and Revise" solidifies the book's feminist comments and demonstrates that Irish theatre "does not have a clear beginning, middle and end" but should instead be thought of as a series of repetitions of key themes in Irish culture (204). This "Repeat and Revise" concept structures the whole of *Irish Drama and Theatre Since 1950*. Lonergan employs several methodological strategies throughout the text, including robust archival research, close readings of dramatic texts, and performance histories.

The book begins with 1950, despite Lonergan's aversion to straight chronology, joining recent scholarship in challenging the notion that the 1950s were a stale period in Irish theatre. The first chapter isolates three case studies to demonstrate the theatrical innovations happening in Ireland at this time, including An Taibhdhearc's 1949 commission of Siobhán McKenna to put on her Irish-language translation of George Bernard Shaw's *Saint Joan*, retitled *San Siobhán* to rebrand the work as uniquely belonging to both McKenna and Ireland. The second chapter's approach to the trend of "post-Catholicism" that emerged in Ireland after the 1950s, for instance, includes a detailed account of Frank Carney's 1946 *The Righteous Are Bold*. Lonergan reveals this drama to be an important index of how views on the treatment of women progressed in Ireland throughout the twentieth century. Where Carney's melodrama leaves sexist, Catholic-inflected social beliefs about femininity "troublingly untroubled" (48), Máiréad Ní Ghráda's 1964 legal drama *An Triail* just under two decades later challenged the "impossible circumstances" patriarchal cultures impose on women (55). Ní Ghráda's play ultimately proved "excit[ing]" for audiences who desired to see playwrights express a "willingness to grapple with difficult issues" (57).

The remaining chapters explore a host of issues domestic and international, all with an eye for their recurrence throughout Irish history. Chapter 3, "Internationalizing Irish Theatre," traces the numerous interactions Irish theatre had with playwrights from around the world and concludes with an examination of two Chekhov adaptations by Marina Carr (*Sixteen Possible Glimpses*, 2011) and

Lucy Caldwell (*Three Sisters*, 2016). Studies of difference in Irish theatre (chapter 5) and new directions in Irish theatre, particularly those responding to the Great Recession (chapter 6) round out the book, pointing to how the theatre recapitulates anew old themes like Irish-English conflict and corruption in the church. Even in a book that emphasizes cyclicality, Lonergan establishes that however far Irish theatre still has to go, it has made headway on issues of gender representation and challenged powerful institutions like the Catholic Church.

Written at a level that specialists and nonspecialists (of theatre or Ireland) alike can appreciate and available in an affordable paperback, *Irish Drama and Theatre Since 1950* offers scholarly contributions to those deeply familiar with this subject and also to those looking to broach the field for the first time. The photograph on the cover of the book—taken from the 2011 musical of the film *Once*—evokes a familiar Ireland: a group of people in raucous enjoyment, folk instruments in hand. The story Lonergan tells in his historical survey, however, is anything but one-dimensional.

—BRICE EZELL
University of Texas at Austin

Mixed Faith and Shared Feeling: Theater in Post-Reformation London. By Musa Gurnis. Philadelphia: University of Pennsylvania Press, 2018. Pp. 272. $55.95, cloth.

Mixed Faith and Shared Feeling effectively challenges several misconceptions about playgoing and religious life in early modern London. The average Puritan, it turns out, was not the avid antitheatricalist one might have assumed. The book presents an image of London's theatregoing community as confessionally diverse, with devout Calvinists, recusant Catholics, and even your pious Puritan brushing shoulders at the theatre. Musa Gurnis's first monograph offers a meaningful exploration of the mixed-faith landscape of post-Reformation London theatre.

Employing a cultural materialist framework, the book focuses on the playhouse as an agent of cultural change, not a mere reflection of dominant cultural ideology. It foregrounds plays as events that "*refract* the confessional material they stage" (1). One of Gurnis's particular strengths, perhaps reinforced by her own professional experience as actress and dramaturg, is her sensitivity to theatre as a collection of moments, perceived or felt from an array of vantage points. Ultimately, readers gain a strong appreciation for how early modern playgoers, and even playwrights, routinely engaged with dissimilar belief systems. Readers are left with a strong impression of how multifaith, ideologically diverse audiences were not only prominent but also key to commercial success.

The book has a two-pronged argument indicated by its title. First, it establishes "mixed faith" commingling as central to London's post-Reformation theatre. Then, it describes how theatre allowed audiences to explore various religious beliefs through acts of "shared feeling." The latter might include adopting confessional viewpoints that weren't one's own. Shakespeare's *Measure for Measure* (1603–1604), for example, offers a way by which Calvinist anxieties toward predestination became a point of dramatic entry for spectators from an array of faith backgrounds (chapter 5). Through such experiences, theatre offered, as Gurnis describes, "imaginative processes that allowed playgoers to engage with the always-changing tangle of religious life" (1). The argument is persuasive and conscientious not to suggest some utopian fantasy. An analysis of Middleton's *A Game at Chess* (1624), arguably the most popular play of early modern London, illustrates how shared feeling could strengthen ideological boundaries, even functioning as a call-to-arms against a Catholic minority (chapter 4). The circulation of shared feeling in the theatrical forum reflected, quite often, the rough contours of its ideologically heterogenous audience.

The book has a strong structural logic. It starts with a bird's-eye view of London's playhouses, surveying the varied faiths of playgoers. Then, it isolates individual case studies, productions highlighting a promiscuous array of religious beliefs. The opening chapter features a particularly impressive feat of archival research. It traces seventy known playgoers from diverse confessional backgrounds. It is rich, compact, and marks a significant challenge to any scholarly "reluctance to imagine godly people inside theaters" (19). Chapter 2 lays the groundwork for "shared feelings" in the theatre: the "orchestration of collective and ideologically elastic experience" (53). Gesturing toward reception theory, Gurnis focuses in on the theatregoer's perspective. A firsthand account of Brome and Heywood's *The Late Lancashire Witches* (1634), a play that humorously dramatized real-life events, shows how theatrical amusement could displace religious agendas. By examining Spanish Match plays of the 1620s, the chapter also unpacks how topically related plays may have inspired divergent feelings that strengthen or blur confessional lines. The following chapter, "In Mixed Company," considers the surprisingly collaborative ideological spirit of early modern playwrights. Gurnis details how mixed faith authors effectively worked together to shape religiously loaded martyr plays, such as with the band of playwrights Drayton, Hathway, Munday, and Wilson's *I Sir John Oldcastle* (staged 1599). The closing two chapters, mentioned earlier, offer in-depth analysis of two theatrical productions from markedly different confessional perspectives. Ultimately, readers are left with a strong appreciation for how the interaction of differing faith perspectives could be central to the post-Reformation theatrical event.

The project engages almost exclusively with early modern scholars and makes quite limited use of critical theory, despite its theoretically rich topic. At times this may be detrimental to the study. Performance scholars of affect theory could offer useful definitions and insights as to how feeling circulates at the theatre for commercial gain. Public sphere theory is the focus of the Epilogue, yet further scholarship, like Stephen Wittek's work on public making in *A Game at Chess*, may have enhanced Gurnis's image of theatre as a cultural and political agent if incorporated earlier on. Despite the relatively short length, the book is able to offer a wide scope of case studies on an assortment of religious plays from an array of affective registers. One is likely to find its emphasis on Shakespeare's contemporaries refreshing, allowing us to dust off a number of less familiar plays.

In sum, *Mixed Faith and Shared Feeling* will serve as useful reading for scholars of early modern drama, culture, and religion. Gurnis establishes a well-reasoned, historically grounded argument about feeling in the theatre—an otherwise slippery subject. The book does an excellent job of blurring the confessional and ideological lines of the post-Reformation London stage while demonstrating the oft-surprising emotional pleasures along the way.

—THOMAS FISH
Kennesaw State University

Haunted City: Three Centuries of Racial Impersonation in Philadelphia. By Christian DuComb. Ann Arbor: University of Michigan Press, 2017. Pp. 1–187. $24.95, paperback.

In January 2020, the Froggy Carr Mummers Club danced down Broad Street in Philadelphia with their trademark "frog-face" umbrellas painted orange to match their black-and-orange costumes honoring Gritty, the media star and mascot of the Philadelphia Flyers. But the organization (which dates back to the 1930s) was disqualified from awards after at least one of its members was found to have been wearing blackface as part of their costume. The act drew condemnations from the Mayor of Philadelphia, other mummer groups, and the press—

though one mummer told local media that wearing blackface "wasn't racist" to him or the African Americans he knows.[1]

The Mummers Parade—which dates to the colonial history of the city and draws from a variety of European working-class traditions—is a Philadelphia institution; as someone who grew up in Eastern Pennsylvania, I recall watching local broadcasts of the parade every New Year's Day. But as evidenced by the recent controversary over Froggy Carr, the parade has a long history of problematic representations of race, gender, and ethnicity. In his expansive and personal book from the University of Michigan Press, Christian DuComb charts the complicated history of the Mummer's Parade in the City of Brotherly Love from performances that grew out of public tensions over racial identity in late-eighteenth- and early-nineteenth-century Philadelphia to the formation of a contemporary performative space featuring competing visions over representation.

One of DuComb's guiding themes is how performances "haunt" the various spaces of Philadelphia, as the history of racialized and gendered performance imprint on the collective memory of the city. Drawing on the work of scholars like Joseph Roach and John Kuo Wei Tchen, DuComb outlines how Philadelphia mumming and other racialized performances coarticulate "blackness and orientalism" and why such representations often "play out either across women's bodies or in conjunction with male-to-female transvestitism" (11). For him, this specter of performance carries an additional weight in the make-up of Philadelphia as a historical place. As he writes, "Ghosts can and do appear through presenting those aspects of the past that remain stubbornly *in place*"—both in terms of the performance institution of mumming and the geographical place of Philadelphia, "where specific performance histories both shape and index changing social relations in the city, the nation, and the broader Atlantic world" (19).

One of the surprising aspects of DuComb's work is his broader scope of the development of racial performative haunting in Philadelphia. I suspect that, for many scholars, the starting point of such an exploration would be the intersection of Irish immigrants and African Americans, as well as the rise of the minstrel show, in the mid-nineteenth century. While DuComb dedicates portions of several chapters to this better-known historical genealogy, including an engaging analysis of minstrel parade performances in the years prior to the Civil War, some of his strongest chapters are concentrated on the development of these questions of Blackness and performance in the broader Atlantic world. In chapter 2, DuComb shows that performative events like the Meschianza, street burlesques, and various dance performances before, during, and after the Revolutionary War drew on a complicated web of Anglo-American and European co-construction of Orientalism, Blackness, and gender that "*all haunt each other*" in one place: Philadelphia (57). Indeed, one of the consistent ironies that DuComb frequently notes is that for a city whose culture is often seen historically as insular, one of Philly's best-known cultural events offers a historical genealogy that is far from provincial.

I found the most engaging chapter to be "The Minstrel Wench and the Mummers Wench: A Performance Genealogy." Here DuComb traces the development of the "wenches" archetypes (male Mummers dressed as women and/or dancing to minstrel-era dances) and then analyzes the significance of those archetypes in contemporary performance, centering his research on trends post-1964, the year blackface was banned in the parade by the city. Much of this chapter incorporates DuComb's own ethnographic observations of Mummers Parades, and his attempts to place a historical genealogy on the gendered and racialized performances give him "Mimetic vertigo" as he's overwhelmed by the "mirrored hallway" of representation that he sees (135). For DuComb, the larger point is that contemporary Mummers often view their performances through an ahistorical lens: men who perform as female wenches ignore the potentialities of gendered satire and focus on the "fun" of performance, while Mummers who have worn blackface in performance evoke a historical "tradition" of blackface in past Mummers Parades to explain their choices. While there are moments where such performances may be transgressive, DuComb argues that more often than not, these ahistorical performance frames showcase reactionary views to diversification, immigration, and globalization and create dystopian performance spaces.

Despite the problematic history of the parade and its lingering issues of representation, DuComb does see something beneficial to Mummers performance: "This may not be utopia, but the rush of a wench brigade strutting in front of City Hall sends both the performers and the audience into a joyful abandon where boundaries between people blur and anything feels possible" (141). As such, he issues a call to action to his readers: "join the festivity" (142). DuComb, who details his own participation with a progressive Mummers club, the Vaudevillians, proposes participation as the best antidote to the Mummers' reactionary performative norms, thereby inviting others to "claim the parade as a site of political protest, and to counter dystopic performances of racial and gendered impersonation, which attempt to justify their presence by denying their past" (142).

Note

1. Drew Smith and Brian X. McCrone, "Mummer in Blackface Defends Himself After Mayor Jim Kenney Disqualifies Froggy Carr Wench Brigade," NBC10 Philadelphia, January 2, 2020, https://www.nbcphiladelphia.com/news/local/i-talk-to-black-people-mummer-in-blackface-defends-himself-after-mayor-boots-brigade/2269419/.

—PAUL GAGLIARDI
Marquette University

Memory, Transitional Justice, and Theatre in Postdictatorship Argentina. By Noe Montez. Carbondale: Southern Illinois University Press, 2017. Pp. 239 + xi. $45.00, paperback.

Noe Montez's *Memory, Transitional Justice, and Theatre in Postdictatorship Argentina* joins the rich archive of theatre and performance scholarship on politics, memory, and state violence in Argentina. A substantial study of theatre produced in the late twentieth and early twenty-first centuries, the book engages with the legacy of Argentine theatre criticism from the dictatorship and democratic transition, namely, works from Catherine Boyle, Jean Graham-Jones, Ana Elena Puga, and Diana Taylor. Montez anchors and contextualizes each chapter within Argentina's post-dictatorship history, giving an illuminating account of the complex shifts in approaches to transitional justice, which he defines as "the practice of responding to human rights violations and state-sanctioned violence through governmental action" (5). The detailed analyses of productions draw on the author's background as a theatre historian, director, and dramaturg and comment on venues, audiences, "directing, design, and performance, in addition to the text" (13). Written with English-speaking readers and audiences in mind, Montez presents an accessible compilation of archived, filmed productions and pieces that toured internationally. The selected repertoire also foregrounds emerging artists from the last few decades and introduces readers to innovative practitioners and techniques. Together, the chapters consider how theatre producers have used the stage as a space for negotiating policies, memory, and modes of memorializing those lost to violence.

The first chapter turns to the Menem administration (1989–1999) and their attempts to reunify the nation through policies centered on "reconciliation and forgetting" following the nation's transition to democracy (1982–1983) (17). Through an analysis of four plays and productions by El Periférico de Objetos, Javier

Daulte, Marcelo Bertuccio, and Luis Cano, Montez illustrates how a new generation of theatre producers subverted official discourses of reconciliation through experimental, postmodern forms and nonlinear narratives. Montez examines how the performances explore approaches to representing violence and the unreliability of memories while developing spaces for critical reflection by placing "interpretive responsibilities on spectators" (54).

The second chapter depicts the work and legacy of Teatroxlaidentidad (Theatre for Identity), a play festival and workshop founded in 2000 by the Grandmothers of the Plaza de Mayo, an NGO dedicated to reuniting children kidnapped during the dictatorship with their birth families. Montez traces the lineage of the festival from its positioning as a descendent of the antiauthoritarian Teatro Abierto (Open Theatre) through its expansion to international tours.

The majority of the chapter is dedicated to productions by Patricia Zangaro, Héctor Levy-Daniel, and Mariana Eva Pérez that emphasize the centrality of heredity and biological identity in the Grandmothers' collaborations with artists. Montez's compelling discussion of Pérez's *Instrucciones para un coleccionista de mariposas* (*Instructions for a Butterfly Collector*) (2002) exemplifies a shift in recent productions to challenge the Grandmothers' strong use of genetic language and idealized kinship narratives (99).

In the third chapter, Montez takes up theatre produced during the Cristina Kirchner presidencies (2003–2015), a period marked by increased legislative and judicial reforms and accountability for state-sanctioned violence. Montez maps a turn in theatre to address the experiences of children raised during the dictatorship and the aftermath of collective societal harm as seen in productions by Damiana Poggi and Virginia Jáuregui, Federico León, Mariano Pensotti, and Lola Arias. In response to the inconsistent and muddled accounts of the dictatorship and the years following it, Montez recounts how cultural producers of this era frequently used forms of self-documentation and personal artifacts to explore the construction of memory and the self (109–10). He argues that the theatremakers of this generation do not merely provide subjective testimonials but also "speak to a larger cultural need to document the self" amid histories of disappearance (111). The plays of this period reflect the transitional policies and practices centered by the Kirchner administrations as the artists explore the relationship between personal memories, self-documentation, and the archive.

The fourth chapter considers how performances have contributed to and disputed narratives surrounding public memory and the contested Malvinas War (1982). Montez describes the government's amplified calls to memorialize the veterans of the Malvinas War during the Kirchner administration, which coincided with the thirtieth anniversary of the conflict. In a discussion of works from Julio Cardoso, Patricio Abadi, Mariana Masover, and Lisandro Fiks, Montez identifies four key elements employed in writing about the Malvinas War, including "allegory, farce, war narratives, and postwar explorations of memory and trauma" (151). Throughout his analysis, he shows how the theatre generates a space for greater understanding of Argentina's historical relationship with the Malvinas territory and offers multidimensional representations of veterans.

In *Memory, Transitional Justice, and Theatre in Postdictatorship Argentina*, Montez illustrates the myriad ways that theatre creates memory narratives and shapes political and social policies. Through a sustained look at local and touring productions, Montez convincingly shows that contemporary Argentine theatre serves as a model for using cultural production in transitional justice practices in the national and international spheres. The book promises contributions to scholarship in memory studies and Latin American theatre and performance as it illuminates new aesthetics and forms of politically engaged performance that reaffirm the power of the arts to incite social change.

—ELIZABETH GRAY
Pennsylvania State University

Imagining Cleopatra: Performing Gender and Power in Early Modern England. By Yasmin Arshad. New York: Bloomsbury/Arden Shakespeare, 2019. Pp. 337. $110.00, hardcover.

Queen Cleopatra VII (69–30 BC), the last Ptolemaic ruler of Egypt, has held a prominent position in popular culture for centuries. From serious representations such as Joseph L. Mankiewicz's *Cleopatra* (1963) to more lighthearted send-ups like Gerald Thomas's *Carry On Cleo* (1964), Cleopatra has become one of the most recognizable figures from ancient history. As Yasmin Arshad's groundbreaking study reveals, similar sentiments are also true of Cleopatra's legacy in early modern England. However, while acknowledging that "the image that dominates popular culture now derives mainly from Shakespeare and is that of the sultry siren of the East lounging on a burnished golden barge" (1), Arshad's important monograph, through its in-depth examinations of three literary works from the period, reveals a far more controversial and contentious figure than present-day readers might expect to find.

Introducing *Imagining Cleopatra*, Arshad states that it is her intention to "look back beyond Shakespeare's Cleopatra to understand the sources and cultural contexts that produced her" (2). Arshad examines three noteworthy texts from the period: Mary Sidney's 1590 work *Antonius* (her translation of Robert Garnier's *Marc Antoine*); Samuel Daniel's 1594 closet drama *The Tragedie of Cleopatra*; and, finally, Shakespeare's *Antony and Cleopatra* (1606–1607). In this beneficial approach, readers are encouraged to consider Shakespeare's play as a product of a lengthy period of Elizabethan/Jacobean popular fascination with Cleopatra rather than, as a comparatively narrower and more familiar study might offer, in a wider early modern context.

Each of Arshad's five chapters provides a fascinating account of how its key text addressed the subject of Cleopatra in its particular immediate context, with chapter 5's analysis of *Antony and Cleopatra* serving to demonstrate how Shakespeare's tragedy, although often viewed as a definitive portrayal of the character, was in fact heavily inspired by the dramatic works that had come before it. Chapter 1 considers how Sidney appropriated Garnier's work for the purposes of topical commentary in 1590, reading this "first dramatization of the Cleopatra story in English" through the lens of Sidney's personal and political history (29). Chapter 2 similarly reads Daniel's *Cleopatra* topically, examining both the original 1594 version, a work noteworthy for its sympathetic portrayal of Cleopatra's elegance and suffering in defeat, and the revised 1607 version, which Arshad emphasizes was heavily influenced by the accession of James I in 1603 and the nostalgia for Elizabeth that this event widely generated. Chapter 4 follows these revelations in delivering an account of the effectiveness of Daniel's closet drama in modern performance, first at Goodenough College, London (March 2013), and later at the Shakespeare Institute in Stratford-upon-Avon (November 2013) and the Great Hall of Knole House in Kent (June 2014).

Two of the most fascinating aspects of Arshad's monograph deserve to be singled out for special recognition. The first of these is in chapter 3, where Arshad examines an undated portrait of a Jacobean lady that she convincingly identifies as Lady Anne Clifford posing in character as Cleopatra. The quality of Arshad's stringent detective work and accomplished literary analysis in reaching this conclusion is impressive, not least in her discovery that the painting's inscription is "excerpted from different parts of Cleopatra's final speech" from Daniel's play (112). As Arshad concludes, "the painting furnishes possible evidence of a performance of *Cleopatra*, and even stronger evidence of a Jacobean lady wanting to role-play as Daniel's Cleopatra" (142). Arshad's revelations in this chapter make for valuable insights into a particular individual's experience of Cleopatra in early modern England and for our received perception of the essential "unperformability" of Renaissance closet drama.

Second, the book's inclusion of eighteen black-and-white images allows for an unexpected level of insight into the wider history of the reception of Cleopatra, taking the study beyond exclusively textual sources and enabling consideration of paintings, objects, statues, and performances. Particularly noteworthy is Arshad's early inclusion of a trio of images that highlight the conflicting representations of the Egyptian queen during this period. Here we are presented with Guido Reni's ca. 1628 depiction of a beautiful young Cleopatra holding her asp to her exposed breast (20), Sebald Beham's ca. 1530–1550 engraving of a misshapen, haggard-looking Cleopatra (21), and Gaspard Isaac's sixteenth-century (otherwise undated) caricature of an elderly and comically ugly Cleopatra, next to similarly negative representations of Helen of Troy and Lucretia (22). As Arshad puts it, "these works indicate how divergent and multi-layered views were of Cleopatra in the period" (22), but they also help us to remember not to treat Cleopatra as a wholly singular entity defined only by the image of "the sultry siren of the East" through which twentieth- and twenty-first-century audiences have tended to imagine her, following on from performances of Shakespeare's famed tragic heroine. The reality for early modern audiences, as shown by Arshad's study, was much more complex.

Imagining Cleopatra is an accomplished and varied scholarly work that provides a necessary and unexpected interpretation of a popular figure so often tempered by the famous work of Shakespeare. By examining the character from a literary-historical perspective, Arshad enables consideration of Shakespeare's play in light of the major English works that preceded it, illuminating Cleopatra in a way that will be highly beneficial to students, scholars, and theatre practitioners alike. Arshad's monograph also encourages readers to interpret Cleopatra not just through the lens of literary analysis but also through that of political history, art history, and the interpretation of museum objects. The infinite variety of Arshad's study is a vital new contribution to this field of study, throwing fresh light upon one of the most familiar rulers in ancient history.

—WILLIAM DAVID GREEN
Shakespeare Institute—University of Birmingham

Occupying the Stage: The Theater of May '68. By Kate Bredeson. Evanston, IL: Northwestern University Press, 2018. Pp. ix + 216. $34.95, cloth.

Kate Bredeson's *Occupying the Stage: The Theater of May '68* is not only an excellent history of the often overlooked French theatre companies that engaged in the worker and student protests of 1968 but also remains topical in light of the worldwide protests seen since the book's publication in 2018. In four succinct chapters, Bredeson discusses the occupation of the Odéon Théâtre in Paris, the development of a new working style by the Théâtre du Soleil and the Théâtre de l'Aquarium, the creation and legacies of the non-Parisian theatres Théâtre Universitaire de Nancy and the Nouvelle Compagnie d'Avignon, and censorship of Théâtre du Chêne Noir and the Living Theatre as local French authorities began reacting to the revolutionary fervor of 1968. In so doing, Bredeson lays out a history of French theatre, and the theatremakers within it, from 1959 to 1971 that, she argues, forms a "stand-alone paradigm called 'The Theater of May '68'" (3). *Occupying the Stage* considers "how offstage production practices—in combination with plays, onstage performances, and their reception—contribute to upholding or dismantling present worlds" (5), providing a thorough analysis of how theatre companies and theatremakers used theatrical performance to join and change the 1968 protest movement across France. Through these different case studies, Bredeson follows how the revolutionary feeling of the 1968 protests led to a move away from the postwar Absurdist theatre and traditional theatre organization toward experiments with collective creation, with theatre productions that engaged with social and political issues, and with theatre spaces to engage workers, students, and non-elites.

Bredeson's first chapter focuses on the more well-known 1968 occupation of the Odéon Théâtre in central Paris, analyzing the Odéon as part of a "genealogy of occupations" (22) where "theatre buildings can be resources in ongoing political and social movements" (61). She considers how the theatre building itself was a site for assembly, speeches, housing, and other needs while also being frank about how the occupation reinforced certain hierarchies as it attempted to dismantle others. Bredeson's analysis of the theatrical assemblies held within the Odéon emphasizes the labor and purpose of large, durational gatherings of protestors, utilizing speeches and open microphone techniques and other such strategies often seen in other protest movements worldwide and beyond 1968. Unfortunately, the limitations of the Odéon occupation are replicated throughout Bredeson's book. As Bredeson acknowledges in her introduction, the 1968 movement was entrenched in white patriarchy. Although Bredeson engages the work of some women, especially that of Ariane Mnouchkine, *Occupying the Stage* is limited by the movement's own shortcomings and the omission of womxn and BIPOC perspectives from the archives.

In the second chapter, Bredeson provides a close analysis of the Théâtre du Soleil and the Théâtre de l'Aquarium, clarifying how these theatre companies sought to combine their theatrical skills with the demands of the workers' movement and explore new ways to make theatre. The time spent detailing how these two theatre companies moved away from entrenched theatremaking into working with audiences, developing lived experiences, and exploring new ways to self-organize is rewarding. Any reader interested in the development of collective creation, revolutionary and protest theatre, and street theatre will find this chapter illuminating. Particularly fascinating and inspiring are Bredeson's play analyses, notably that of the Soleil's 1967 *La Cuisine* (or *The Kitchen*), which beautifully interrelates the political aims of the production with the political ramifications of the 1968 movement, racial justice, the French class system, and more.

In *Occupying the Stage*'s third chapter, Bredeson considers two non-Parisian theatres, the Théâtre Universitaire de Nancy and the Nouvelle Compagnie d'Avignon, tracing the creative impulses and successful development of these theatres from the 1960s in general and 1968 in particular to their long-lasting legacies within French theatre. Citing how these two theatre companies "enacted grassroots decentralization projects using the tactics of location" (100), Bredeson provides a reading of the 1968 theatrical movement away from the capital. A welcome and refreshing take on how location informs theatrical creation and political movements, this chapter addresses gaps in French theatre history as well as the larger history of the 1968 movement in other parts of France.

Bredeson's fourth chapter considers the backlash experienced in Avignon against the theatre of 1968, focusing on the censoring and banning of productions by the Théâtre du Chêne Noir and the Living Theatre. Through analysis of how each theatre company engaged with the artist/activist tactics of the 1968 movement in their dramas, Bredeson elucidates how theatremakers lived and breathed the 1968 movement as they shocked the local population and government officials. This chapter engages not only each individual production but how the Théâtre du Chêne Noir and the Living Theatre collaborated with each other to bring their lived experiences of censorship to the stage. Further, this chapter studies the resistance from local inhabitants, French authorities, and established theatremakers who were uncomfortable with the new ideas and practices developed by the up-and-coming (and often quite young) generation that threatened to change how theatre worked.

Occupying the Stage provides important context to the misunderstood and overly simplified 1968 protests and workers' movements throughout France. It also is an excellent example of how play and performance analysis and a theatre lens can elucidate larger social and political moments. By centering play analysis and theatre history methods, Bredeson brings together an examination of "the role of art in revolution as a key instrument in the disruption of social systems" with "the knowledge that art can work to liberate passions, emotions, and thought" (171). Through careful consideration of individual theatre actions and performances, Bredeson weaves together how theatre companies explored acting spaces, hierarchies, collective creation, language, and more to create new utopic possibilities within (and beyond?) the theatre world.

—**ALÍCIA HERNÀNDEZ GRANDE**
Northwestern University

Playing Sick: Performances of Illness in the Age of Victorian Medicine. By Meredith Conti. London: Rutledge, 2019. Pp. xiii + 196. $155.00, hardcover.

Meredith Conti's *Playing Sick: Performances of Illness in the Age of Victorian Medicine* offers a persuasive and comprehensive discussion of the dramatic representation of illness during the Victorian era. Specifically, it centers the performance of illness on the Victorian stage by analyzing embodiment, symptomology, and medicine against the representational strategies devised to portray them. Although Conti's focus is tripartite—ultimately settling on tuberculosis, drug addiction, and mental illness, "three of the era's most pervasive and provocative illnesses" (2)—by examining competing biomedical and sociocultural understandings of contagion, sickness, and public health, she also considers the broader landscape of illnesses shaping the medical and artistic innovations of the Victorian period and conditioning onstage representations of suffering.

Conti opens with an allegorical eclogue featuring a dramatic exchange between Cholera and Typhus from an 1853 edition of London's *Times.* Although this date is passed over quickly, the eclogue's publication during the highly fatal third cholera pandemic (1846–1860) is noteworthy—and, as Conti notes, a mere year before a massive outbreak devastated London's Soho district. This dialogue reveals how "epidemiological horrors" like typhoid and cholera thrive in terms of contagion and popular reception, emphasizing how transmission is abetted when science-based guidelines for mitigating contagion are ignored.

This opening example, presenting personifications of Cholera and Typhoid, effectively grounds *Playing Sick*'s focus on epidemiological devastation, the dramatization of illness, and its artistic commercialization to introduce fundamental themes: the confrontation of miasmatic and germ theories of disease; aestheticized representations of illness versus the medical and artistic realism increasingly in vigor as the Romantic period turned toward the Victorian era;

and socioeconomic issues that designated certain illnesses as morally superior, nobler, and even inspirational, thereby worthier of pathos than baser ailments afflicting the poor and apparently exclusive of public sympathy and idealization. By understanding illness as "a collaborative, almost alchemical construct that blends biomedical, sociocultural, and individual theories and experiences, and actors' embodiments of illness," Conti presents theatrical representations as a vibrant and much "trafficked site" for contesting, negotiating, and renegotiating nineteenth-century "illness narratives" (2).

The book's three sections on consumption, drug addiction, and mental illness divide cogently into chapter pairs. Part one gives readers "Rosy Cheeks and Red Handkerchiefs: Performing Camille's Consumption Before, During, and After the Contagionist Turn," and "Foreign Invaders: The Transatlantic Consumptives of Sarah Bernhardt and Eleonora Duse," which parse the creation and theatrical history of Dumas's 1848 *La dame aux camélias* and the representational strategies (including physical aspect, acting style, weight, and even diction and accent) of the actresses portraying the titular character. These strategic approaches were informed by the "etiological shift" sparking a move from miasmic theory toward germ theory upon the discovery of tuberculosis's bacterial cause (and communicability) during the late nineteenth century. Rather than perpetuating idealized mythologies around consumption as an inherited illness felling only the most remarkable individuals of society's upper echelons, who languished in artistic spells until their tragic, romantic deaths, tuberculosis and its "graphic realities" became understood as a highly contagious "disease of the masses" (15), far removed from an elite, aesthetic ideal.

Part two studies addiction with "Early Dramaturgies of Drug Addiction in Stage Adaptations of *Dr. Jekyll and Mr. Hyde* and *Sherlock Holmes*," and "Master, Martyr, Monster: The Addict Archetypes of Richard Mansfield and William Hooker Gillette." Taking the invention of the hypodermic needle (1853) as a decisive moment that drastically altered personal drug use—home hypodermic kits became widespread, for example—and led to the establishment of a disease-based model of understanding addiction some decades later, these chapters identify archetypes: "the reluctant victim, the criminalized fiend, and the controlled habitué" (15–16). Helpful, albeit brief, is Conti's mention of cocaine's origins and the discriminatory practices that cast the drug usage of Latin Americans and minority laborers as "proof" of moral and/or developmental faults. She then shows how the medicalization of addiction and the increased criminalization of addicts contributed to the preponderance of "antagonist-addicts" on the popular stage (134–35).

The final section begins with "The Madwoman in the Theatre: Normalizing the Disordered Female Mind in Ellen Terry's Lyceum Repertoire," and concludes with "Abortive Masculinity, Social Decay, and Neuroticism in Henry Irving's Mad Roles." While Conti passes over a point with absolute relevance by making only fleeting mention of race and discriminatory sociocultural and medical practices—in this instance, she explains how African and Native American women were not read as hysterics given what was considered their biological and emotional primitivism (151)—this section has compelling foci. First, attention is given to the fin-de-siècle's psychiatric revolution and development of the "talking cure," along with the nineteenth century's limited, abusive, and repressive understandings of mental illness. Second, Conti deftly elucidates the lexicon surrounding madness and corporeality to parse differentiations between "hysterics" and "madwomen" and psychopathologies of mental illness that aligned men with perversion rather than hysteria, thereby encouraging representations of male madness symptomized by enfeeblement and death, as well as new "mediocultural" representations of gendered madness.

If one were to voice any quibbles, the discussion of illness as related to nervous conditions arrives late, despite the fact that Conti's treatment of the "emotive umbrella of 'nervousness'" is astute (210) and has been proleptically signaled throughout. Likewise, straightforwardly engaging disability studies theory would be useful, especially given the wide-ranging scaffolding of Conti's introduction and scholarly determinations. Lest the inclusion of disability analysis seem anachronistic, many recent disability theorists robustly treat the same issues of power, embodiment, biomedical uncertainty, representation, and sociocultural misprisions that Conti also prioritizes. Given the careful attention to terminology understood as offensive today (although "invalid" merits further elaboration), this omission becomes more surprising.

Dexterous and erudite as it seamlessly analyzes historical theatrical representations, creative agency, and evolutions in prevailing medical and epidemiological views of health, contagion, and the body that renegotiate etiological understandings of illness, *Playing Sick* has high stakes and yields high returns. It offers a riveting, meticulous analysis of physical and mental illnesses on the Victorian stage and their attendant "mediocultural" concerns—a term Conti aptly foregrounds—to better illuminate the complex, rich relationship between performers, directors, and playwrights; between medicine and literature; and between epidemiological realities and theatrical culture.

—ALANI HICKS-BARTLETT

Brown University

Staging Memory and Materiality in Eighteenth-Century Theatrical Biography. By Amanda Weldy Boyd. New York, NY: Anthem, 2018. Pp. v +209. $115.00, hardcover.

Staging Memory and Materiality in Eighteenth-Century Theatrical Biography is a persuasive text that examines the rise of theatrical biography by considering its roots, ramifications, and roles in eighteenth-century literary and theatrical culture. Amanda Weldy Boyd places theatrical biography in a broader literary context by considering its exchange with the novel and the role of the reader in enacting a type of material memory-making when consuming these texts. She clarifies that the art of collecting was undertaken by both the biographer and the reader: The biographer gathered anecdotes and trivia, while the reader could undertake scrapbooking and marginalia. Using case studies of theatrical biographies of well-known actors, Weldy Boyd acknowledges the ongoing archival impulse of literary tradition. This text argues for the importance of theatrical biography as a genre that was popularized at the same time as the rise of the novel and yet has still to receive thorough critical engagement, particularly in relation to materiality.

Staging Memory and Materiality consists of three chapters and an epilogue. Chapter 1 focuses on biographies of David Garrick, specifically the work of Thomas Davies, and the role of the biographer in eighteenth-century literary and social circles. Weldy Boyd explains how Davies associated his 1780 book with "his own reputation as a gentleman by publicly claiming authorship" (8). Chapter 2 examines three biographies of Charles Macklin "in order to determine the extent to which theatrical biographers were actually able to represent their subjects' onstage antics" (8). Chapter 3 rounds out this examination by discussing the career of James Boaden, whose significance, Weldy Boyd writes, comes partly from "our ability to track the changes in his approach over five biographies spanning almost a decade" (9). This structure follows a logical progression: from the origins of this genre through the popular topic of Garrick's life to the increasing emphasis on the biographer as artist. However, Weldy Boyd also adopts an overarching focus on theatrical biography as object and vehicle for artistic representation, and materiality as an aid for memory that allows the reader to understand the significance of these case studies.

Throughout her study, Weldy Boyd delineates the under-recognized relationship between the trends of scrapbooking, epistolary correspondence in the novel, and theatrical biography. She further covers the reciprocal relationship between theatrical biography as a literary form and portraiture, periodicals, and archival reading. She writes that using "contributions to that archive as a way of asserting one's own presence in addition to that of the archive's subject, can be seen in readers' interactions with these texts" (7). This archival reading practice is exemplified by the eighteenth-century exercise of extra-illustration: the "burgeoning trend of binding or rebinding an individual copy of a book to include illustrations, newspaper articles, playbills, or other related phenomena" (50). The reader could therefore create a new textual artifact and mark "the text as a permanent locus in which one could store objects of value" (7). Weldy Boyd documents this role of the codex as a material locus in her study of Queen Charlotte of Mecklenburg, whose extra-illustration in Davies's biography of Garrick shows her "focused interaction with the text, not sprinkling Garrick memorabilia indiscriminately between any two pages" (53). Yet, it was not the case that eighteenth-century theatrical biographies were simple texts that became more complex solely due to reader interaction. Weldy Boyd explains the role of epistolary correspondence in the novel and in theatrical biography as part of an authorial "quest for perceived authenticity" (6). She argues, "The novel becomes heavily invested in mock biography, and biography borrows from novelistic techniques in order to compete" (6). Weldy Boyd addresses the role of theatrical biography as a material artifact for the reader and also offers an examination of the process of the biographer, particularly as an author building on the work of others.

Chapter 2 explores the effects of multiple authors writing about one theatrical figure and highlights the fact that later biographies feature more prominently than their subject the authorial voice and opinions of the biographer. Focusing on representations of the actor Charles Macklin, chapter 2 explores the "biographer as artist" (61). In the final chapter, centering on James Boaden, Weldy Boyd continues examining the situational fame of the biographer relative to their subjects and the dual "artistic anxiety" (3) that theatrical biographies contain. Biographers, such as Boaden, navigated the generic and temporal aspects of capturing both the actors' lives and their performances while maintaining their own authorial voice. These anxieties, Weldy Boyd claims, "manifest in biography primarily through concerns about originality and competition: the theatrical biographer recognizes the need to be perceived as an artist" (3). Weldy Boyd positions the efforts of eighteenth-century theatrical biographers as straddling the realms of literary, material, and theatrical history and form.

The relative brevity of the text (150 pages) means that while Weldy Boyd makes engaging claims about the role of theatrical biography in the eighteenth century, these could be explored further in a longer text, addressing, for example, the generic traits of these texts using multimodal literary theory. In her introduction, Weldy Boyd addresses the lack of female theatrical biographers in her book. She explains that the "main accounts of eighteenth-century female biography are actually autobiographies, and thus do not participate in the same phenomenon" (10), leading to gaps in the study. However, she achieves her aim of examining "what the biographer is doing, how he perceives his role, and how his readers received these efforts" (3–4). She not only outlines the biographical writings of specific eighteenth-century authors but also begins to delve into the broader practices of biographical research and memory practices in the eighteenth century. This book is successful in its assertion of theatrical biographies as multimodal spaces of storage and creation for memory and authorial voice. *Staging Memory and Materiality* is informative about eighteenth-century biography, reading, and theatrical forms and practices. It is also a pleasure to read, with content that appeals to literature, theatre, and history scholars and those working at the intersections of these fields.

—ROSE HILTON
Sheffield Hallam University, UK

The Drama of Celebrity. By Sharon Marcus. Princeton, NJ: Princeton University Press, 2019. Pp. vi + 318. $29.95, hardcover.

In concluding her detailed study of celebrity culture, Sharon Marcus notes that "most histories of celebrity culture emphasize change over time and variations across media; this one has highlighted continuities" (216). *The Drama of Celebrity* not only generates "a new theory of celebrity culture" (3) but also argues that there isn't anything "new" at all about modern celebrity. Instead, the interactions of modern celebrity culture are rooted in the eighteenth and nineteenth centuries, when "the modern meanings of the words 'celebrity' and 'star' first became widespread" (9). Alongside this new theory, *The Drama of Celebrity* carefully traces the beginnings of "celebrity culture" as we know it to the historical theatre, revising the work of such critics as Richard Dyer, Leo Lowenthal, and Walter Benjamin, who find these beginnings in the film industry and Hollywood studio system.

One of the major questions Marcus's study seeks to answer is: "Why did modern celebrity culture emerge when it did?" (10). Throughout the text, this question is answered by noting in the eighteenth and nineteenth centuries specific advancements in technology, new communication practices, and a growing focus on individualism. Marcus's primary archival methodology—much of the text takes as evidence a range of understudied theatre scrapbooks—emphasizes the basis of celebrity culture in these specific shifts. What Marcus terms "the golden age of theatrical scrapbooks" stands as physical evidence of the centrality of specific "technological advances in photography and printing" (97) and indicates the continuity of the mediated interactions sought by fans. In the nineteenth and early twentieth centuries, fans curated, edited, and repurposed images, much as fandom today relies on the sharing of star- and media-created content across various online and print platforms.

Through this exploration of historical continuity, Marcus defines "the drama of celebrity" as the theory that celebrity culture is formed from the triangular relationship between the media, the public, and the star. Contrary to previous theories such as that of Joseph Roach that position stars and fans alike as "helpless before It," that unnameable factor of celebrity (48), Marcus's theory emphasizes the agency of all three sides of the triangular relationship. These three factors are more conventionally addressed as separate contributors to a culture of celebrity; Marcus argues, in contrast, that the three must interact, working either in conjunction or in opposition. "Celebrity culture exists," she concludes, "only when publics, media producers, and well-known individuals engage with one another. If one group were to drop out or ignore the others, celebrity and fandom would disappear" (217). The triangular relationship located at the center of "celebrity," then, is one of power but also one of relative equality. The power held by any of the three elements at a given time can never be so all-encompassing as to eclipse the contributions of the other two.

Each chapter dissects a form of this triangular relationship, and each notes a specific power balance between the three elements. Evocative titles such as "Defiance" (chapter 1), "Savagery" (chapter 3), and "Merit" (chapter 8) locate the point of interaction between the three elements and the balance of power addressed in that chapter. "Defiance," for example, highlights the attraction of a rebellious star and traces the effects of a celebrity's deviation from social expectation on their fans and on media representation. "Intimacy" (chapter 4) details the many ways fans have sought to create a sense of closeness to celebrities, from collections of merchandise to stalking. The second chapter, "Sensation," is particularly persuasive. Here Marcus most thoroughly connects the text's varied streams of analysis, linking the triangular relationship of celebrity culture, and the mutual exchange of that relationship, to the argument for historical continuity. In the eighteenth century's "rise of overpowering acting" (51),

Marcus locates a power dynamic between fans eager to allow "their autonomy, reason, and individuality [to] melt away under the influence of the stars" (51), stars equally eager to "dominate" from the stage (45), and media that encourages, supports, and even allows for both sides of the equation. As the chapter title highlights, this exchange of sensations stands at the heart of this variation of the drama of celebrity.

The most convincing organizational aspect of the book—which relates less to the overall theorization of celebrity than to the specific emphasis on historical continuity—comes in Marcus's use of Sarah Bernhardt as a central figure throughout the text. In each chapter, Marcus illustrates the permutation of the triangular relationship in question through a specific example from Bernhardt's career. In fact, the text might be read as a partial biography of the actress, one that focuses not on her life as a whole but instead on her celebrity. In opposition to more conventional biographical structures, Marcus positions Bernhardt in relation neither to private networks nor to public events but instead to "fans and haters, reporters and reviewers, editors and publishers, photographers and publicists" (16). This central figure in part accounts for the success of the "Sensation" chapter. As evidence of the tripartite exchange at the centre of this chapter, Marcus turns to an example of Bernhardt's performance theory to support the implication that the choices underlying a star's public presentation on and off the stage are equally central to the creation of "celebrity." The attention to detail evident in Bernhardt's onstage characterization is paralleled in her offstage "performance," the creation of her public celebrity image.

The text begins and ends by deliberately subverting the reader's expectations about celebrity. In an opening anecdote, Marcus highlights a 1960s French actress, identified only by her first name: Catherine. Marcus clearly expects readers to anticipate Catherine Deneuve as the figure discussed, and when she reveals that the actress in question is the lesser-known Catherine Spaak, readers must reevaluate their initial reaction. Similarly, in the opening paragraphs of the conclusion, Marcus lists characteristics of a leading American political figure. The revelation that the figure described is Davy Crockett rather than Donald Trump again forces the reader to revisit what they've just read. In playing with readers' assumptions in this way, Marcus draws attention to the study's two main themes: First, celebrity culture is in fact a historical continuity wherein little has changed from the era of Crockett's celebrity to the era of Trump's. Second, merely capturing one element of the triangular relationship—the press, in Spaak's case—isn't enough to ensure celebrity. Celebrity culture as we know it, *The Drama of Celebrity* argues, relies equally on the media, the public, and the stars themselves, as it has done since the eighteenth century. The balance of power between the three elements may shift, but in Marcus's thorough revisioning of how we think of celebrity culture, that balance must nevertheless exist.

—CATHERINE QUIRK
Concordia University

BOOKS RECEIVED

**Indicates assigned for review*

Aronson, Arnold. *The History and Theory of Environmental Scenography, Second Edition*. New York: Methuen, 2018.

Damodaran, Sumangala. *The Radical Impulse: Music in the Tradition of the Indian People's Theatre Association*. New Delhi: Tulika, 2017.

*Davis, Tracy C., and Peter W. Marx, eds. *The Routledge Companion to Theatre and Performance Historiography*. London: Routledge, 2021.

*Durkin, Hannah. *Josephine Baker and Katherine Dunham: Dances in Literature and Cinema.* Urbana: University of Illinois Press, 2019.

*Eichin, Carolyn Grattan. *From San Francisco Eastward: Victorian Theater in the American West.* Reno: University of Nevada Press, 2020.

Forsgren, La Donna. *Sistuhs in the Struggle: An Oral History of Black Arts Movement Theater and Performance.* Evanston, IL: Northwestern University Press, 2020.

Franks, Matthew. *Subscription Theater: Democracy and Drama in Britain and Ireland, 1880–1939*. Philadelphia: University of Pennsylvania Press, 2020.

*Gibb, Andrew. *Californios, Anglos, and the Performance of Oligarchy in the U.S. West.* Carbondale: Southern Illinois University Press, 2018.

Godfrey, Mollie, ed. *Conversations with Lorraine Hansberry*. Jackson: University Press of Mississippi, 2020.

Guynn, Noah D. *Pure Filth: Ethics, Politics, and Religion in Early French Farce.* Philadelphia: University of Pennsylvania Press, 2019.

*Houlihan, Barry. *Navigating Ireland's Theatre Archive: Theory, Practice, Performance.* Oxford, UK: Peter Lang AG, 2019.

Johnson, Jake. *Mormons, Musical Theater, and Belonging in America.* Urbana: University of Illinois Press, 2019.

*Kennedy, Seán, ed. *Beckett Beyond the Normal.* Edinburgh: Edinburgh University Press, 2020.

*Lemon, Rebecca. *Addiction and Devotion in Early Modern England.* Philadelphia: University of Pennsylvania Press, 2018.

Magelssen, Scott. *Performing Flight: From the Barnstormers to Space Tourism.* Ann Arbor: University of Michigan Press, 2020.

Maley, Patrick. *After August: Blues, August Wilson, and American Drama.* Charlottesville: University of Virginia Press, 2019.

*May, Theresa J. *Earth Matters On Stage: Ecology and Environment in American Theater.* London: Routledge, 2021.

McAvinchey, Caoimbe, Lucy Richardson, and Fabio Santos, eds. *Phakma: Making Participatory Performance.* New York: Bloomsbury, 2018.

*McAvoy, Mary. *Rehearsing Revolutions: The Labor Drama Experiment and Radical Activism in the Early Twentieth Century.* Iowa City: University of Iowa Press, 2019.

McHugh, Dominic, ed. *The Oxford Handbook of Musical Theatre Screen Adaptations.* New York: Oxford University Press, 2019.

*Mielke, Laura L. *Provocative Eloquence: Theatre, Violence, and Antislavery Speech in the Antebellum United States.* Ann Arbor: University of Michigan Press, 2019.

Minton, Gretchen E. *Shakespeare in Montana: Big Sky Country's Love Affair with the World's Most Famous Writer.* Albuquerque: University of New Mexico Press, 2020.

*Picon-Vallin, Béatrice. *Le Théâtre du Soleil: The First Fifty Years.* Trans. Judith Miller. London: Routledge, 2020.

*Purcell, Carey. *From Aphra Behn to Fun Home: A Cultural History of Feminist Theater.* Lanham: Rowman and Littlefield, 2019.

Rabinowitz, Stanley J., ed. and trans. *And Then Came Dance: The Women Who Led Volynsky to Ballet's Magic Kingdom.* New York: Oxford University Press, 2019.

*Robert, Yann. *Dramatic Justice: Trial by Theater in the Age of the French Revolution.* Philadelphia: University of Pennsylvania Press, 2019.

Rodgers, Amy J. *A Monster with a Thousand Hands: The Discursive Spectator in Early Modern England.* Philadelphia: University of Pennsylvania Press, 2018.

Ruwe, Donelle, and James Leve, eds. *Children, Childhood, and Musical Theater.* London: Routledge, 2020.

*Schmitt, Natalie Crohn. *Performing Commedia Dell'Arte, 1570–1630.* London: Routledge, 2020.

Schweitzer, Marlis. *Bloody Tyrants and Little Pickles: Stage Roles of Anglo-American Girls in the Nineteenth Century*. Iowa City: University of Iowa Press, 2020.

Shandell, Jonathan. *The American Negro Theatre and the Long Civil Rights Era*. Iowa City: University of Iowa Press, 2018.

The Books Received list is updated regularly and is available at https://matc.us/theatre-history-studies-4/theatre-history-studies-the-matc-journal/theatre-history-studies-books-available-for-review.

CONTRIBUTORS

ANGELA K. AHLGREN is an associate professor in the Department of Theatre and Film at Bowling Green State University, where she teaches performance studies and theatre history. She is the author of *Drumming Asian America: Taiko, Performance, and Cultural Politics* and articles on taiko, performance, and pedagogy. Her current research includes a study of Asian aesthetics and racial politics in American modern dance since the Cold War and an ethnographic study of stage managers, gender, and invisible labor in the performing arts. She is currently serving as VP of Awards for the Dance Studies Association and cochair of the Articles in Progress/Pitch Your Book sessions for the Mid-America Theatre Conference.

JANE BARNETTE is an associate professor in the Department of Theatre and Dance at the University of Kansas, where she teaches courses in dramaturgy, theatre history, and script analysis and seminars in theatrical adaptation and the performance of gender and sexuality. Her book, *Adapturgy: The Dramaturg's Art and Theatrical Adaptation*, explores the powerful alchemy of dramaturgically savvy adaptations for the stage. Jane is a director, a dramaturg, and a theatre historian whose research includes Chicago-based touring theatre at the turn of the twentieth century, American pageantry, and depictions of witchy characters onstage as well as in popular culture.

DAVID BISAHA is an assistant professor of theatre history and theory at Binghamton University, SUNY. David's research specializes in the history of scenic design in the United States and in the more recent history of immersive and participatory performance. His book project, "American Scenic Design and Freelance Professionalism," is a history of scenic design praxis among twentieth-century designers and artists in New York City. At Binghamton, David teaches theatre history and acting/directing theory in the MA and BA programs.

CHRYSTYNA DAIL is an associate professor of theatre history at Ithaca College. Her book, *Stage for Action: U.S. Social Activist Theatre in the 1940s*, is a part of the Theater in the Americas series published through Southern Illinois University Press. Her essays and reviews have appeared in the *Journal of American Drama and Theatre*, *Theatre History Studies*, *Arthur Miller Journal*, *Theatre Journal*, *Theatre Annual*, and *Performing Arts Resources*, as well as in the edited collection *Working in the Wings: New Perspectives on Theatre History and Labor*.

REBECCA K. HAMMONDS is an independent scholar currently based in West Palm Beach, Florida. Her ongoing research investigates the construction of literary and scholarly (or "bookish") female characters in American musicals in the face of the genre's abiding connection with spectacle. She holds a PhD in theatre from Bowling Green State University and an MA in theatre from Regent University.

JESSICA ANN HOLT earned an MFA in directing from Baylor University. In addition, she holds a master's of theatre studies in production and design from Southern Oregon University and a BFA in acting from Utah State University. Jessica is a director, designer, actor, and educator.

LISA JACKSON-SCHEBETTA is an associate professor and chair of the Theater Department at Skidmore College. She is the author of *Traveler, There Is No Road: Theatre, the Spanish Civil War, and the Decolonial Imagination in the Americas*. She has published in *Theatre Journal*, *Theatre History Studies*, *Journal of American Drama and Theatre*, *Modern Drama*, and *New England Theatre Journal*, among others. She is the immediate past president of the American Theatre and Drama Society and a former American Association of University Women fellow.

ODAI JOHNSON is the author of numerous books and articles—most recently, *Ruins: Classical Theatre and Broken Memory*. He teaches at the University of Washington's School of Drama.

LINDSEY MANTOAN is an assistant professor of theatre and resident dramaturg at Linfield College. She researches contemporary US character, on both the national and the individual levels. She is the author of *War as Performance:*

Conflict in Iraq and Political Theatricality and coeditor with Sara Brady of *Vying for the Iron Throne: Essays on Power, Gender, Death, and Performance in HBO's "Game of Thrones"* and *Performance in a Militarized Culture*. She is an occasional contributor to CNN.com.

SCOTT PROUDFIT is an associate professor of English at Elon University. He is the associate editor of *A History of Collective Creation* and *Collective Creation in Contemporary Performance* and the coeditor of *Women, Collective Creation, and Devised Performance*. Before obtaining his PhD from Northwestern University in 2008, he worked with the Actors' Gang and the Factory Theater in Los Angeles and with Irondale Ensemble Project in New York. In addition, for almost a decade he worked as an editor for the newspapers *Back Stage* and *Back Stage West*.

MAMATA SENGUPTA is an assistant professor of English at Islampur College, West Bengal, India. Her research interests include performance studies, orality and audience reception studies, folkloristics, and gender studies. Sengupta received her MPhil and PhD on postwar British drama and is presently working on the intersectionality between religion and performance.

JONATHAN SHANDELL is an associate professor of theatre arts at Arcadia University. He is the author of *The American Negro Theatre and the Long Civil Rights Era* and coeditor of *Experiments in Democracy: Interracial and Cross-Cultural Exchange in American Theatre, 1912–1945*. Other publications include articles in *Visions of American Tragedy*, *The Cambridge Companion to African American Theatre*, *African American Review*, *Journal of American Drama and Theatre*, and *Theatre Topics*. Jonathan is past president of the Black Theatre Association (BTA) and received his MFA and DFA from the Yale School of Drama.

